HOME ALONE

A HOME ALONE

Eryn Grey with Gia Summer

Copyright © 2014 by Eryn Grey with Gia Summer.

Library of Congress Control Number:		2014914231
ISBN:	Hardcover	978-1-4990-6091-1
	Softcover	978-1-4990-6092-8
	eBook	978-1-4990-6090-4

All rights reserved. No part of this book may be reproduced or transmitted in any form or by any means, electronic or mechanical, including photocopying, recording, or by any information storage and retrieval system, without permission in writing from the copyright owner.

This book is designed to provide information on *home alone* only. This information is provided and sold with the knowledge that the publisher and author do not offer any legal or other professional advice. In the case of a need for such advice, consult with a professional in that field. This book does not contain all the information available on the subject matter. This book has not been created to be specific to any individual or organization or their needs or situations. Every effort has been taken to make this book as accurate as possible. However, there may be content or typographical errors unintentionally.

Therefore, this book should only serve as a general guide and not as a source of subject information. This book may be dated and is intended only to educate and entertain. The author and publisher shall have no liability or responsibility to any person or entity regarding any loss or damage incurred, or alleged to have incurred, directly or indirectly, by the information contained in this book.

Any people depicted in stock imagery provided by Thinkstock are models, and such images are being used for illustrative purposes only.
Certain stock imagery © Thinkstock.

This book was printed in the United States of America.

Rev. date: 08/14/2014

To order additional copies of this book, contact:
Xlibris LLC
1-888-795-4274
www.Xlibris.com
Orders@Xlibris.com

DEDICATION TO MARSHA WHITFILL

We dedicate this book to Marsha Whitfill, confidential intermediary, Harford County Department of Social Services. Marsha spent countless hours sorting through mountains of paperwork and was instrumental in reuniting them after thirty years.

Marsha coined the phrase they lacked the "where with all" to keep the family together.

We will be forever grateful for her heartfelt compassion and empathy.

Eryn and Gia

CHAPTER 1

Who could forget what Beverly and Diana went through the first years of their lives? Beverly was four and Diana was seven when they were abandoned by their parents. But Beverly and Diana never forgot the feelings of how heartbroken they felt until someday they would be reconnected. Beverly had that reoccurring memory of Diana, so fragile, dark hair, big brown eyes, holding her doll all soiled and raged. Diana recalled Beverly as a slight, sad blonde with a twinkle in her blue eyes and a dust of freckles across her nose. As their tiny hands were squeezed so tightly together their knuckles were white like little marshmallows. The 1950 Chevy Impala pulled up to this old white farmhouse; they swung open the door without saying a word; they both had tears rolling down their pink cheeks as they tore their tiny sweaty hands apart. Diana and Beverly were inconsolable as they were separated from each other, still crying for their mommy. But the social worker had a job to do. They were being placed in different homes. They never forgot that day.

In August 1982, on the West coast of south Florida, it was a hot sunshiny day. Beverly was ready to mail the letter she had thought about sending most of her life. Beverly never forgot her big sister Diana; as a result, she always had hopes and dreams of reconnecting with her someday. Although years had gone by without a word, she wondered if this was a dream or if it was possible to fulfill her aspirations. Beverly was very strong willed and full of determination.

That was what was running through Beverly's mind as she wrote her letter, licked the envelope, and placed the stamp on it. Now she was ready to send it to the Welfare Department in Bel Air, Maryland, as she remembered that is where she had been taken as a small child. As

Beverly walked to the mailbox she watched the kids playing in the yard; it was a beautiful day, and the sky was so blue, she knew this was the right day for her letter to be sent for Beverly's journey to begin.

Farther north in the Panhandle of Florida, as the waves of the gulf rolled on to the beach and the light willowy sea oats blew in the slight breeze, Diana, who had been searching for many heartfelt years for her sister had just finished her letter in August 1982. Diana also had a very strong vision of that day in the Chevy Impala where she and her sister were so tragically torn from each other's hands. She being the older child had suffered many more deep heartbreaking memories of the family that they once had. She longed to make a family once again, starting with her sister, never understanding why they did not try to place them together; instead, Diana was placed with their six-month-old brother. She had come to a point in her life when it was the time to write this letter and send it to the Welfare Department in Bel Air. As she peered out the kitchen window she saw the mailman coming. Diana ran to meet him with her letter. He chuckled and said, "Must be pretty important."

Diana replied with a big smile and a skip in her step, "This is the one I have waited my whole life to send."

It was just four days later that these two letters reached the department of social services in Bel Air, Maryland. They were both placed on the desk of Marsha George. Can you imagine when she read the two letters, one from Beverly, thirty-three, married with two children, and the other from Diana, thirty-seven, married with two children telling the same story, from thirty years ago! It was unbelievable that these letters crossed after so many years and were received by the same social worker. What a wonderful blessing for Beverly and Diana, and they did not even know it yet.

The letter was on the way, and now the waiting started. Beverly was so excited that she could hardly keep her mind on her everyday life. Taking care of two boys and it being summer, they wanted to do something every day. All Beverly had on her mind was wondering how long it would be before she got an answer to her letter. She wondered,

"Will they be able to find my sister and where she lives?" Beverly decided to take the boys, Scott and Blake, to the park for a while; when she got back, the mail would be there and she would check it then. Diana was hoping she had given enough information in her letter that would identify the family as she remembered them. She definitely recalled there were two boys, James and Joseph, and Beverly and herself. Their dad's name was Willy, but Diana could not remember their mother's name. Diana was very concerned that was going to be a problem in putting them together. So the Panhandle was filled with worry, and the southwest coast of Florida was starting to rumble and they did not know why.

Scott, with his golden blond hair, went whizzing by on his mongoose BMX. Beverly walked to the mailbox with such anticipation that there would be some information or acknowledgement from the state that she could hardly open the box. Beverly quickly shuffled through the mail: bills, advertisements, subscriptions, and there it was—Welfare Department of Md. The tears just began to pour down Beverly's face, and she had not even opened it yet. It could be bad news.

Scott yelled, "What's wrong, Mom?"

"Oh, nothing, you go on and play." Beverly went inside, and she thought for a minute, should she wait till her husband Luke got home? He had so much wisdom when it came to this subject, or should she call her best friend Janet that was her confidant from day one with this journey. Beverly waited for Luke to come home, and they read it together.

The letter was to acknowledge that they had received Beverly's letter and that they had a few questions that would need to be cleared up. She gave a big sigh! "I guess that is better than nothing." But the question that Marsha asked Beverly was quite puzzling. So Beverly began to wonder if this was the right family that Marsha had found or was she on the wrong track? Beverly explained, "When we were abandoned, they put my sister Diana and our six-month-old brother Joseph in the car together." Now why would she ask Beverly that question? Beverly finished up a few more questions, but after she sent that letter off to

Marsha, she just could not get that thought about three children out of her mind. Could there have been more? No, Beverly knew because she only remembered Diana and the baby.

Meanwhile, Diana was on pins and needles, waiting as it had been weeks since her letter was sent. Diana was much more patient than Beverly. Diana's husband Vito asked her if she had been to their post office box lately with a snicker. "Yes, honey, every day!" Like she would not go down there every day since she sent the letter. Vito was headed down to the docks to work on his thirty-foot catamaran; he was having some new sails replaced for his voyage down to the Florida Keys, and he said on the way back he would check the box. Diana said, "Okay, Vito, but don't be too long."

As soon as Vito pulled in, Diana went running out to the car, and much to her surprise, Vito was waving a white envelope in his hand. The tears started to roll down her face. Vito said, "You haven't even opened it yet."

Diana said, "Oh, go on!" Diana opened it to find a "Thank you for your letter, and we will be happy to assist you." They went on to say, "There is a question about you mentioning four siblings in your letter, and we just want to make sure with you that we are correct with four." Diana thought that to be odd but sent back the letter stating, "Yes there were four. However, James was living with our mother's sister named Katie as he was sick with asthma and needed to live in a different climate." She sent off the letter, thinking they must have found something or they would not be verifying that information.

Beverly grew very impatient and could not wait for another letter. "What is going on?" Beverly was the type to pick up the phone and call and talk to this person and maybe get just a little hint from her as to whether they had found out any connection to her sister at all. So Beverly called, and she gets through to Marsha; she introduced herself, and they got acquainted. She found Marsha very sweet and easy to talk to about this subject. Although she did not give her a real answer, she did tell her she was working very close with another lady in the office that was helping her with this case. She said she understood how it feels, and she knew how excited Beverly was to get this information and how long she had waited. She expected to get a letter out very soon.

Another month passed, Beverly felt she could hardly make it without some news when she got a call from Marsha, which was the call of a lifetime. Marsha said, "Beverly, you need to be sitting down." Beverly anxiously listened for what she hoped was the news she had been waiting all her life to hear. She wanted to just give Beverly a small amount to digest until she could send a letter explaining all the information she had located. Marsha explained to Beverly that she had located her sister! Beverly was overcome with excitement and joy! Marsha enlightened her that Diana wrote a letter the same time, same month, same year she wrote a letter. Beverly was overtaken with emotion. How could this be happening? The only difference was her sister spoke of four siblings, and Beverly spoke of three, so Marsha explained that she had to make sure with further investigation that they were sisters.

Now Marsha was going to write a letter to both of them explaining all of this in detail. She would put her identifying information at the bottom. Marsha also would call Diana today to tell her the same information about locating Beverly. Beverly immediately was concerned about how long this was going to take. Marsha clarified that she would get the letters drafted by the middle of the week and they would both get them on the same day. Marsha realized this information would be emotionally difficult to digest, "so feel free to call me with any questions at any time."

While Marsha imagined that Beverly's contact with Diana will be a joyful and a longed-for reunion, she also expected this entire process may trigger many mixed emotions. It was the beginning of "opening up the floodgates" for better and worse. Marsha told Beverly, "Whenever I have a gain, such as finding your sister, there is always a corresponding loss. I will not know what the loss part for you girls will be, perhaps your loss of innocence or identity as you knew it." Marsha felt compelled to mention, while sharing this information, "In addition to the joy of your reunion, you may experience a renewal of grieving over your initial separation from family."

She added, "Please wait a day before you call each other to digest the information that is contained in the letters."

It was now the middle of October, and without a doubt Beverly and Diana were anxiously waiting for their letters to arrive. They both had been through so much, but little did they know what was in store for them in the future. All they could think about was "Finally we are going to meet each other. We had longed for, hoped for, dreamed about, prayed that somehow we could enter each other's life." Beverly had told her adoptive parents what she had done before she wrote her letter and her father, Harvey, was okay with it, but her mother, Margaret, warned her that this was the wrong thing for her to do. Beverly tried to explain that she just wanted to find her sister, not her mother. But she did not believe her, which once again made Beverly have those same feelings of displeasing her mother. But the desire was so strong, and she was an adult now. Why couldn't she understand? While Diana's mother, Ruth, had already passed, she had an even stronger desire to find her biological mother, more than Beverly. Even before she passed and as far back as when Lewis and Ruth adopted Diana, she had told her parents that she had a sister and she wanted to find her. At the time of her adoption they tried to find Beverly, but she was already in the process of finalizing her adoption with Mr. and Mrs. Simpson. Diana had taken legal measures on her own to find Beverly but to no avail. She had even written to the same agency at one time and never received an answer to her letter. Diana and Beverly would not have to wait long.

On October 19, 1982, Beverly received a parchment envelope with Harford County on the upper-left corner around 3:15 p.m. on a typical rainy afternoon in southwest Florida. Diana also received her letter on October 19, 1982, but it was a much different day as Diana had to wear a jacket as she drove with Vito to the post office. There it was! Diana felt like she had been waiting for this all her life.

Vito said, "Open it."

Diana said, "Let's just get home and have a nice cup of hot chocolate with marshmallows in front of the fire." They drove home with Diana squealing all the way. As they sat together to read the letter, Diana had a hard time containing her feelings. She cried, she smiled, and she read every word like each word was the most important thing she had ever read. So much joy overcame her. Diana could not believe her dreams were fulfilled. At the bottom it was written by hand: "I am suggesting to both of you that you wait for two days before contacting each other making sure each has gotten my letter."

Diana wondered, "Did Beverly get her letter yet?" Should she wait two days?

Meanwhile, Beverly had this parchment envelope; there was not much she was afraid of, but opening this letter was catastrophic. "Okay, pick Scott up from school. That is first. No, call Janet first because she is going to have to be the one to open this envelope." Beverly called Janet, and what a reaction she got when she told her it was here. Beverly told Janet she was going to pick up Scott and bring him over to play with her son, Johnathan, as they were best friends, while Janet reads her the letter. Janet said, "*What?* Don't you want you and Luke to read it together?"

"No. I am shaking like the willow tree in my front yard, and I can hardly contain myself. You have to do it for me."

Beverly arrived at Janet's; the boys rode off on their dirt bikes so they could be alone. Beverly said, "Okay, open it!"

Janet began to read with tears flowing down her pudgy pink cheeks. Beverly, of course, joined her. It was real! She knew she had a sister. It wasn't just something she had made up. She remembered that dark-haired little girl and that lady tearing their little hands apart. She didn't make it up. Everyone made her think she was crazy because everyone said she made up stories about having another family. Now Beverly said, "I even get to meet her." Beverly expressed to Janet, "Does she want to meet me, and has she been looking for me too?"

Janet explained how they were getting these letters at the same time, and on the advice of Marsha, she said, "We should wait for two days before calling."

Beverly said, "Are you nuts? Wait for what? I will call Luke and get him over here, and he can call for me first and get her husband on the phone to smooth things over, and then we will get on the phone. We will be making a trip next weekend if she has anything to say about it."

Luke made his way over and finds Beverly bouncing off the walls. By then Janet had started some snacks for the boys and Luke. Beverly was too overwhelmed to eat, and Janet and she were dissecting this letter. Beverly wanted to make sure she did not miss anything that Marsha put in this letter. Beverly was the type to read between the lines. There was a lot of "identifying" information that could not be shared with us, and that would mean because of the persons' names that they did not know. Beverly had already asked Marsha if she could get a copy of her parents' divorce papers. She said, "Yes, it is public record. Just send a letter to the courthouse in Harford County, ask how much, and you can get a copy." That is just what Beverly did; she called the courthouse, got the amount for the copy ($ 6.50) and address, sent the check, and waited for a copy of the divorce papers.

Beverly was now pestering Luke to get on the phone to call her sister. Finally he said, "Here goes." Beverly's face was still wet with tears. Luke said "Hello." On the line was Vito, Diana's husband. They had a little chat about the situation, and that was a good opening for two girls that had not spoken in thirty years and had not believed this day would ever come.

Vito went to Diana and put his hand very lovingly on her shoulder and said, "This is the call you have been waiting for. It's your sister." The tears began to flow like Niagara Falls. Diana had to get her composure.

"Okay, this is it. Hi, Beverly! What do you say? I can't wait to see you. What kind of things do you like? Do you like hot stuff? Do you like gardening?"

Beverly jumped in, "Whoa with the questions. You're my sister finally. It is hard to believe we found each other. Look how we did it at the same time! That is really amazing." Beverly told Diana how she would see girls walking down the street and she would think, "Maybe that is my sister."

Diana said, "Me too! Where do we start to know everything that has happened in our lives?"

Beverly said to Diana, "The first thing is to see you face-to-face. We can't wait. Luke and I will talk about it, but what about the last weekend of the month? Would that work for you? You can give us some directions, and we can look on a map, and we can drive up in our Toyota wagon. That is only about ten days away, and that is about as long as we can wait, right, Diana? No longer than that for me." It seemed like the questions went back and forth for at least two hours as Beverly and Diana could not let go of the little bit of happiness that came from just hearing each other's voices.

Beverly began to reflect on what Marsha had said that this was going to open up many memories good and bad and to be ready as they went through this journey to look at this as a healing process. Diana and Beverly both felt that first meeting each other was the biggest step toward that journey and that they were ready; good, bad, or no matter how ugly, they were ready to go forward.

The ride up US 19 from Clearwater toward the Panhandle of Florida on Friday was filled with excitement and anticipation as to how the weekend would be when Beverly would first set her eyes on Diana. It was going to be a six- to seven-hour trip, so with a four-year-old and a twelve-year-old, you had to keep them somewhat entertained and stop for bathroom and eating breaks. At times when Scott and Blake got to fighting, Beverly was drifting off in her mind thinking about what she was going to say to Diana and didn't even hear them. It seemed like it took forever to get there. Beverly remembered when they pulled up in the yard, she got out of the car to greet Diana, who came running to the car, just about 5'2 with a pretty print blouse on and jeans. The first thing she said was "You're so tall!"

Beverly was 5'6; maybe that was all she could think of to say at first. With the tears flowing like a river, they hugged and did not want to let go. Right away, Scott and Diana's son, Eddie, got acquainted, and her daughter Lynne took to Blake; he was so cute with that golden blond hair and dark brown eyes. Luke and Vito knew they better get out of the way because they knew there was a lot to talk about.

Beverly shared with Diana what it was like living in the same town they were born in until her last year of high school and then on to Florida. Diana had moved to New Jersey and then on to Florida. Beverly explained how hard it was for her as her adoptive parents never told her she was adopted, although she remembered things, places she had been and houses she had lived in. Mrs. Simpson kept telling her she was a dreamer and that she made up things. Beverly said she would just accept that answer because she did not want to be sent back to a foster home. Beverly said she was bullied by kids at school because they would tell her, "Those aren't your real parents." But fear kept Beverly from saying anything; she just kept it bottled up inside. Beverly said she knew she could never ask about her sister as she feared what her mother would say. Diana said she did not have that problem. Her parents were open and honest with her. Because their youngest brother, Joseph, also adopted with Diana, was only six months old when they were abandoned and about three by this time, there was no need to tell him. They both went on for hours, recalling what they remembered about their childhood. It was amazing how their memory of that last month's together had made such an impression on their innocent little minds.

Beverly made a Mexican dish, and Diana made her famous chocolate cake. They all sat around the table trying to guess what each other's favorites were, and it was unbelievable how close they were alike. From dinner the conversation started up again and lasted until the wee hours of the morning. With a big squeeze and a hug, almost thinking, "Am I dreaming? Will she be here in the morning?" they went to bed smiling and happy.

They woke up to the smell of hot brewed coffee. Beverly knew Luke was up because he walked around with a cup in his hand all the time. Beverly was not too sure of Vito yet. "But being from Italy, I'm sure the Vito would come out sometime soon." Beverly came downstairs, and Diana was in the kitchen, cooking bacon, and she said the kids were outside running around like a bunch of Indians. Beverly could see them running around the yard and some white stuff hanging everywhere.

Diana said, "Go out in the front yard and take a look." They opened the front door, and the whole yard had been rolled with toilet paper! Yes, Eddie's buddies had thought it funny to roll his house with toilet paper during the night. The kids thought it was hysterical. It was funny because you should have seen the look on Eddie's face when Diana said, "Your friends, you clean it up."

"But, Mom!" Eddie whined! "Come on, Lynne, will you help me?" Scott and Lynne felt bad for him and they all got together and had it done before breakfast.

It was a cool but sunny day, so Diana and Beverly packed the kids in the car with a picnic lunch, and off to the beach they went down by the bridge. The sky was blue, the clouds were puffy like pillows, and nothing could be more perfect for them. They continued their conversation right where they had left off. Diana began to bring up questions about their mother and father. For some reason Beverly could only remember situations with their father and not many with their mother. Beverly could sense Diana really wanted to meet their mother very much. She had much more of an attachment to her than Beverly did, and Diana, being the eldest, had a closer connection with her. Beverly took this opportunity to explain how strongly she felt about not wanting to have anything to do with their mother. Diana was very respectful of Beverly's wishes and assured her that she would never push that on her. Beverly said, "When and if Marsha finds her, I would like to send her a letter for her to give some answers to questions she has about why she gave us away."

Beverly explained to Diana, "When you have the opportunity to meet her, you have my support," but Beverly was concerned that "you will not let our mother upset or hurt you after all these years."

They took pictures so that they could remember the first time they saw each other in thirty years. Some people said they thought they looked alike, but some said they didn't. Diana was short with dark hair and dark eyes, and Beverly was blonde with greenish-blue eyes and was taller. Even they could not understand why they looked so different, but that was part of the journey to find their roots. "Who do we look like? Who walks like us? Who smiles like me? Who is quiet and more reserved like Diana? Who is more outgoing and always making jokes like Beverly? Maybe someday we will know the answer to those questions that have been such a burning desire to know all our lives."

It was sad having to leave, but Diana and Beverly knew this was the tip of the iceberg for them. They had already made plans that Vito and Luke did not even know about. This was just the beginning. Beverly rode home with so much to digest. She had just met her real sister that she longed to meet. It was real, and it brought happiness, loving feelings of joy to her heart. No one could take her away from Diana ever again. Diana too leaned back on the recliner with her dog Bruno beside her and thought about all the wonderful memories that were brought up as they sat up like two teenagers would do. It was a start for Diana to have time with her real sister that she was robbed of so many years ago. Diana had such a bitter feeling all her life just as much as Beverly did that they had been separated. But would they ever be able to find out why? Diana reflected on how they laughed and giggled about things that normally weren't funny. This was a wonderful reunion, and nothing was going to break up the happiness Beverly and Diana had this weekend and the many more to follow.

CHAPTER 2

It was hard settling back into a normal life after such a magnificent weekend. Beverly and Diana were anxiously waiting to see if there was even a possibility of finding their mother. Marsha was working diligently on finding their mother through their parents' divorce documents, which contained identifying family information. Beverly had already sent off for a copy of the divorce documents as they were public records, and she was waiting for them to come for herself and Diana.

The suspense was building every day, and Beverly and Diana kept the telephone lines hot, calling back and forth every time they thought of some little thing they remembered. No matter how insignificant or how late it was, they were on that phone. Luke and Vito hadn't said anything yet, but it was coming. You know, with Vito being Italian and all… he was probably going to complain even if he didn't care.

Beverly was going to visit her mom and dad because she had not seen them since her visit to meet Diana. Her stomach was starting to roll over just thinking about what her mom was going to say. Dad would be fine. Beverly wished they could have talked about her life as a child and not waited till she was sixteen. Beverly's parents pretended they were her only family when she knew different but was never allowed to talk about it. She just wanted to get it out and talk about what happened to her that she remembered and why did they take her sister away. It was all a secret. So now Beverly did not want to hurt her mother, but that burning desire to know was so strong that she chose to finally act on that yearning even with the fear of hurting her mother.

The drive to Bradenton was about one and a half hours, and Mr. and Mrs. Simpson lived on a lake near the mobile home park Mr. Simpson used to manage. They all met at the door, and of course, Blake was the center of attention at first. Without barely a hello, Mom blurted out, "So how was your sister?"

"Oh, Mom, she was great! We talked and talked and had so much fun." Beverly knew what was coming up next and could see the sharp curl on her mother's lip as she asked if Beverly was going to see her mother. Beverly exclaimed immediately, "You are my mother. Diana wants to see her. That is her business."

Mother annoyingly said, "She will get you to meet her."

Diana and Beverly talked about it, and she knew how sensitive Beverly felt; therefore, she respected her feelings. Beverly even brought some pictures of Diana at their first time meeting each other. Mother looked at the pictures and enlightened Beverly that "neither of you look like each other." She went on to say emphatically that they absolutely did not look like their mother. Beverly let her mom know "We both have their families, and Diana would like to meet you, and she wants me to meet her father, as her mother has passed." Mother expressed her pleasure in meeting Diana and said she would love for Beverly to bring her down real soon for dinner.

Beverly knew that when she came to visit, it would be difficult for her mom; she would not be happy and was undeniably certain to bring up the past about her biological mother. Beverly knew that she was looking out for her so that she doesn't get hurt. "But when you choose this journey, you have to know that there will be good and bad consequences. There will be things you wish you didn't know, but is it all worth having the closure in your life that has been missing?" she mused.

When Beverly got home, Luke said, "You better call Diana. She sounds like she is in labor. She was so excited." Beverly called Diana only to find that she got a letter stating that Marsha may have found their mother. Diana was jubilant to say the least.

Beverly said, "Wait a minute! Maybe I got a letter too." She went to the mailbox to find a letter from Marsha. Together they began to dissect every word very carefully.

Marsha had located her in Louisiana, and to properly approach her, she got in touch with the social services in Louisiana. Her name was Arlene Johnson, and they gave her a call and would get back with Marsha. Beverly and Diana felt like school kids. "This is our mother! They really found her." Hopefully she would be surprised when she got the call. Beverly and Diana wondered what she would say. Beverly said this was so overwhelming for her she felt sick. Diana felt more excitement after waiting all these years and wondering what her mother had done with her life. It would be difficult to wait, but the girls had to be patient and wait for their mother to answer.

There were so many questions the girls had unanswered running through their minds; however, they may not always get the answers they wanted to hear. But they were so hopeful that they did not let in those thoughts of getting their hearts shattered. Children from abandoned homes have many dreams as Beverly and Diana have had, which are like fantasies. For some reason, as a child, the bad thoughts about your mother do not always come to mind; you can't process that they don't want you. It's hard as a child to understand you are not wanted and loved or that your parents could just abandon you. Although, you have to be prepared for what the circumstances are when and if you reach the biological parent as to how you may feel.

It seemed like months, but it was not very long before Beverly and Diana got a startling letter. A letter they had never expected to receive. Marsha had located their mother in Louisiana. When the social worker from Louisiana called Arlene and expressed to her that there was a request from a Maryland agency on behalf of two young women now in their thirties, and would she know anything concerning them, there was a short pause, and Arlene replied she could not understand who that could possibly be. The social worker gave her the opportunity to think about the information and come down to the office if she would like to discuss it further.

After reading this reaction, Diana was hurt thinking, "Why would she deny us after all we had been through to find her?" Holding back tears, Diana wondered, "Does she have feelings at all? Were we bad little girls and that's why she did not want us?" She decided that after she gets her composure she will call Beverly to see if she has received a copy of the letter.

Beverly was already at her boiling point. She felt hurt and sad that they were just nobody to their mother. Beverly was still in wonderment as to how can you forget your two firstborn children or at least act like you don't have any memory of them. "Whatever happens, we have to remember this whole situation is not our fault. How could she reject us like this? It is so discouraging after so many years."

Diana called Beverly, wondering if she too got the letter and how she has reacted. As soon as Beverly came to the phone, they both broke down. Beverly suggested, "We'll make a trip to Louisiana, and then maybe she will know who we are if we face her."

Diana exclaimed, "We both better calm down and think reasonably as we have no idea what she may be thinking or what her situation might be."

Beverly got defensive and expressed that "We were the ones she left for days, with no food, a six-month-old baby and ourselves to survive alone in that shack."

"Now, Beverly, we have to get past that and give her some time. Maybe it is just such a shock. She never thought we cared enough to even try to find her."

"There you go again being all nice, Diana, and forgetting what she did to us."

"Beverly, she can't forget that easy." That was her mom too, and she had so much hatred built up in her all these years after what she did to them and no answers as to why. Beverly did not want to hate anyone, but she could not get the feeling of rejection from her own mother out of her mind. Diana, on the other hand, being older, always had the feeling of wanting the family back together, which really was a natural feeling. Even though things were not good, that still was the only family she remembered. Beverly felt like she needed to find out for her own sanity why her mother would walk away from three children and leave them *home alone.*

About two weeks went by, and they got a call from Marsha. Arlene had gone down to the social services to speak to Mrs. Hayes, who had given her the call. She explained that it had been a shock after thirty years to hear from her two daughters! Yes, it was her two firstborn, and she wondered how they found her. Mrs. Hayes explained that she received a letter from Bel Air, Maryland, from these two women looking for their biological mother and needed some information about her. Arlene began to explain that the reason she had hesitated was because she was ashamed to admit she had never told her husband of ten years that she had any children. She further explained that before she could go any further with this process, she would have to sit down with him and explain some things about her past that she really never wanted to reveal. Arlene, however, said that this just might be what would move her to reveal this deep dark secret. She would need the help of her sister Jenny to collect her thoughts and approach her husband with all this information. Mrs. Hayes said she understood her situation and she could get back with her when she was ready. Mrs. Hayes relayed the information to Marsha so that she could give Diana and Beverly an update on the situation with their mother's reaction.

Diana took the bull by the horns this time when Marsha called her, and right away she knew what she was going to do. She was not waiting for any letter. Beverly was okay with having her questions answered by Arlene in a letter form and mailed through the social services. Diana had no intention of waiting for a letter. Diana had longed for the time to meet her and see her, still thinking about getting the family back together. They put their heads together and knew Jenny's family still lived in Aberdeen; so they looked up the number, and Diana called her mother-in-law to get her phone number. She was quite surprised to hear from Diana as the story of these children being given away was a long-forgotten part of their life. Reluctantly she gave her the number, and Diana called and got Jenny on the phone. Her first reaction was she never thought she would hear from us. Jenny asked Diana tearfully if she would give her an hour or so to prepare Arlene. "You have to know this is a shock to us. It does not seem real."

Diana said, "Sure, take your time and call me back when she feels comfortable to talk."

Diana heard the phone, and with much anticipation she ran to the phone, picked it up, and heard this squeaky little voice say "Hello, this is your mother." Diana let out the breath she was holding, and said hello. There was a short silence and then through the tears Diana began to talk. Diana had thought she would have so much to say, but she could not find the words. She wanted to ask her so much, but now was not the time; so she just asked about her family, told her about hers, and they exchanged how nice it was to hear from each other. Arlene asked Diana how far was it to her house and she said it was not far. She said Jenny and Arlene would like to ride down in a week "and visit you and meet your family." Diana began to get excited.

"Really! *Oh!* That would be wonderful! We have plenty of room, and you will love the beach." Diana thought, "Now we can catch up on so many years of our childhood that our mother can share with us."

Diana hung up the phone, feeling like she was in a dream world. Was she finally after all these years talking to her mother? Never did she think that day would come. Diana felt numb. "Vito, will you pinch me to see if this is a dream?" Diana knew she should call Beverly to let her know that she talked to her. She wondered what her reaction would be.

Beverly was happy for Diana as she knew this was what Diana wanted so much in her life. But she still had to warn her once again that she needed to tread lightly as "you don't know how things will go once you meet. She may not be as receptive as you expect. People change a lot over the years and you may not recognize her. Diana, you have to be ready for anything that might come up that may throw off your expectations." Beverly told Diana, "I am here for you and always will be and will back you up. My only fear is to see you get hurt any further than you have been over the years. We are opening a big can of worms, so to speak. Now we better be ready to deal with them. The best part is we have each other. We both need closure from being abandoned and left *home alone*. Maybe Arlene will be able to fill in some of those gaps of times and places we can't quite put together." Beverly and Diana would love to be able to have some baby pictures. "Wouldn't it be great if she had some picture for us? This is the time we have waited for. Now it has come, it is hard to believe. We may learn about our real family!"

It was a beautiful fall sunny day in the Panhandle in Mexico Beach, Florida, about 72 degrees. Mexico Beach is a quiet little town of about thousand two hundred people with no traffic light and reminds you of Mayberry. It was going to be a special day for Mexico Beach even though the beachgoers had no idea what was happening in their little town. Diana had made her special chocolate cake, and Vito had gone to the fish market to get some grouper so they could stuff it and marinade it with his secret recipe. Lynne and Eddie were excited to meet the grandmother they never knew but had heard their mother cry over many a time. They too needed to see what this was all about, what could make their mother hurt the way she did at times and yet she had such a drive in her to meet her mother.

Diana kept checking out the window to see if she was coming. She did not know what she was driving, so she really did not know what to look for but just a different car down their street. Diana was wearing out the carpet from the door to the window. Then she saw a long sleek car turn the corner; she ran out the door to get a better look. It looked almost new and had beautiful shiny wired wheels and was as tan as the sand on the beach. Could that be her? As she rolled closer very slowly and as they looked like they were looking for someone, Diana could barely contain herself. "That must be her!" She stepped back by the door so they could pull in the driveway, which was right in front of the most beautiful blooming pink rain tree that soared above the top of the stilt home. The door opened, and this tiny woman stepped out, Diana first noticed her designer shoes in powder blue, then a white tiny poodle with a pink bow and painted nails named Pierre! Arlene seemed to make such a fuss over her dog. Diana wondered how she thought about her children. As Diana approached her, she saw that Arlene had a lovely blue matching outfit; on one hand her eye caught in the glistening sunlight what she thought to be a three-carat diamond ring and a cigarette hanging from her mouth. Diana felt her insides drop. Of course a hug was in order, but it felt distant. Jenny, Arlene's sister, came over and gave her a very big welcome! All the emotions that Diana had been holding inside just began to flow. She cried, and she wanted her mother to hold her and tell her it was all right. It was unbelievable that she was here. However, all the old feelings began to raise their ugly head, feelings of anger, resentment, and bitterness. Diana's frame of mind of low self-esteem began to creep back up.

The dinner was very tasty, and Arlene was impressed with Vito's grouper dish. He was so proud his chest got all puffed up, and the kids were teasing him. So everyone went to the living room for a chat while Jenny stayed in the kitchen with Diana to help with the dishes. Jenny began the conversation by telling Diana that Arlene was very nervous about this visit and wanted to let Diana know to be careful with what she said to her, as she had been through a lot. Diana paused for a moment to think about that and wondered just what that meant. Jenny went on to tell her, "She has had hard life, she is not well, and I stay with her a lot to give her the support that she needs." Jenny said to Diana that she was sure she had a lot of questions for her, but she was not sure if she was going to be able to give Diana what she needed. Diana felt disappointed, but this whole thing was awkward. And although she was filled with excitement and joy to see her mother, she also wanted some answers as to what happened so many years ago.

It was time for the coffee and chocolate cake. Eddie could not wait another minute. Lynne helped her mom cut the cake and serve it. Lynne got her chance to tell her mom that Arlene seemed a little apprehensive about talking about herself. "She just keeps asking about us and Daddy and you, Mommy."

Diana told her, "You have to understand this is the first time she has seen me in thirty years. It was a shock first of all, and there are a lot of mixed feelings that have to be worked out. It will take time to build a relationship with her, and that is if we both agree to make this work."

Diana told Jenny, "This will be a long journey. Wondering where your sister, brother, mother, and father are and what happened to them all these years has left quite a gap in my life. This is just a start to fill it."

After the cake, the kids and Vito left the girls alone to talk. You could feel the tension in the air. Diana had to ask some questions about her life. The first thing was to ask about James, the brother that lived with her sister Katie. She seemed okay with that question. Arlene said she would call Katie and explain that she had met Diana and would like to introduce her to her brother. They decided it wasn't too late to do that right now as James lived next door to Katie. Arlene called Katie and talked to her for a few minutes to explain and then gave the phone to Diana. She was pleasant but short with her and said she recalled her as a young girl. "Let me get James for you, and you two can talk."

James was a quiet, mild-tempered young man; he got on the phone and began to talk about his military career and said that he was single and lived in a cabin he had built. He was friendly but not overjoyed to hear from her. After the call, they went back to their conversation and talked about how Arlene ended up in Louisiana and Jenny followed her there.

Arlene had very little information to offer other than the present ten years with her husband. When Diana tried to ask a question about the past, she seemed to hesitate; a foggy look came over her face, and she said she didn't remember. Diana was getting the picture after hearing that a few times. Either she had blocked out the past, or she did not want to share it because it was too painful. Diana could see in her eyes there was a lot there, but she could not get her to open up. Maybe that was enough for one day. Diana suggested they get a good night's sleep and hit the beach in the morning or go shopping. Arlene spoke up, "Whatever we do, I must go to the meat market and get a fresh steak for Pierre!"

Diana said, "That will be no problem," thinking, "This dog eats steak!" She added, "Good night! See you in the morning, Arlene. I am so glad you and Jenny are here finally. We have waited a long time to see you once again."

After breakfast, the girls hopped in the fancy new car, and Arlene threw the keys to Diana and said, "You drive. You know your way around here."

Diana asked, "Where do you want to go?"

Jenny spoke up, "Well, let's ride around and see the area, and if there are any garage sales, we will stop."

Arlene, in her little squeaky voice, said, "But don't forget the steak!"

Diana thought, "She remembers that for sure." Things were still very tense; you could just feel it in the air. Lynne went along to give Diana the support she needed also. Diana had all these thoughts, questions, feelings, and needs going through her mind, and she could not express them to her mother. But was this her mother really, or a stranger she was really just getting to know? Diana had to hold it together and all those feeling that wanted to come bursting out because now was not the time. Diana could see this was going to be a slow process with Arlene. Her mind drifted back to what Jenny had said about her having a hard life and that she would have to be careful how she approached her with questions. It still puzzled Diana as to why Arlene would have a hard time talking about their family. Diana had to put it out of her mind for the day so she could enjoy the visit and make the best of what she had for now.

The rest of the time Arlene and Jenny spent there was very quiet and enjoyable, but you could still feel the strain between them. It was a chilly morning, and of course, Pierre had a little red sweater with a matching hood. One thing was for sure—Arlene took a lot of pride in her dog. Everyone came out to wave good-bye as they got in the car for the ride home to Louisiana. Arlene and Diana seemed to hold on to each other nervously, almost like they might not see each other again. Diana told her that she would come up there to meet her husband sometime after the first of the year.

Vito put his arm around Diana as he saw the tears start to roll down her cheeks. He wondered, "Are they happy tears, or did she get the answers she wanted?" Diana had built up so much for this visit; in fact, it had been years in the making. All the times she wondered, "Where was she? What does she look like? Why did she do this to us?" and the many more times of feeling being unwanted had all just manifested themselves in one day. Diana felt like she did not get any of her questions answered. Why not? Diana knew it would be hard for her to talk about her life back when they were children, but couldn't Arlene imagine how much it would mean to Diana to know about her past with her biological family and what it was like? She knew it was probably going to take more than one visit to get some answers about what it was like and what she has been doing all these years.

Beverly called Diana to see how her visit went with her mother. Beverly always called her that to Diana. Diana said it was distant. Beverly started firing questions as she always did. Diana said, "Slow down. It was not like that at all. She was not able to tell me anything about the past."

Beverly came back a little harshly and asked, "Well, why not? Can't she talk?"

Diana quickly came right back at her with "Yes, she can, but she does not remember." Beverly really wasn't buying that for an answer.

"You mean she was there for three days, and you got nothing out of her?"

"No, Beverly, it was not an interrogation." Diana was quick to let Beverly know that it hurt her deeply that she could not seem to be more loving and happy to see her. Beverly thought to herself, "That's why I just want my questions answered and learn about why she did this to us on a piece of paper."

CHAPTER 3

A few weeks passed, and a letter came from Marsha; it always was nice to hear from her. Enclosed was an 8½ × 11 lined sheet of school paper numbered 1 through 10. This was from Arlene in answer to the questions Beverly had written to her to be answered for her, including health questions. Needless to say, she was shocked by the content of the letter, and it was not what she was expecting. Beverly was hurt. First of all here was an opportunity for Arlene to at least write something to her daughter after thirty years. "Hello, Beverly, I am sorry how things turned out. How is your family?" Anything at all! Here was another letdown. Again Beverly felt "she didn't care about me just like she didn't when she left me so many years ago. What did I do that was so bad?" The feelings of abandonment were welling up inside. She just wanted Arlene to care. Her adoptive mother had told her she was no good and that she was a drunk, and "Beverly, you are making a mistake to try to find her." Beverly's feelings were as close to hatred for her as could be, and that is why she did not want to meet her as Diana did. Also she was struggling with her mother's feeling. Beverly tried not to let her attitude toward Arlene show to Diana, but she knew. Beverly read what she wrote; it did not answer her questions, so downhearted, she put it in the file, and it is still there today.

Beverly had to move forward from these feeling of rejection that she felt from her mother not giving her any kind of explanation for what happened when she left them. There was a lot more to think about because they were planning a camping trip with a lot of their friends, especially her friend Janet. Diana and her family were going to join them at a campground in northern Florida near a beautiful lake that was surrounded by cabins. They would be sitting around the campfire at night talking for hours. Now the girls had a lot to talk about while the guys were doing their thing, so to speak.

Just in time for the camping trip, the divorce papers of Arlene and Willy had arrived. Beverly was so excited to open the big manila envelope because it was so thick. When she pulled out the copy, there it was all official stamped and dated August 16, 1956. So she sat down and began to read. It was written like question and answer. The judge would ask Arlene a question, and then she would answer. She stated her name and where she lived and worked then answered some questions about her husband. But then there it was right on the second page; the question came up: "Do you have any children from this marriage?" The hardest words to read came next like hitting a brick wall. The tears began to flow so hard Beverly could barely see the paper. "Do you want to keep any children from this marriage?" It was the first time Beverly saw Beverly Ann and Diana Lynn associated with their mother. Then it went on to say that she gave them up for adoption. That hurt so bad, she will never forget that moment, the pain—it all came crashing down on her. She felt as though she was being thrown away again, discarded like a piece of trash. Beverly knew why she never felt loved by her mother; now she saw it with her own eyes.

After getting herself back together, she continued to read on and could start to put some pieces together, and names of relatives that she had forgotten were in the paperwork. That would be helpful for Diana and her for their research in finding some of their relatives to find out what happened to them. Also, they should have some cousins and maybe somebody will have pictures.

They got the travel trailer all set for the weekend and made a lot of food. Janet and Beverly were the food-makers: big salads, macaroni salad, chocolate chip cookies, brownies, hotdogs, hamburgers, steaks, and not to forget the s'mores. Everybody was anxious to meet Beverly's sister. When they got there, Beverly wanted to surprise her with the divorce papers, so she put a car out by the road with a sign on the windshield Divorce Papers Are Here! The copy was lying right under the sign. Diana could not wait till they got in the campground; she made Vito stop so she could grab the papers and then come in. Needless to say, Beverly had to go through the whole shock again with Diana. But they went off in a quiet area to read it, and everyone understood. They both had a good cry and decided they would put this on the back burner for this weekend so that they could enjoy their friends. They hugged and were happy to have each other because even that was a giant step in itself to have two sisters together after thirty years.

Diana was a little quiet, but of course, next to Beverly anybody is quiet. She got along great with everybody and really enjoyed making new friends. Eddie and Lynne had a great time on the motorbikes and fit right in with all the different age kids that were there. Every time Diana and Beverly would see each other, they just could not get enough of each other. There was so much they had missed, how could they make it all up? It was hard to know where to start.

Beverly was not real sure of Diana's personality as she was a little quiet, and Beverly just loved to be the life of the party. So it was a challenge for Beverly and Diana to get to know each other not just as friends but on a deeper level. That was going to take time. Beverly began to think it was going to take a long time to develop that closeness that sisters had for each other. But she was impatient, and she wanted it now. Beverly could see she would have to wait.

The time together went great, and Beverly and Diana were already making plans to get together again soon. It seemed like they were on the phone cooking up something all the time. But now they had more information to work with, and that meant they could play detective. In fact they both had come up with a lot of names that they did not know before they got the divorce papers, which enabled them to get phone numbers. Also the date when their parents were married and for how long they were married was made clear. This also helped Beverly and Diana to begin to fill in the blanks of parts of their life that they had wondered about for so long. Remembering things but not being sure if that really happened can really play crazy things with your mind. Beverly was always living in a dream world as she remembered being in other places, and her adoptive mother would tell her, "No, we would never live there." It was very confusing to her. Whereas, Diana's adoptive parents shared with her all about her adoption. Beverly's parents thought they were doing the right thing at the time by not telling her she was adopted. But deep down Beverly knew.

Diana called and said she was coming down for a visit. Beverly was so excited because she was ready to make some phone calls. The first call they were going to make was going to be to their father's elder brother Benjamin. They remembered living at his farmhouse but they had not remembered his name until they saw it on the divorce papers. They were hoping he would have some pictures of them playing at the farm. So Diana was driving down for the weekend, and the phone lines were going to be red hot!

Beverly lived in the older section of St. Petersburg, so it was quite a drive for Diana to come so far from the Panhandle. But there was no stopping these girls. Once they got a little information, it was like they were bursting with excitement to call one of the names on those divorce papers. So that is what they did. The first name was Benjamin Clark, who lived in Street Maryland. Now Beverly remembered her father's brother and that he had a farm. "We used to go to and play on his porch. We wondered if he still lived there after all these years." Street Maryland is a very small town as Beverly remembers. "So let's call the operator and see if they have a number for him."

As they were dialing, Beverly and Diana could feel a lump in their throat come up. Ring! Ring! Ring! And then an older man said, "Hello."

Beverly said, "Hello." Beverly started by saying, "Do you know Willy and Arlene Clark?"

He said, "Yes, Willy is my brother."

Beverly then said, "And they had four children together."

There was a silence, and then she could hear a sniffle as if he had started to cry.

Benjamin then said, "Which one is this, Beverly or Diana?" Beverly almost dropped the phone. Diana was listening in; they started squealing and jumping up and down. "This is their Uncle Ben."

He said, "I never thought I would hear from you girls again." Beverly could tell the tears were rolling down his face. He began to tell them how much their father loved them. He did admit that he did drink, but he said he used to take them places and always brought them to the farm. The girls asked if he had pictures, and he said yes. So they talked a while about their father and then told him, "We would get back to make arrangements to get together somehow." As time went by, Beverly and Diana thought many times about their Uncle Ben, but their journey was so full of activities it seemed they would never get back to him. Unfortunately, he passed away the next year, so they did not speak again. But little did they know that their journey with Uncle Ben's family would not end there.

Diana and Beverly kept on the trail of everyone they could remember in the little town where they came from by trying to call where they may have worked. Beverly had lived there until she was sixteen, so she remembered relatives working at the diner, A & P store, Green Derby, and the Bata Shoe Company. That was just to name a few. Diana and Beverly would call and ask if they knew Arlene or if they knew her sisters. Sometimes they remembered them! The girls would get so excited; it was like going back in a time capsule. Just to know they were there, they were related and part of that family. Even though they had good families, there was just a piece missing. It is hard to put into words. You wonder what things would have been like. Have you missed something and it became like a fairy tale or a dream? Just to hear someone's voice from the past or their name can bring excitement which sounds so simple but can mean so much. It is so childlike. Thoughts of your childhood you have carried with you and wondered about for so many years and then you feel as though you may get some answers. You still feel cautious because you may get hurt, but you don't want to stop because the answers are more important at this time in your life. Beverly and Diana decided this was their time to make this journey.

After spending days on the phone and going over names and trying to put together from the divorce papers what they thought took place when their parents split up after ten years of marriage they thought they had all the answers. As the years went by, they found out how wrong they were.

Diana had to go back to the Panhandle to work and Beverly was sad to see her go. She was planning another trip to see Arlene, and Beverly told her to have a good time on her visit. Diana did not express anything at the time, but Beverly could since she wished they were together with their feelings about Arlene. Beverly understood Diana. She was the first child, and she had tried so very had to keep the family together. While Beverly unfortunately just remembered the bad things about her as a four-year-old. As Beverly grew up in the same small town, she saw her, and kids at school said things about her mother, so she did not have a nice picture of her mother. Diana was trying to be understanding and so was Beverly, but again there seemed to be a wedge that began to come between them. Diana was going her way that would involve Arlene, and Beverly by her own choice was pulling away because of her feelings about Arlene. Beverly really could not explain to Diana how she felt, and that was why they were not drawing closer as sisters at this time.

Diana had been back home and to work at the hospital sharing with her friends about her visit with Beverly. There was so much to tell about the camping trip and how well the kids got along and all the wonderful talks they had, staying up all night like teenagers. Everything seemed to be falling into place, and Diana was excited with the success they had made so far in finding out about some of the relatives. She was happy that she got to spend some much-needed time with her mother after all these years. It was hard to express her feelings to others. It was something Diana just couldn't talk to everyone about. Diana was still processing all of it herself. She had mixed feelings at times exactly how she felt, but as time went on and she got to see her more, she knew that bond will grow.

Arlene had a birthday coming up in March now in 1983, and she was going to visit Diana at her house for a nice party and dinner. Diana was very thrilled that they were going to cook together. That was something Diana loved to do, and she found that they had that in common. Arlene also liked to start sourdough bread. There was so much to learn, but they had plenty of time to get to know each other as Arlene seemed willing to drive to the beach often to see Diana. She also liked peppers, and she canned some and brought some extra to send to Beverly. They had a lovely time. Eddie even got in the act and took Arlene fishing. They caught some fish and brought them back and cooked them up that night for dinner. It seemed like Arlene was game for pretty much anything. Again Diana was busy in the kitchen, and they cooked up the fish like mother and daughter, and Diana could feel some affection from her but not over done as one might understand as this was all so new.

Looking from afar was Lynne watching and not too happy with the situation. She had seen her mom struggle with her feelings for many years. Lynne was very cautious with what she saw going on. She was not going to let anyone hurt her mom. Lynne was a sensitive but strong child and knew her mom's feelings, so she was very protective of her. Maybe she came across as little standoffish, but she had her guard up for her mom. All in all, the visit went off like a family visit should; everyone hugged, even Lynne, and then Arlene left after a few days.

As time went by, Diana was getting more anxious each time for another visit with her mother. Although she did not seem to be able to get her to talk much about the past, she kept trying to ask her what life was like for her as a child. Arlene would always give the same answer that she could not remember; everything was foggy. It was so hard for Diana to hear that because she had such a desire to not only bond with her mother but get to know about her life. It seemed to be such a secret. The only thing she would talk about was her brother James that her sister Katie took at about one and half years old. Diana remembered that time because she heard the family talk about him being very sick with asthma, and he needed to live in a different climate. Although when the subject came up, Arlene seemed to get quite unhappy about James being with her sister. She let Diana know that it was an ongoing battle with Katie, and she let Katie know that she was James's mother every chance she got. That had to be hard on Katie as she had raised him as her own all those years and put him through college. That was the only family secret that she would tell Diana about, and she was not interested in what went on in the family. If only she would just let

Diana know about her childhood and told her about their father. Diana wanted to know about what she did as a child, what their grandmothers and grandfathers were like, but Arlene just had no information about anything in the past, just about the present. Diana called Beverly and reported to her with much sadness that "we may never know where we came from if we depend on our mother."

A few months went by. Diana and Beverly spoke on their phone regularly. However, both had jobs, and it was hard to get a real sister relationship five hours apart started. But they still were eager to keep in touch; the bond was there, not ever to be broken. Both were interested to see if Diana was going to be able to build a relationship and get closer to Arlene. As they spoke on the phone, Beverly noticed that Diana called her "Arlene." She asked her if she called her "mother" when she spoke to her. She hesitated and then said no. Beverly asked her why. She said she did not know why. Beverly found that to be odd because she was the one that was most sensitive throughout the abandonment, knew the most, wanted to get the family back together the most, and asked about her mother more than anyone. But when years later she was able to meet with her she did not call her "mother." Beverly did not want to question or press the issue too much but could understand that Arlene just did not give her that warm fuzzy feeling when they met. She had a mother as Beverly did also that brought her up and gave them both a wonderful life, and out of respect it just did not feel right.

It would be easy to say that every time Arlene called, Diana hoped that this time she would have something more to tell her. So each time she got her hopes up when the phone rang and it was Arlene. Arlene called to say she had some great news for her. Diana was all ears. "What is it?" James was getting married in Maryland, and Arlene was invited to the wedding. Obviously that was big news in of itself because of all the problems between the sisters Katie and Arlene. Arlene asked Diana if she would like to attend and meet her brother. Diana said sure she would "but you better make sure it is all right with the family." Diana was all excited; not only would she meet her brother but see him get married for the first time. What an exciting time. Maybe things were starting to look up. Diana clarified with Arlene, "You make sure you have permission before we go any further and call me back."

Diana could hardly go to work without telling everyone about the good news. She was so excited she was bursting with happiness. This was the starting of more happy times since she met Arlene. About a week went by, and Diana got a phone call from Arlene. Arlene in her little squeaky voice said to Diana, "James doesn't want you to come to the wedding."

Diana said with tears starting to well up in her big brown eyes that she understood. "He has never even met me, and the wedding is a big event to meet your sister for the first time in thirty-five years." Arlene told her she was sorry, but it was part of this ongoing problem with her sister Katie that probably would never be resolved. Diana hung up and could only feel she was letdown again. How many more times could she take it? She tried so hard to make this work with Arlene, but every turn seemed to have a road block. Diana felt she must go forward to satisfy her heart and feelings about her family that were never fulfilled as a young child. Diana remembered asking over and over about getting her family back together. Was she still thirty-five years later trying to bring them together?

Months went by, and Diana thought things had calmed down, and she got a call from Arlene. She would prefer to come to visit her in Mexico Beach as she liked the shopping and wanted to see Eddie and Lynne. Diana said, "Sure, can you come for a week?" Arlene said that would be great. She wanted to do some cooking with Diana and bring some canning that she had prepared down to her family. Diana knew there was something in her little voice that sounded different.

Arlene began with "I want to tell you something, and please don't be upset with me."

Diana came right back at her with "The only thing you could tell me that would hurt me is that you had more children and gave them away too." There was not a word spoken.

Slowly in her squeaky voice, Arlene said yes, she did have more children. "Diana, are you there, and can you forgive me?"

Diana said, "Maybe when you come down in a week you could explain. See you soon."

Arlene came for her visit, and Diana was quite on edge. How could this be? She had given it a lot of thought, and she was trying to get close to this person and have some kind of relationship. Yet she seemed to be pushing her away. They talked about James's wedding and how nice it turned out. Things again seemed strained, but they cooked and shopped and finally Diana had to ask about the other children. Arlene said she had met a soldier and had a son with him, lived overseas for a while, and he kept the boy. Then she met a doctor and had a one-night stand, had another son, and the doctor kept him. It probably was hard for Arlene to be honest to reveal her past like that, but she felt she needed to share that with Diana. Diana felt she did not need to hear anymore but felt like she was leaving more out.

Arlene finished her stay as usual with more shopping and cooking, enjoying Eddie and Lynne, and leaving Diana with more questions than answers. Diana was still hoping that the more time she spent with her the more she would open up and talk about her life not only when they were a family but also what happened after she had her other families. One thing was for sure—the questions like: Where did I come from? Who do I look like? Why did they give me away? (It seems that all adopted children have them, and they want the answers too.) "The one person, my own mother, who should be able to finally give me the answers to my questions has been found, but will she give me the answers?" Diana wondered.

Diana had a lot to think about after her last visits with Arlene. If she were to go back and ask herself if this was what she expected, the answer would be definitely no. Diana had hoped for more feelings to be shown, some kind of mother–daughter attachment to have begun to grow. Maybe that was too much to ask for this early in the relationship, but a lot of time had passed and she had friends she had more of a connection with; she developed friendships in a shorter time. You think all your life if you just get the opportunity to find your mother, you know how it will be. You will ask all these questions, and she will have all these answers to your questions. All the hurt you felt for years can begin to heal because she will make it feel better. You will learn why you were put in a foster home, and maybe it was for a good reason. Your mother will be able to make it all better because she is your mother, and they nurture their children. But what happened when Diana did not get those answers and it began to confuse her thinking and feelings? Maybe things weren't turning out like she thought they would. She recalled Beverly had warned her about letting Arlene hurt her or take advantage of her kindness. Diana could not take any more heartache. But the questions about family were just constantly on her mind, and it was like a battle she was fighting. Sometimes Diana sat at her desk at work and felt like she was not really there. Diana acknowledged she must ask for help. She could not handle these feelings alone. Her therapy session began here.

Diana was making progress with the doctor, and she did not see Arlene except talked to her on the phone very briefly in almost a year. She was using medication, but she did not like the way the medication made her feel. But for right now the doctor felt she needed the medication. Diana had many sessions with the doctor to try and evaluate how an adoptee should put in perspective finding their biological family after so many years. After much counseling, Diana began to feel somewhat better, but still had those lingering questions haunting her, feeling powerless as her mother, damaged from a hard life, could not answer.

Arlene had been married to Ralph for ten very happy years, and early one morning she called Diana to tell her he had passed away. Arlene was heartbroken as she loved and cared for him so very much. Her sister Jenny was there with her, helping her to make funeral arrangement. Arlene wanted Diana to come up to Baton Rouge for the funeral and spend a week with her. Diana said she would and made the arrangements with Arlene to make plans for time to spend a week to help her out.

Diana made the trip to Baton Rouge for the funeral. Ralph had a lot of friends that attended, which made Arlene feel good. They had a dinner at Arlene's and Ralph's home where Arlene had prepared all kinds of homemade dishes. Things calmed down within a few days; however, there was a lot of paperwork to be done as far as death certificate and other documents. Diana said she was familiar with all that, so she would handle the insurance for Arlene and any other paperwork she needed to fill out. Arlene was in the dark so to speak because Ralph had taken care of all the household business. Therefore, Diana had quite a lot to show Arlene as far as paying bills, insurance, taking care of the car and notifying those needed with the death certificates. Arlene felt overwhelmed. There was so much to do that Diana's visit kept getting extended. In the meantime, Arlene kept complaining that she wasn't feeling well. Diana thought it was from all that had taken place, and she needed to rest. Jenny would be there when she left, so she felt it was time to let Arlene have her grieving period and her rest.

The next morning, Diana got up and began to pack her car, and Jenny came running out to the car with a look of panic on her face. Jenny told Diana she went in to check on Arlene and thought she had a stroke. They called 911, and within five minutes they were there to pick her up and take her to the hospital that Ralph had just died in not two weeks ago. Diana followed in the car with Jenny. As they rode in the car and talked, Diana said this has all been too much on Arlene. She is so small and fragile. It was hard on her to lose her partner of ten years so abruptly when he was ten years younger and had not even been sick. Sure enough, after the doctors examined her, she had a stroke. It was a mild one but she would need therapy as it had affected her speech. Diana stayed on to help because Arlene was being stubborn about doing her therapy and just wanted to get home. It took Diana and Jenny both to get her to go to her therapy. After they brought her home, things began to change. Arlene's speech was so bad she was almost not being understood. But Diana was still having a time with her not getting her to therapy.

After a few days at home Arlene had Diana take Pierre down to the boutique to be groomed and have his nails done. She told Diana to take him and go to the market and get some steaks because they were out for Pierre. As Diana was riding in the car she began to think here she was taking time off from work, helping her mother she hadn't seen in thirty-eight years, who treated her dog Pierre with more affection than she did her own daughter. That really hurt. Diana felt like she cared more for her dog and her drinking than the first child she brought into this world. She couldn't understand how a mother could feel that way about her children. Diana felt like someone punched her in the stomach; all she wanted was her mother to give her love and attention that she never had from her.

Things got worse with Arlene's drinking. Diana had noticed before that she would take a drink with Ralph when he was alive, but now she would drink starting in the morning and last all day. Diana was getting very concerned about the amount of alcohol she was consuming and suggested to Arlene that maybe she should get some help with her alcohol problem. Arlene spoke right angrily to Diana and told her to mind her own damn business as she did not have any drinking problem! Diana was shocked that she would speak to her that way and spoke no more about it to her. Obviously she was an alcoholic and not willing to admit it.

Diana decided to take Arlene to Mexico Beach with her to finish her recovery there to get back to her family. So along came Arlene and Pierre to Diana's so she could try and get her some speech therapy there. Again she refused any help at all. Diana found her very stubborn and between the ways she treated the dog, talked to her about the drinking, and would not go for therapy Diana was close to another breakdown. She returned to therapy once again and explained the obstacles that had come up with Arlene. The doctor gave her some very good advice when he told her, "Diana, you need to put all these things including Arlene in a box, put them on the shelf, and leave them there." He explained emphatically, "You don't want to hear this, but you must back away. You have to get healthy, or you are no good to yourself or your family."

Diana came back from the doctor knowing that she had some decisions to make, and they were tough ones. She had wanted things to work out so badly with Arlene, and she tried with all she had to make some kind of relationship with her. But no matter what she did, it just did not seem to work out. The doctor was right; she had started having the panic attacks again as before, and her health was important for her family's well-being. That night she cooked dinner without Arlene helping as usual as she had been drinking most of the day and was not capable of doing anything. Diana hated for her children to be around the alcohol because they did not have that in their family life, and she was very sensitive to it because she remembered it as a small child. Diana remembered the times Willy and Arlene were drunk and were fighting, leaving Beverly, Joseph, and her *home alone*. It all came back when she would drink to excess, and Diana did not want to be around it or be reminded of those unhappy days. This was supposed to be different.

Diana woke up in the morning and began to make breakfast for the family, and Arlene had not gotten up yet. She figured that she probably had a bad night after all the drinking she had done. Little did Diana know that during the night Arlene went to Diana's phone book and looked up Beverly's phone number, which Diana had promised not to share with her. Diana respected Beverly's wishes. Without Diana's knowledge, she called Beverly in the middle of the night. Beverly later told Diana how she was very drunk on the phone and said to Beverly, "This is your mother."

Beverly said back to her, "No, you are not my mother. She told Beverly she wanted to be a grandmother to Beverly's two boys. Beverly told her that was not possible and not to ever call again. That was the one and only time Beverly ever spoke with Arlene.

After Arlene got up, Diana explained to her that she was not feeling well herself and needed some time to sort things out. Arlene said she understood and asked if Diana could she take her back to Baton Rouge. Diana was willing and told her to get some things together, and they would leave in the morning. Arlene was happy with that because it would give them time to get some steak for Pierre. Once again the dog got more attention from Arlene, and she had no idea how upset she had made Diana. Arlene didn't seem to understand what Diana was going through, putting her emotions out there to find her, not knowing what she would find or how she would be received. Diana was trying to keep it together as she never expected her mother to have such little feeling for her after all these years.

Diana did not hear from Arlene for several months after she took her to her home to Baton Rouge. It was a good break for her as she could start to work on putting things back in the box and on the shelf. However, her visits to the therapist became more frequent. Diana was trying to create the bond that was broken, and Arlene just was not showing that same compassion that Diana had. The relationship with Arlene was like watering last year's flowers, and it made Diana feel more distanced rather than close to her mother. Work was helping get things back to normal. Diana felt that it was time to make a trip to see Beverly, so she called and they made plans for the next weekend.

It was a bright sunny day as Diana drove down Route 19, singing along with the radio as she approached New Port Richey. She met Beverly at the auto dealership that she managed; there always was a lot going on where they were busy selling cars. Beverly had to direct the salespeople, and Diana was excited to see her little sister in action, running those salespeople around getting those automobiles ready for customers to take delivery of their new vehicles. Diana arrived late as Beverly was usually late working her car deals because customers came in late. So they would go to dinner after she closed up the dealership.

Sometimes they did not get a lot of time together, but they both cherished every minute they shared. They were still learning about each other, and that was still difficult. Beverly really spoke her mind, and Diana seemed to step back and observe before she spoke. But things went well after not seeing each other for over thirty-eight years now. They went to a restaurant for a bite to eat before they went to Beverly's for the night. They both ordered a few appetizers. Diana ordered her iced tea with lemon, and Beverly ordered a mixed drink. They sat and talked about her visit with Arlene and how things had been going with her and her drinking. Diana brought her up to date about Ralph passing and Arlene having a stroke. Diana excused herself and went to the restroom when the drinks came. Beverly did not think too much of it at first until the time seemed to go on and on. Beverly thought of checking on Diana as she had been gone for some time. She found Diana in the restroom sobbing. Beverly asked her, "What is wrong? Did she say something to upset you?"

Diana had to get her composure first. Through her tears she explained to Beverly that she just could not bear to see her drinking.

Diana had just been through weeks of Arlene being drunk all the time. Beverly assured Diana that she doesn't have an alcohol problem and she doesn't ever get drunk, "so you don't have to worry about me having a problem." Beverly was extremely sorry as she did not know how much her having a drink affected Diana. Actually the evening was ruined; they left and made their way to Beverly's condo.

The rest of the evening was very strained between them. Beverly spoke up and asked Diana just what it was about her having a drink that caused her that much pain. Diana told her that she remembered the drinking when they were children, a vision embedded in her mind, and now she was watching Arlene drunk and arrogantly saying she has no problem. The thought of losing Beverly to that horrible disease made her sick. Beverly put her arm around Diana and reassured her that she only drank socially and was not going to turn out like her mother and father as she remembered them drunk and fighting. Diana felt better, although she was not quite sure that she trusted Beverly as many of the times she had visited she always seemed to enjoy her drinks. Diana wanted this relationship to work with Beverly and not feel disconnected like she did with Arlene.

The next day, they went shopping, and it was so much fun to see how many times they would pick the same colors. Diana giggled when they picked up the same lipstick. Beverly got all the products to color Diana's hair, and they also bought out the Lancôme counter of makeup. They had lunch and were ready to go home and beautify. Later on in the evening they put on their jammies, made some popcorn, and watched movies just as if we were two sisters growing up in a happy home.

It had been a happy visit but a stressful visit at the same time said Diana as she sat with her therapist and answered the questions he asked about how she was doing. She had been through a lot with Arlene's drinking, arguing with her, and not being able to get any closer to her than she was before. Then she related the experience that she had at Beverly's. Diana took Beverly's drinking as her responsibility, and of course, the doctor told her to let that go. Diana had the uncanny way of still trying to mother everyone as she did in the early days when they were left *home alone*. She was the eldest and was left with much more responsibility than any small child of seven should be. The doctor reminded her to separate herself from things and people that made her feel sick. "You don't need to deal with them, so put them in the box on the shelf and deal with them later."

A few months had passed, and Diana got a disturbing call from Arlene that Jenny had passed away. Jenny and Arlene were very close. In fact, wherever one moved, the other followed. She was quite distraught over her loss and did not know what to do. Arlene did not have many friends in Baton Rouge, and she really did not feel comfortable there without Jenny and Ralph too. Diana asked her what she could do to help. Arlene told Diana she really felt like she would rather be close to James as he is her son. Even though Katie didn't like her to be around, she wanted to be near him.

Soon after Arlene sold her house, she asked Jenny's son to come down from Maryland and pick her up and move her back to Aberdeen. She moved to the projects on Swan Street. It wasn't long after she met up with one of her old drinking buddies, Benny. He moved right in as Arlene had the money to pay for the alcohol, and he could live off her inheritance. Just as the statistics prove, he got a DUI and lost his license, so they had a hard time getting around and getting their alcohol. Soon she was going to need Diana again to help her get around. Diana had no idea she was drinking to the extent that she and Benny had been consuming alcohol. This became the beginning of the end of her relationship as she knew it with Arlene. Diana had tried with all her heart to try to be a daughter, and instead, she felt like her world with Arlene was crumbling.

Diana had asked Arlene, when she was sober, would she have her up to meet James and Katie. Arlene finally was sober enough to make the arrangements and called Diana. Diana was excited as she felt if she got to talk more to James and Katie, maybe they would have pictures of them as children. James picked her up at the airport, and they had a great time laughing and just getting along fine. They had a wonderful lunch at a little crab shack that James knew about. When they walked in, the smell of crab and old bay seasonings brought back those childhood memories of the seashore. James had built his own log cabin. It was something to see. He had done all the work by hand, and the craftsmanship was wonderful. James was very talented. They had dinner with Katie and the rest of the family, where Diana was able to ask if there were any pictures. Katie was quite reluctant to share any pictures or answer any family questions with Diana. James was not interested in the subject and left the room. The more inquisitive Diana got, the more Katie pulled away. She accused Diana of digging up bad memories. That was not at all what Diana's intentions were. All she wanted was to satisfy her need to see what their childhood was like, what they looked like, something that their mother, who had used alcohol for so many years, was not able to share with them.

Finally, Katie brought out a big box of pictures. Diana was beaming. She knew part of her life was in that box. Katie began to pull out and identify some of the photos, saying, "This was your grandfather. This was your grandmother." This sent chills all over Diana. She was feeling part of the family. As Katie pulled out some photos, Diana thought she recognized some of Beverly, and she set them aside. Many times, she just inquired, "Who is this?" Sometimes Katie would tell her, and often she would be reluctant to say. Diana knew something seemed strange, and there seemed to be a secret. So she asked if Arlene had more children than the four of them. Katie snickered. Diana asked, "Were there two, or were there more?" as that was all Arlene had told her about. Katie once again would not answer. Katie then asked Diana about the photos in the stack by her arm, and she said she would like to make a copy before she goes.

Katie snapped at her and said, "Those are my pictures!" Roy, Katie's husband, spoke up and told Diana that he would make sure copies would be made and sent to her. He kept that promise, and Beverly and Diana would have some pictures as very small children on a farm with Katie. They were very excited when they arrived from Roy. James insisted that Diana spend the night there before he went back at his cabin; she was relieved that he had a calming effect over her. Their day had turned out to be quite an incredibly frustrating day. The flight home was peaceful, and Diana had a lot to share when she got home.

Not long after, she went back to work with stories of her new adventures. Some good, some not so good. Diana also had another session with her therapist and, of course, a lot to talk about. She really was not very pleased with the medication but knew with everything going on, it was best that she take what was prescribed. Diana had a chat with Beverly and did not mention her drinking, although she wanted to ask her about it. She let Beverly know there were pictures coming. Beverly was very happy to hear that. She questioned Diana how she was able to accomplish that feat. Diana told her the whole story, and Beverly agreed, "There has to be something underlining between Arlene and Katie that we don't know about." Diana agreed because Arlene did admit they fought constantly over the years over James. However, James grew up with Katie from the time he was one and a half. "We must be missing what the big secret between them is and may never know." Diana wanted to make time to come and see Beverly and bring the pictures when they arrived.

Diana was giddy with a phone call from James. He wanted to thank her for the visit to Maryland and said he enjoyed meeting her so much that he wondered if he could meet his other two siblings, Beverly and Joseph, as they also lived in Florida. Diana beamed with excitement; she was sure she could arrange that meeting, she told him. She explained to him that she would call, check everyone's schedule, and see if it would coordinate with his plans, and then they would make definite plans. Diana got off the phone; it was an incredible feeling, all four siblings together! She could hardly wait to call Beverly. She would be the one that would have the hardest time taking off. Diana knew Joseph worked and lived near the church where he was employed and had flexible hours; whereas, Beverly worked weekends. But she was going to have to take off this weekend as this was a real family affair!

The flight for James had built a lot of anticipation for meeting his siblings all together for the first time. James really did not know what to expect; he knew nothing of their personalities, families, or employment. But he was going to learn quite quickly. Diana was to meet him at the Tampa Airport, and they were to go to the automobile dealership that Beverly managed. Diana was right on time. They chatted on the way over, and Diana was very proud of her sister being the manager of all these salespeople. They walked into the store and past Beverly's desk, which was behind a large glass partition. Beverly could immediately see the resemblance—the color of his hair and the same squinty eyes when he smiled. It was difficult to know exactly what to do; to be honest, it was like meeting a stranger. Beverly felt like she should show some sort of affection, so she got up and gave him a hug and asked him to take a seat while she finished up this transaction. The whole process felt strained, but they got through it, and things began to lighten up on the way to Beverly's house.

Diana, Beverly, and James spent some time getting to know as much as they could about each other before they left to go to Joseph's in Daytona. Beverly was divorced and wanted to share some pictures of her two sons. She had been in the automotive business for more than ten years and had a lot of stories to tell. Beverly had worked as a salesperson for two years and then sales manager, then general sales manager. It was different in those days to have a female manager in the automotive business—a very tough business for a male and even tougher for a female.

They arrived in Daytona Beach and pulled into Joseph's quaint house, and his two boys came out running to meet us. This was also the first time Beverly had seen Joseph since he was six months old when they were abandoned. Everyone said their hellos, and it was just a jolly time. You would have thought this was a festival gathering. Food was everywhere, and there were flowers and games for the children; excitement was in the air. James seemed to have some jet lag and asked if he could go in the living room area and rest. The rest of them were in the kitchen or dining area. Some were playing games. Diana was making her chocolate cake for James, and Joseph was cooking some fish he had caught earlier in the day. It looked like they were going to have a feast. Debbie, Joseph's wife, and Beverly were chatting away at the table, and Joseph and Diana were in the kitchen, working on the food. Diana, being the most sensitive of them all and the most motherly, instinctively got to talking about their days of being left home alone before they got picked up. She was describing how they had to eat out of garbage cans, scrounge for food wherever they could. They had to go to the bar next to the shack they lived in and get milk for Joseph, who was six months old. Beverly and Diana would take turns going out for food. She was explaining to Joseph, who really could not remember how terrifying those days were for them as children. Diana expressed that Beverly also wanted to know why their parents left them. "It is something we can never forget, and we have also been searching for answers. It just never goes away."

As Beverly was sitting at the table, she felt James's hand on her shoulder, and he whispered in her ear, ever so softly, "Please ask Diana to stop talking about what happened to all of you." Beverly did not know that he was even listening to Diana and could see that he was visibly upset. She went to Diana and took her aside to let her know that James was upset with the conversation. Nothing more was said about their childhood. They had a lovely dinner and great chocolate cake and took some lovely pictures of the four of them together, which was amazing after so many years and miles apart.

It was not the same trip back as the trip over. They got to Beverly's and spent the night, and there was not much conversation. However, James did mention that he would like them to come to Maryland if they could and visit him in December. They both agreed that they might be able to arrange the time to do that. The next morning, Diana took James to the airport and then went on to Mexico Beach. Although most of their time together was new and exciting, the last part seemed to leave an emptiness that just did not feel right. But Diana was thrilled to show all the pictures to the family of all of them together to see the resemblance. Some thought Joseph and Beverly looked alike, and others thought Joseph and James looked alike. All in all, Diana was glad she had the opportunity to have the family she had lost years ago together once again.

The phone rang, and Vito answered. The voice on the other end was James, and he asked for Diana; however, she was not home from work. He asked Vito if he could take down a message that could be relayed to her. Vito got a pen and paper and was ready. James told Vito, "Please ask Diana not call or write to me ever again. Not for any reason do I want to hear from her." Then he quoted a scripture for her to read. He said, "Thank you, and good-bye." Vito was shocked and knew this message would tear Diana to pieces. How would he give her such a message? It was her brother, and he had no choice. He would be there for her and support her in any way he could. Diana came home at her normal time. When she came in the door, the kids were upstairs in their rooms, which was very different as they were usually running around asking, "What's for dinner?" Vito was sitting at the dining room table and asked Diana to join him. Her face turned white. "Has something horrible happened?" she thought. Vito began to tell her about the phone call from James. He could barely get through the words as the tears came flowing down her pink cheeks. Diana was devastated. However, she picked up the phone and called James; much to her surprise, he answered. Diana explained that she would abide by his wishes; however, she longed for the chance to once again speak as brother and sister. There was an eerie quiet moment on the phone. Then Diana spoke softly to James putting into plain words, "Don't forget this little crumb."

He finally replied, "You are not a crumb." Without another word, they both said good-bye. All kinds of things started going through her mind. She thought, "Maybe because we talked about their abandonment and he did not go through it. That could be his reasoning. Maybe Katie put him up to this. She does not want us involved with him." All kinds of thoughts were swirling through her head. What could she do but abide by his wishes? Once again, Diana felt like she lost her brother she had just found. Sometimes this process was just unbearable.

Many years had passed since Diana had heard from Arlene. Beverly and Diana only spoke occasionally, and her therapy sessions were starting to get less and less. Diana had called Beverly back when James had called, and Beverly sent him a letter; she read the letter she wrote to him—how she felt from her heart, and her way of thinking was that she understood that if he felt he did not want to keep in touch. That was his choice. Beverly told him she respected his choice and would not bother him; however, if he ever felt differently, "here is my phone number. Let me know." Beverly was not as sensitive as Diana was, because from a male's point of view she could see it might be different.

Diana knew she had opened up a can of worms with this journey to find her mother and siblings. But which was worse—to have the desire to know where you came from, or the fear of what you might find? Diana chose to stay on this journey until she got her answers to where did she come from?

The days passed, and no more letters came, no more information about the family. Beverly and Diana had exhausted all they could by using the names on the divorce papers, and it seemed like they had come to a dead end. Diana had tried so hard to bond with Arlene, and she just had to accept the fact that she was an alcoholic and was not willing to get help. That was the way she was willing to live out her life. But if she needed Diana, she still would be there for her when not one of her other children were there. It was painful for Diana, but she kept putting herself through the pain to fulfill her desire to bond with the mother she never had.

Diana was at work when she got a call from Arlene that she had broken her hip, and she needed her help. Arlene was having a hard time getting to the store and to get her hair done. She told her that Benny had lost his license and could not drive her around. Diana said she would see if she could get a week off and come to Maryland and help her. Of course, Diana was going to go. When she got to Baltimore Airport, Benny had sent one of his friends to pick her up and bring her to Arlene's house. When she arrived, both Arlene and Benny had been hitting the bottle pretty hard all day. Diana hated it; she did not even like the smell of it. Arlene right away wanted Diana to use her car to go out and get more alcohol. Diana did not want to do it, but Arlene put up a fuss, and so down to the local package store they went.

The next day, Diana asked if she could show her around where they used to live. Arlene took her to Havre-de-Grace where the shacks used to be by the bridge, but they had been removed. Diana next wanted to go out to Ray Osborne farm, but Arlene could not remember where it was, nor could she remember the hospital where Diana was born. They then went to the grocery to pick up some food because Diana wanted to make something special for Arlene. She was so skinny from not eating and just drinking all the time. Diana was really worried when she opened her purse, took out her flask, and took a drink right in the grocery store. The next day, she took her to get a new outfit and to get her hair done at the beauty shop. Hopefully, this would make Arlene feel better about herself. The evenings were much the same. Benny and Arlene drank until it was time to go to bed. Diana felt very lonely.

A week had gone by, and Diana had done as much as she could. She got up early with Benny and was sitting in the kitchen while he was making breakfast. They had been talking for quite some time as Arlene had a late night and slept later in the morning. Arlene came in with her walker and mumbled something. Diana turned to her, and Arlene motioned to Diana and Benny, accusing them of fooling around behind her back. Benny was quite a bit younger and more Diana's age, but that was far from the truth. Arlene was quite nasty to Diana and further called her names. Diana had asked for a picture of her grandmother, and Arlene said she could not have it. Diana took it anyway and they had a fight about that the night before, so she thought, "Maybe this is her problem." Diana was done with the drinking, and this way of life was not how she was brought up. She got her things together, called a taxi to take her to Baltimore Airport, and said her good-byes.

After she got home, Arlene called with an apology for how she treated Diana and what she had said to her. Diana accepted her apology and thought that was the end of it.

A few weeks later, she got an envelope in the mail from Arlene. Diana was happy that things had calmed down and she was getting something from her mother. Diana opened it to find her picture, which she had shared with her mother after thirty years, with a big mark across it and torn in half with no explanation enclosed!

Diana was done! She had taken all the pain she could stand. This had become unbearable. Diana once again felt like a throwaway child. She felt unloved, unwanted, and a castaway. These were the same feelings Diana had felt when she was seven, going to the first foster home. Diana felt she had come full circle. Diana never saw Arlene again.

CHAPTER 4

Beverly Spirals Out of Control

About a year had passed since Beverly and Diana had met in 1982. So much had developed in both of their lives. Now in September 1983, Beverly went through a divorce from Luke, and her life began to spiral out of control. As Beverly looked back over the years, she was well aware of the impact her journey to find her biological family had on her life. She never knew how painful her life would become.

Beverly was brought up in a Christian home with regular Bible study and married a Christian elder in their religion. Luke had been married before and had two children by his previous marriage. They had also had two wonderful boys together. There were the typical problems with going back and forth that go on with stepchildren. However, they had both boys at the beginning, and the young one, Wayne, cried constantly for his mother. Beverly was only eighteen at the time and had only been told of her adoption when she was sixteen. Although her parents did not tell her until then, she had horrible memories of past experiences that haunted her. She had not fully processed the shock of the information in her mind and was having nightmares. Beverly tried very hard to take the place of Wayne's mother, but he was so confused at one and a half, it just seemed impossible. Wayne was uncontrollable and had to be rocked until his father got home, and then Beverly could make dinner. One day this became so unbearable, Beverly felt she could not go on; she put Kent (the elder one) down for a nap, left Wayne on the rocking chair, and went to the kitchen. The only thing Beverly remembered was the blood dripping from her wrists. The windows were open, and a neighbor heard the children crying and came over to check on them. The neighbor called 911 and Luke.

Waking up strapped to a gurney was a feeling that Beverly never wanted to repeat. Luke was on one side, and a doctor with a very gentle voice was asking her, "What seems to be the problem?" Of course, Beverly was not able to tell him the reason she did such a terrible thing to herself. But when the doctor said she needed to be admitted, all she could think of was a room with padded walls. Beverly told Luke to call her father for advice as to what to do, as she had full confidence in his decision. Luke did, and her father had a private nurse stay with Beverly round the clock at home until he could get to Tallahassee to assess the situation. The doctor gave Beverly some medication, and she was released. She slept for days until her father arrived, and the boys, Wayne and Kent, were sent to live with their mother.

This was Beverly's first experience with a psychiatrist. She was very uneasy as she had heard all kinds of stories about this kind of doctor. Beverly had many sessions with him before he finally got her to open up about her adoption and the things that had happened in her early childhood. No one had ever let her speak about the things she remembered as a young child. One in particular was when she was left home alone with her six-month-old brother, Joseph, and he cried all the time; she was four, and her sister Diana was seven. His diagnosis was that the memory of trying to help and quiet her baby brother reminded her of Wayne, and she had lost control because she did not have the ability to stop the crying. It was starting to make some sense to Beverly. Of course, the doctor encouraged Beverly. He said, "It might take some time with the help of medication and therapy to overcome some of your fears and feelings of not being worthy. All this will take time, but you will get better as you go forward with your therapy."

Beverly continued to have therapy and take her medication. Wayne stayed on with his mother, and that was best for him. Luke and Beverly had regular visitation with him as they moved back to St. Petersburg area so they could have visits. Kent felt more comfortable staying with their family and continued until he was eighteen.

Beverly and Luke did all the things that a normal Christian family would do and their children felt loved very much. Beverly, on the other hand, still carried all her demons and kept them bottled up inside. She did not confide in any of her friends what she felt inside about her self-worth. Beverly had not shared that she had been adopted and that was the root of her problems. She had a hard time feeling loved and did not know if what she felt for Luke was even the kind of love you should feel between a man and a woman. Beverly knew she had resentment somewhat toward her parents for not telling her about her adoption, and maybe that was why she chose to get married so quickly. She got caught up in wanting a family of her own, vowing never to do what her mother did to her.

The alcohol began in Beverly's life; she had never had anything to do with it as a teenager or in her married life, and one night, as she was working in the Bath Boutique and Flower shop they owned, it all began. Luke still worked his regular job, and Beverly managed their boutique located out where several restaurants were, and it was designed to look like an old boatyard. It had pathways to different shops selling shells, T-shirts, imported hammocks, paintings, and their Bath and Flower Boutique. It was quaint, and people would mingle around, waiting to be called for a table at the fish house restaurant. Beverly was happy showing her salesmanship, working nightly there, running the shop. She got to know some of the other shopkeepers. After some time, several of them would go to the restaurant after closing and have a drink and relax. Many times they would invite Beverly, but she would always thank them and go home to the family.

The gentleman that worked across from her shop was very kind and always said nice compliments to her. Beverly began to notice that he would tell her almost every day how nice she looked or comment on her perfume. She started feeling more confident about herself as she was not used to a man showing her attention. One night he invited her after work to play Pac-Man with the group. Beverly did not see any harm in that, so she went along. It was fun and exciting. All the others were having a drink; she was offered but declined.

Several months passed, and Beverly spent more time after work playing Pac-Man and was enjoying herself. At first her conscience told her that she should be home with her family and, most of all, with her husband. But as time went on, she began to enjoy her first drink and then her second and one night, her third. She could hardly stand. Her friend offered to help her back to the store until she sobered up. After they got to the store, he began to kiss her neck very gently. Beverly could not at this point reject his advances. He continued on until they were on the floor, and all she could remember was saying no, but he went on. Beverly was totally violated. As a Christian wife, she had to go straight home and tell Luke. She cried all the way home. How could she betray God, Luke, the congregation, and all their friends like this?

As Beverly arrived home, she climbed the oak stairs to the bedroom she shared with Luke. He immediately awoke to hear her sobbing. Beverly asked him to meet her down by the fireplace as she had something to tell him. It took a few minutes to rinse her face in the bathroom, being careful not to wake the children, before she met Luke by the fire. She slipped into the rocking chair and looked at him; he was looking at her with his caring eyes but at the same time wondering, "Where have you been, Beverly?" Beverly began to speak. Although her voice was shaky, she explained that the group of shop-owners had stayed after closing to play Pac-Man, a video game, and had a few drinks. Luke right away could not understand that his wife would be associating with this group of people after work and drinking. Beverly went on to say that she had a few times stayed after, but this time she had drinks and had too much. One of the shop-owners knew she could not drive and helped her to the store. Beverly told Luke that she had committed a sin against him and never did she think this would ever happen. "He was overpowering me, and we violated the marriage arrangement." Beverly pleaded with Luke to forgive her. She knew that she should not have been in association with him, or this would not have happened. Luke was devastated. He went upstairs, and Beverly stayed downstairs on the couch.

The kids got up the next day went to school, Luke went to work, and Beverly had to open the gift shop. It was difficult to say the least to see the shop owner, Raul opening his shop too. He came over to see how Beverly was doing and apologized for what had happened. Raul hoped that Luke and Beverly would be able to work things out. Little did Raul know the consequences Beverly would have to go through when she would go before the elders of the congregation.

A week went by, and a committee was formed with the congregation of elders so that Beverly could let the elders know of her sin. She poured out her heart and was very repentant of her sin of adultery. Beverly told the elders that she would not see this man, Raul, in a romantic way anymore and would completely cut off any conversation with him. As a result, they asked Beverly to try to work out her marriage to Luke for three months. Beverly told the elders the problems in their marriage, and they said they would work with both of them, and they did. As the months went on, Beverly grew farther away from Luke. She could not have him touch her as she felt dirty. Beverly felt as though he could never forgive her and would always remind her of what she had done.

At the end of three months Beverly once again went before the committee of elders, and they asked, "What have you decided?" Beverly told them she had broken it off completely with Raul the person she committed the wrong with, but that she was going to divorce Luke and go on with her life. The elders then, to Beverly's surprise, told her they would disfellowship her from the congregation, not for the adultery but because she did not respect God's marriage arrangement. Not having God's spiritual guidance at the time, Beverly made a very poor decision. She did not respect their decision, repent of her sin and return to the congregation; she decided to leave the congregation. This was a huge mistake, and it led to Beverly spiraling further out of control.

Beverly got an apartment not too far from their home and took only her clothes, one sofa, and one car. She left everything to Luke. When the divorce came finally, they split custody, and Beverly had the children half the week and Luke the other half. But because Beverly had left the home, the children had Luke's home as permanent residency. Beverly remembered Luke standing at the door, telling her that she would never amount to anything. Those words rung in her ears for many years, and she was not going to let them come true. Beverly also kept the gift shop so that she had an income, even though by this time the whole complex was starting to fail; she tried to hang on to the only way she had of making an income.

Many weeks, months went by, and Beverly picked the children up for visitation or if they needed to go to the doctor on a regular basis. This process was very difficult as Luke made it so stressful for Beverly when she came to the door. Luke had moved on with his life rather quickly and remarried, but he still seemed to have utter disgust for Beverly. Beverly knew she had wronged him, but it would seem that time would heal things. But nothing Beverly did seemed to please Luke. When Scott had band practice, Beverly had to take him. "You want him to take tennis lessons, then, Beverly, you will take him. If you think Scott needs braces on his teeth, you take him and pay for them too." Beverly felt so bad for the mistake she had made toward Luke that she continued to be the one to care for any of the extra needs of Scott and Blake. At times the stress was unbearable, and Beverly would use the nights she did not have the boys to medicate herself with alcohol to relive the pain of the hurt she felt. Little did she know this was just the beginning of a long road of drinking which she never wanted to go down because it eventually reminded her that she would become just like her mother.

It was about a year after the divorce and loss of the business that Beverly had to look for a new career. The only training she took in school was business courses, and she had sales training from the gift shop. Beverly decided one day to just look in the newspaper to see what jobs were offered. She looked in the employment section and noticed a sales position for an automobile dealership. It said to call JR for an appointment. Beverly thought that her father had sold mobile homes all his life and she had been around that, so maybe she could sell an automobile. Remember, Beverly had none of her family or friends to confide in as she was removed from the congregation and could not speak with them. It was very hard not to associate with any of your family especially. But Beverly knew she could change her way of life and go back to the congregation, but she still had that arrogant way of thinking and was not ready to change because she was still drinking.

Beverly called JR, and he was surprised to hear a woman on the other end of the line but made the appointment for the next day. Beverly dressed appropriately in a suit and entered the Nissan dealership; with all eyes on her, she approached the receptionist and asked for JR. All the salespeople knew what she was there for and could not believe a woman would apply. Beverly filled out the application and had a very nice interview with JR, and he said he would be making a decision by Friday. Beverly made it very clear that she was a quick learner; she could get the product knowledge down, meet and greet a customer, and with the manager's help have the customer driving a new car. JR was impressed!

Beverly was a nervous wreck all week waiting and hoping, knowing this would be a good career for her. She could hardly wait until Friday. As the day went by, she was very anxious. Beverly thought she might go have a drink, but that was not a good idea if JR should call her. By 1:00 p.m., Beverly felt that was long enough; she had grown impatient, and she thought maybe she should let them know she really wanted the job. So she called and asked for JR. The receptionist told Beverly he was out to lunch but she would leave him a message that she had called. Hours went by and no call. Beverly began to wonder if that meant she did not get the job or if they had not made a decision. She wanted to know before she let this opportunity go by. Beverly called again at around 4:00 p.m. and asked for JR. The receptionist put Beverly right through to his office. He picked up the phone and told Beverly that she certainly is aggressive "and that is a quality that you must have to be successful in the automotive business." JR told Beverly to report to the dealership on Monday morning at 9:00 for a meeting. Beverly was so proud that she did this on her own, and she was going to make a success of this new venture.

Beverly certainly did just that. She sold cars barely for two years and won a Silver Star award from Nissan, and then JR was leaving, recommending Beverly to take the position as sales manager. Beverly progressed rather quickly and was eager to learn new positions in the automotive industry, so she accepted that position. Before she moved into that position she went to a seminar to get her award at a banquet put on for salespeople for outstanding achievement. It was at that banquet that she met another salesperson, Michael, from a nearby dealership that had won the same award. Beverly had talked to Michael on the phone many times when they would exchange cars between dealerships. She found him to be a charming, interesting, and always a pleasant guy to talk to when they spoke. Beverly thought it would be nice to meet him face-to-face. As you can imagine, that is what happened. Beverly and Michael met that night; they were instantly attracted to each other. There was quite a bit of drinking, but they had a great time and Michael took her number and called the next day.

Michael and Beverly dated for one year and had a wonderful time in their courtship. Although there always was a lot of drinking associated with whatever they did, they managed to control it enough to enjoy their time together. In August 1987, they were married in a small ceremony with Michael's family and only Beverly's sister, as her family would not attend. Beverly was very happy as for the first time she felt as though she had someone she loved deeply and felt he loved her equally as much. But this is not a "happily ever after" story. With all the love in the world you have for someone, if alcohol is present, it can destroy that love, no matter how deep it is between you. When Beverly and Michael were sober, it was fine, but as soon as they got home from work or went out with others, they would drink too much. Then a fight would ensue, and sometimes it would become physical. Pushing and shoving. Slapping and punching. Black eyes and marks on Beverly's neck. Michael would have shirts ripped off him. Someone would get hurt. Michael took the first step and left Beverly. Beverly did everything in her power to get him to come back as she loved him with all her heart. Michael moved on to another woman quite soon, which hurt Beverly deeply. Beverly began to drink and party even more to cover her broken heart. The one thing neither Michael nor Beverly tried was to stop drinking and work on their marriage.

Beverly at least had her job, and that was a lot of pressure to keep all the salespeople in line as it was. But as her marriage had fallen apart, her work was starting to feel the effects of her mood changes. She would get aggravated more easily and would get phone calls from Michael, and they were not always pleasant. One of the other managers started complaining to the general manager. They were very fond of Beverly as she was able to keep their profits up and were hesitant to let her go. But one day they had enough of complaints, and that is just what they did. Beverly was once again discouraged beyond belief. She had lost not only the man she loved but now the job she loved too. The thoughts began to go through her head of worthlessness. No one ever really cared for her. "You always were tossed around from place to place, and here you go again." Her first thought was to pick herself up and leave the area but not to stop drinking.

Luke had moved to North Carolina with Blake, obviously to get him away from Beverly. He even tried to get Beverly to sign her rights away for the boys. Something she knew her mother had done and she never would do. Luke knew that, so how could he bring Beverly a document for her to sign away her rights? Scott stayed with Beverly at the time, and Blake went with his father to North Carolina. Beverly would fly Blake back and forth for his visits, but he was so sad when Beverly put him on the plane that it broke her heart. Beverly's first thought after leaving her job was to go be near Blake and work at a dealership there. She made the trip to the beautiful smoky mountains and thought, "This is a lovely place to live." Beverly found a small Nissan dealership up on a hill about the same size as the one that she had come from. Beverly walked in asked for the general manager, sat down and talked to him, and told him her background and experience. Mr. Hines said in about one month he would have an opening for a business manager position. Beverly told him she might need a little training, but she would love the opportunity. They shook hands, and Beverly went to look for a condo; she would go back to Florida to get her things and would be ready for work in a month.

Not long after Beverly arrived, she began to visit with Blake. She would go to the next town closest to Asheville and pick him up and bring him to her condo for the weekend. They had some great times together. They drove up to Boone, which was a college town up the mountain, and it was a windy road with rocks, water running down the rocks, little bridges, and beautiful crisp green mountains all around. It felt so good to see Blake happy and not sad anymore when he had to go back on the plane. However, this did not last for long. One Saturday, Beverly came home from work and found a note and no Blake. His father had picked him up and taken him home. Once again Beverly felt powerless. Blake had written the note, but the content sounded like it came from Luke as Blake was only eight. It was Blake's way of saying he could not have any association with his mother until she came back to the church. Beverly was devastated; she knew what she had to do—repent and turn around and go to the church. But Beverly was beginning to see she had a drinking problem and she had to fix that first, but did she have the power to do it alone as well as straighten out her life?

Beverly once again felt abandoned in her life. She knew it was not her eight-year-old son's fault, and really she could only blame her reckless lifestyle for the things that were happening to her. Once again, Beverly tried to find happiness in going out to bars and drinking with the other managers at the dealerships locally. The General Sales Manager Zeke and Beverly had become very close as they went out all the time after work. Zeke even took Beverly on his dates with other girls he had been dating. That seemed strange at first, but the girls in the accounting office let Beverly know that he was definitely interested in her and not the other girls.

About six months went by, and Zeke asked Beverly to move in with him as platonic relationship. They found a lovely condo up on the mountain close to the dealership, with a two-car garage, two large bedrooms, and a den in the back, where Beverly could entertain privately. The living area was large with a beautiful barbeque porch on the back so they could have parties together. They both agreed on the rent and moved in right away. Beverly and Zeke had parties and went out together, and everything just seemed to work out just like best friends should. Other friends would see them always together and would ask, "Are you guys together now?" But they would just say that they were friends, although feelings were starting to grow between them. They both started confiding their deepest feelings and were becoming more vulnerable. It was about this time that Beverly got a call from Michael, and she got butterflies in her stomach. She had told Zeke about him, so it was no surprise when Beverly told him he wanted to try to reconcile with her. Zeke knew how broken she had been and felt if that was what she wanted, he would support her.

Beverly and Zeke went down to their favorite watering hole to have a few drinks before Beverly had to meet Michael at the airport. She was very nervous because she really wanted this to work out, and she especially wanted Zeke's approval. Because of her anticipation, she drank a little more than she should have. Zeke told her to slow down as she had quite a drive out to the airport. Beverly agreed she better leave now as it was also getting dark, and she did not want to be late. Michael was one to be on time.

As things went for Beverly, not only was she late, but Michael was standing there, waiting at the gate, and she smelled like booze. He was angry. Beverly tried to apologize all the way back to the bar where Zeke and their other friends were, but he was just barely cooling down when they got there. Beverly really needed another drink. She introduced Michael to all the guys from the dealership. They had some appetizers and had some more cocktails, and Michael said he was going to pay the bill. Beverly was standing by Zeke at the end of the bar. Michael went down to cash out, and two people were sitting there and started up a conversation with him.

There was some discrepancy about the bill. Michael looked like they were just chatting, so Beverly decided to join the conversation. She stood behind him for a few minutes, and he ignored her or just did not invite her into the conversation.

Whatever the case was, Beverly was drunk and got mad and went to the car; she thought about it for a minute and came back in. He was still talking and ignored her. So she said something very off-color and went back to the car. Michael came right to the car with a look of rage. "How could you disrespect me like that?" Beverly on the way to the condo began to sober up and realized what she had done. It was too late! Michael put his bags on the curb and said he was going home. "This is just like before with the drinking." Beverly was shattered to think that she had caused the man she loved to leave her again over alcohol. Michael got a taxi that night and left for home.

Beverly and Zeke went on for the next few months as usual, going out and spending much of their time together. It was Christmas time coming up; Zeke knew that Beverly did not celebrate the holiday, but he did not want to leave her alone. Zeke invited Beverly to go home to meet his family in Virginia for the holiday. Beverly thought that was very thoughtful of Zeke as the dealership would be closed through New Year's Eve. They made the drive together, and it was cold and snowy. When they got there, the family was warm and inviting. The whole family welcomed Beverly as part of their family, which made her feel better right away. They all went out and had a big family dinner and took a lot of pictures. Beverly was happy that she went; it was better than sitting home thinking about how she had wrecked her last chance with Michael.

It was a difficult relationship between Zeke and Beverly and quite hard to explain. They had a love for each other but more in a companionship way. Although they had become intimate, that is when things started to go wrong. Beverly was a monogamous person, and Zeke was not ready for that at the time. They really did not make it clear in their conversations and still were keeping it a secret with their friends. Zeke started going out without Beverly and would come in late drunk and come back to her room and want to talk. Beverly was starting to realize that he was seeing someone else. Zeke went away one weekend. He told Beverly he had to work on his boat. When he came back, he acted different. Beverly and Zeke swapped cars for the night, and in the center console, Beverly found a receipt for a motel down where his boat was kept, a room for two. Beverly knew her suspicions were true. He had taken someone down with him. The next weekend, Beverly found a condo in the next town and made arrangements to have her things moved out. Zeke was going out in the boat, so he would not be home.

Beverly got everything moved to Black Mountain and was very pleased with the place and felt relieved that she did not have any confrontation with Zeke. She felt he would get the message, and they both could go their own ways. But that is not what happened. In the middle of the night, Beverly woke up to someone banging on the front door like they were going to tear the hinges off. She got to the door, and it was Zeke. He was a mess—crying, drunk, and remorseful. Why was Beverly doing this to him? "What about our friendship?" Beverly tried to calm him down first so that he could understand her when she spoke. Beverly told him about the motel receipt and all the other things that led her to believe that he had someone else, so she did not want to be in the way. Zeke denied it all. He told her how crazy she was and that there was no one else but her. Zeke made up an excuse for everything she brought up. It was so late that Beverly took Zeke in her arms to her room and held him lovingly until morning. They kissed passionately, and he left for work and Beverly got ready to meet him at the dealership.

The next few weeks were difficult at work for both Beverly and Zeke. They tried to remain as normal as possible so that the staff did not notice anything was wrong between them. Slowly, Zeke would show up at Beverly's place after work, or they would run into each other outside, and of course, they would be together. As their differences seemed to calm down, Beverly was also in a contest at work to win a trip to Hawaii for the Anderson Group of dealerships that she worked with. Beverly was up against five other finance men; being the only female, she was really trying her hardest to come out on top. Beverly was very focused on the trip at this time and wanted to make the owner proud of her success.

Beverly was working very diligently to sell products in the business office. One of the products that gave her the most points was offering life insurance and accident and health. You had to be licensed in the state also to sell these products, so Beverly had to be board certified. In the middle of all this pressure, Beverly had a call from the previous owner, Mr. Farmington of the dealership in Florida. Mr. Farmington called to see how she was doing and if she was happy at her new position. Beverly was delighted to hear from him as she had much respect for Mr. Farmington and had not wanted to leave his employment at the time. He did not waste any time in offering Beverly her old job back as general sales manager, only she had to move to the Jeep dealership. Beverly was very surprised and impressed that he made such an offer to her. They chatted a while, and Beverly told him about the contest that would be a month away. Mr. Farmington understood she would not give up an opportunity of going to Hawaii. They parted their conversation with Beverly saying she would give him an answer by the end of the month.

"Here we go again with decisions to make, and it means a move, including a move away from ones I love." Beverly wondered if she should include Zeke in her decision. They had a relationship, and he had been her confidant up till lately. Beverly decided to make a nice dinner and have Zeke over as this might be a little too heavy to spring on him out in public or at the dealership.

Beverly prepared Zeke's favorite—chicken and dumplings, turnip greens with vinegar, and topped it off with homemade apple pie with vanilla ice cream. Zeke seemed curious the whole evening; after they finished the third bottle of wine, he knew Beverly must have something important to tell him. They talked a little about their feelings for each other, and basically, they both said they loved each other and were best friends. It was a good beginning for a relationship, but that was all. Beverly began to explain her phone call from Mr. Farmington and how he would like her to come back and the new position he offered her. Zeke was bursting with excitement for Beverly. She was not expecting that reaction from him. Zeke let Beverly know that he always wanted to live and work in Florida around the beaches. He felt like this would be a great opportunity for both of them. Beverly could go ahead, get a place big enough for both of them, and he could follow later. He would start now looking for positions from a headhunter for that area. Beverly could not believe his reaction and was stunned. Zeke agreed to give Beverly the funds to secure a condo or house, whatever Beverly wanted. Beverly was apprehensive and told Zeke that she would be going on her trip to Hawaii before any decision was made because she knew she was going to win this contest.

By the end of the month, every manager was running neck and neck. It was such a close race. Beverly was pressing hard to sell her products in the business office and giving the salespeople spiffs to help get the customers interested in getting a service contract for their automobile. She knew this was a ten-day trip of a lifetime, and she wanted this with all her heart.

It was Friday night, and Mr. Hines came to the office late that evening, which was unusual. When he walked past Beverly's office, she wondered why he was here so late. The next thing Beverly heard was her name called over the loudspeaker system to come to Mr. Hines office. Beverly immediately went to his office, only to find everyone packed in his office, congratulating, cheering, and screaming that she had won the trip.

Beverly could hardly keep her mind on her work until it was time to take the trip. She invited the title clerk, Mindy, who was also single and liked to party, to go with her. Getting ready for the trip was so much fun; she bought new outfits, a new Nikon camera, luggage, and several bathing suits.

They flew from North Carolina to California then on to Hawaii, and what a welcome they had. The trip was sponsored by JM&A

Finance Group, and they went all out for the business managers from states all across the United States. First they were taken by bus to a beautiful hotel with lush greenery, orchids, and waterfalls everywhere you turned. It was breathtaking. When they arrived at their rooms, there was a large bouquet of red roses. Mindy thought they were for her from her boyfriend, so she read the card. Much to her surprise the card read "Beverly, have a wonderful time, love, Zeke." Now Beverly had some explaining to do, as no one knew of their relationship. Mindy, right away before Beverly could say a word, told her that she had suspected it all along; now she knew and thought it was wonderful for them both.

The whole trip was like something out of the movies. The food was prepared to perfection, and they were served as though they were stars at the Oscars. If you bought a postcard of Hawaii it looks exactly as the picture on that card! Mindy and Beverly were treated to a banquet beyond comprehension. This was a trip of a lifetime, and both will never forget the joyous time spent on the islands of Hawaii.

Beverly was high spirited when Mindy and she arrived at the dealership the next Monday morning after the trip. It was hard to control their emotions and settle down to work coming off such an extravagant ten days. But they were suntanned and delighted beyond belief and ready to share pictures of all the joyful times they shared.

It was not long after this that Beverly made the decision to move back to Florida and go back to work for Mr. Farmington. She had thought a lot about it on the beach, and as she could not see Blake and things were not going smoothly with Zeke, Beverly knew she made the right choice. The next day she called Mr. Farmington and discussed her plans, and he was overjoyed. He was happy because he knew his profits would rise, and he knew Beverly could get the dealership in line. They agreed on a date and time, ending the conversation on a cheerful note.

Beverly had already made arrangements to stay with a friend and put her things in storage until she found a place; now all she needed to do was talk to Zeke. After work one night, they met at a small restaurant that was very quiet. Zeke looked very sad, and his eyes were watery. They ate and laughed about all that they had been through together. Not all was good, but much of it was very exciting. Zeke pulled out of his pocket a small box for Beverly to open. Inside she found a shiny gold bracelet that fit Beverly to perfection. She was delighted. Zeke always knew what to buy her; he had such good taste. He went over the plan for Beverly to find a place for both of them and said that he would be looking for a job. Zeke said he probably would be down in a month for a visit, but if a place was found, she was to call Zeke and he would send the deposit. Zeke was so sweet and made Beverly feel so loved. That night when he came to her place, they had some wine, and Beverly began to softly run her fingers through his reddish-blond hair. They talked, and tears came slowly down Beverly's cheeks. Zeke wiped them away gently, and they both drifted blissfully to sleep in each other's arms.

The time came for the moving truck to come and start loading all Beverly's furniture and many boxes for the trip to Florida. It took nearly the whole day to get the truck loaded. Beverly left a blanket, pillow, and something to shower with as she was leaving very early the next morning. She already said all her good-byes. Even to Zeke and that was stressful, as she still did not feel that confident that he would follow her to Florida. Beverly took her last look out the front window at the Smoky Mountains and what a beautiful sight that was every morning driving to work. "This truly is God's country."

Beverly had nothing to do but go to sleep and it was a long drive, so she laid her head down and fell asleep. She had no alarm set but she was sure she would wake up just because of the excitement of the trip. Beverly was awakened by a slight tapping at the door, or was she dreaming? She heard it again and went to the door this time, and there was Zeke standing with tears running down his face. Beverly hugged him and caressed him like a baby. They both stood there without speaking a word. Then their lips met, and it was an enchanting moment. Beverly felt powerless in Zeke's arms and more vulnerable than she had ever felt. If only this could be their everlasting moment together.

The next day was a long hard road to Florida, but Beverly had a gleeful smile on her face as she drove out of Asheville. Beverly was used to a thirty-six-foot truck as she had driven one up there, only she had a sports car when she came up, but she sold that and drove a demonstrator.

She had to make some stops for gas and get some munches, but other than that she would drive straight through. Beverly made pretty good time as she arrived at her friend Melinda's house just before dark.

Beverly went straight to the dealership to meet with Mr. Farmington to go over some paperwork and some of his plans for how he wanted things done at this dealership. So Beverly spent part of the day with him, and then she excused herself as she had some condos to look at for the next few days. Mr. Farmington let her know she should take her time and get settled. Whenever she felt ready to work, she was to let him know and then she could start. Beverly was happy with that. She could get settled and not worry about looking around while she was working. When she got back to Melinda's, a magnificent bouquet of flowers was waiting for her from Zeke. He was not going to let her forget him.

A month passed, and Beverly had found several places and had called Zeke about them. He would tell her go ahead said he would send the money. Beverly did not feel secure enough with him still in Asheville. She thought she better get something she could afford just in case he never came down. Beverly did not want to be left high and dry with a place she could not afford. So that is what she found, a nice condo on a golf course; she moved in, started her job, and was very pleased that she was settled.

Beverly was busy working with the managers and supervising them; little did she know she was going to be taking the place of the manager that was there. She worked some in the Business Office—sales manager, general sales manager, and Used Car Department positions; one thing was for sure, much to Beverly's delight. A thoughtful bouquet of flowers came every week from Zeke. Finally, in the second month he came for a visit. Beverly showed Zeke a remarkably cool time; they explored together Clearwater, the boats, and beaches, and he was delighted with the area. Zeke was ready to come back as soon as he could.

Beverly made the move into her position as general sales manager, had her new office set up, and was putting together a sales team to work with her at the dealership. She wanted to train them and have them on the sales system she had used previously, where she had been a sales trainer. It was an intense sales system, but if followed, the customer was served properly. Beverly hired ten new sales people and spent quite a lot of her time training them to follow this system. It was very effective and sales started to increase, in addition the profit went up also. Mr. Farmington was pleased with the results.

Since moving back to Florida, it seemed that all areas of Beverly's life were falling back into place. Beverly's job was keeping her motivated, her son Scott eloped with a girl from California at nineteen, two dozen red roses came for Valentine's Day from Zeke, and so everything was certainly coming together! On that same day Beverly got a call from Mindy, her friend that worked at the dealership where Zeke worked. Mindy wondered if Beverly had received flowers from Zeke. The reason for her call was to let Beverly know that their friend Sara ran into the dealership and jumped on Zeke's lap, thanking him for the bouquet of roses with kisses and hugs. Beverly knew what that meant. As she had suspected, Sara was the one he was cheating on her with and had been for quite some time. Beverly had no choice; she had to stop this right now. Although she felt dejected, she knew it was over. She called Zeke, thanked him for the flowers, and asked him not to ever call her again. Zeke knew what the call meant, and he never called her again.

Beverly had to go on once again with being rejected and feelings of low self-esteem, but she felt she could pick up and move forward. But she would not be alone. Beverly once again started stopping at the local places the guys would stop at for a nightcap. Little did she realize that she was just covering all her years of pain and rejection by using alcohol so as not to recall the past. Then again she was really on the road to alcoholism or already there, but never stopped to realize the damage it was doing to her life.

It was not long before she had stopped one night with the business manager, Trace, and they happily drank shots that night. Trace was a slow drinker compared to Beverly. She went out and danced a few times, had a couple more drinks, told Trace she was fine, and that she was tired for the night and leaving. Last words she heard Trace call out to her were "Are you going to be okay?" Beverly started down the road; it was not even two miles from the bar, and she saw flashing lights. "It can't be true," she thought, but it was. The officer pulled her over and asked if she had been drinking. She had. He gave her the sobriety road test, and Beverly did not pass. She was taken to jail; this was the most frightening, devastating time in her life she could remember. It was a real jail—handcuffs, fingerprints, mug shots, and behind bars with hookers. Beverly cried; as the tears flowed, the girls told her to suck it up! The next morning they were chained together, taken to court before the judge, and Beverly lost her license. Beverly was so distraught and felt so ashamed. She had made her one phone call to Trace and was hoping he would be there when she got back, and he was.

How humiliating was this situation for Beverly. She went to the general manager, Allan, and poured out her heart to him and begged for forgiveness. Allan was very understanding; he had been in the same situation one time himself. He told Beverly that they would keep this between him, Trace, and Beverly, and it would not be spoken of again. They never talked about it for a very long time. Beverly had a company that respected her work ethic, and that meant a lot to her.

Almost two years had passed and a lot of changes happened at the dealership. Mr. Farmington was building a new facility on his Nissan and Chrysler site. At the finish of that new development, he was going to move the Jeep franchise to that site also and combine all three. When they were completed, Beverly would be the general sales manager of all three franchises. She was honored, and Mr. Farmington was proud to say he had full confidence in her tenacity and ability to do the job. Beverly was excited; she had also been voted as one of the Businesswomen of the Year that year, so she was grateful for the recognition she was receiving.

Nonetheless, Beverly had gotten her license back just a year and a half ago and had attended a school that was required for those they feel have a drinking problem. In that school, Beverly remembered that a very high percentage receive another DUI within a five-year period, which carries jail time. However, it was to no avail. Beverly kept on drinking. Those in the automobile business seem to be in an employment where they will find drugs and alcohol. Beverly was not willing to admit she had a problem.

It was a late Saturday at the dealership and a very busy one. One of the managers was getting married. They all had rooms at the Marriot in Tampa, including Beverly. She, however, was staying late with the last customer, so she would miss the wedding and just make it to the reception. As it was, she parked, went right to the desk, left her bag in the car, paid for the room, got a receipt, and went into the reception. Beverly had missed the food but not the alcohol. Everyone wanted her to catch up because she was staying there, so no worries. The party went on, dancing, drinking, and more drinking. Actually, Beverly was more tired from working so late and decided to leave early. She said she was going to the car to get her bag and go to her room. When Beverly got to the car, she remembered she had left her new puppy locked in the bedroom and felt she could drive as she didn't drink that much.

As Beverly left the Marriot, everything seemed fine, but it wasn't. The last thing Beverly remembered was making a decision whether to make a right on to Tampa road. She came to an abrupt stop hitting the van in front of her. Of course, the police came, and again she was handcuffed and taken to jail. Fortunately, she sobered up quickly, and Allan was on his way to pick her up as he was at the wedding; however, she was not aware he was notified. Not knowing Allan was coming, when they let her out, she took a taxi from Tampa to New Port Richey, which was across the waterway about fifty miles.

Now at home, she had a bloody knee and a large bump on her head. Obviously Beverly felt devastated, shattered, defeated, and destroyed. Allan had worked it out before, but not this time. Beverly had wrecked a dealership automobile, lost her license for five years, shamed the dealership, and embarrassed herself in front of her staff, and would have to do automatic jail time! She had all day Sunday to think about what this would do to her career.

The first phone call was from Allan. Surprisingly he was very consoling and let Beverly know that they were in her corner. "Monday morning the attorneys will be notified, and you will also be assigned one. However, you should get your own also." This was all overwhelming. Allan wanted to mention to Beverly to come into work at her regular time on Monday, "and we will sit down with Mr. Farmington to discuss how we will move forward."

On Monday morning, Beverly met with the owner and general manager to go over the disaster that had happened over the weekend. Beverly was shaking and was frightened as she knew they would have every reason to dismiss her from employment at the dealership. Mr. Farmington spoke first, and when he explained how disappointed in Beverly he was, she was crushed. His feelings meant a lot to her, as he had always been so kind, thoughtful, generous, and considerate; it stung when she hurt him. The conversation went on, and he said that he had already spoken to the attorney and gave her the name of the attorney that would represent her. Mr. Farmington then went on to tell Beverly, "We are going to work this out." Much to her surprise, he wanted Beverly to go downstairs and keep her mind on business. "Let's not discuss this with anyone except the attorneys, and business as usual." Beverly felt like an elephant had been lifted off her.

It was a tough year. Beverly had to be driven back and forth to work, to the grocery, and to therapy. When she had to appear in court, a friend always had to drive. It was at this time in her life that she went to AAA meetings as she was required. At first Beverly would not stand up and say she was Beverly and she was an alcoholic. But after about a year, she heard a story that touched her heart, and she was able to stand, and everyone cheered! Beverly was finally getting it; she had inherited this trait from her biological parents, and she had to stop now. At this same time, she had been away from her faith, which she still believed in, and she wanted to be reunited in the congregation. Beverly began to attend every meeting at the congregation and stopped drinking; now she was on the road to recovery, and what a good feeling it was.

Not long after, the dealership settled with the person that was hit in the accident. Beverly's lawyer was able to keep her from serving jail time. She completed all the designated courses, AAA, and finally received a temporary work license, was reinstated in the congregation, and has not had a drink in fourteen years.

Eventually, Mr. Farmington sold the dealership to another dealership as he was retiring, and they asked her to stay on as general sales manager. They also were very caring people to work for, it seemed, and Beverly worked there until she turned fifty-nine. Her health was not too good, and it was difficult at times working such long hours as she had lupus. Also, she had been caring for her father for about eight years; he was about ninety-two and getting quite dependent. However, Beverly planned to work at least until she was sixty five.

The owner decided he would shake things up a bit and brought in one of his dear old friends. Beverly's sales team was not fond of his sales process, and neither was she. But in her twenty-five years, she had seen so many "hot shots" come and go that she felt he would be another one with his older methods of selling that would not last. But much to her amazement, one day they called her upstairs and let her go. Needless to say, Beverly was shocked after all she had been through and twenty years there; she felt shattered. They offered her a compensation package for her years of service with them. Beverly was still devastated and had to think their offer over.

Within a week, Beverly took their offer as she felt she did not want to work for a company that treated their employees like they were treating her and many others. Beverly turned in her demonstrator, collected all her personal things, and left the keys with a manager that night, and she has never returned to this day.

Life was now very difficult to say the least. Beverly had her father to take care of, no employment, and just the compensation package to live off, along with what was left in her 401K. Beverly had just sold her home in Sugar Mill Woods and bought a new home in Bayonet Point, and renovated it. Therefore, she had put her savings into new Hunter blinds, wood floors, new paint, new fans, fixtures, and refinishing the pool. Therefore, Beverly was tapped out, and this could not have happened at a worse time. She gradually fell into a deep depression. Beverly tried to work out her feelings, but they accelerated to the point where she knew she was not going to drink, but she needed help. Beverly felt distraught over losing her job, and once again the feelings of worthlessness, rejection, and being a throwaway overcame her. So much so that before she took the next step and hurt herself. She called a doctor in the phone book. He listened and talked her through the pain she was feeling, calming her down to the point that she felt she could make it until the morning and come to his office. He told her, "If not, go straight to the hospital."

Beverly had been to a psychiatrist before but had only touched the surface of her childhood. Now she had her issues with childhood, adoption, alcoholism, loss of her job, failed marriages, and removal from her church, and where could she go from here. She spent the next two years with this doctor and made very slow progress with him as there was a lot to cover. Beverly was so distraught over her job and money; it was hard to get past that.

After going through her money in about two years, her mental state had grown to the point that she applied for disability through a policy she had through her company. It was a battle, but Beverly's attorney won and she was put on disability with the State of Florida as well. At this time, Beverly's brother, Peter, was an enormous help as far as their father was concerned. He also helped with the funds they needed to buy food before Beverly received her disability. Without his kindness and generosity, Beverly would not have been able to make it through such a difficult time. Peter was not only her brother but her best friend too.

Beverly felt she needed a new start after her case was settled, and she had to short sale her home. She had visited her son Scott in California just about every year for twenty years. Beverly had one grandchild, and that was Angelina. She was the best thing in her life. Every month she used to send her a box with dresses, toys, stuffed bears, and shoes. Beverly was called OMA for grandma, and Angelina called the box her OMA box. Beverly called Scott and Patty, his wife, to announce she was moving out there as she had expressed she would when she retired to be close to Angelina. Everyone seemed jubilant!

Not long after, Patty helped find a place for Beverly and Harvey to rent. Peter helped to pack them up and they were there in three days. Scott had some of his friends come over and unpack the truck, and then they had pizza and beer.

Beverly had only been there two weeks when she got a high fever, and Patty had to take her to the hospital; she was so sick. She had a procedure done on her kidney to see what the problem was, and from the hospital she caught MRSA. That is a staph infection that can be deadly. It affected Beverly in the kidney. She had a port put in her arm and had to go to an infectious disease center every day seven days a week for two to three hours and have infusions. Beverly was sick with this infection for nearly two years.

Beverly's son Scott was worried about his mother not being able to take care of herself—she was not eating properly—and the future if this was to go on. In the meantime, Beverly's other brother, Warren, who lived in Washington State was willing to take their father, Harvey, to care for him as now he was ninety-six and needed to have some special care. Beverly sold most of her furniture. Scott and Patty got a large home with a casita, swimming pool, putting green, and even extra room for a den that Beverly could use. It was wonderful seeing her son every day as he worked from home. When football season came around, they could cheer together as both Beverly and her son were fans. Beverly enjoyed all her time being able to cook for the family, pick up Angelina from school, take her for ballet lessons, and enjoy a movie on the big screen. It was just like her own little family.

When Beverly first moved to California, she met a lovely lady just six doors down from her, named Rose. They became best friends and still are today. She was a schoolteacher for twenty-eight years and they bonded very quickly. She was witty and liked plants and had a kind soul. Beverly and Rose would sit and talk for hours as she had such a wealth of knowledge from her teaching career; they have a genuine friendship that will not be broken. Rose recommended a psychiatrist as she knew of a very good one in the valley. Beverly started seeing him right away, and this was the turning point in her therapy. Finally, after all these years, she got a diagnosis of her condition. The doctor after only a year of sessions with Beverly diagnosed her as bipolar I disorder and with posttraumatic depression. Dr. G was what his patients call him, and he gave Beverly an assignment to read up at home on her computer to know everything she could about those two conditions. When Beverly came back for her next visit they would discuss the meaning and how she felt they applied to her.

Beverly was apprehensive at first to be reading about her own diagnosis. However, it was just a week away, and Dr. G was expecting her to have that information for the discussion. As Beverly read through countless pages of articles and doctors' reports on their diagnosis of these two conditions, it was like reading her own biography and looking in a mirror. Beverly wondered why no one had ever taken the time to give this diagnosis. They would just tell her she was depressed and give her Prozac and increase it until she was on a very high dosage. After that the doctors began to add other antidepressants to go along with the Prozac, but Beverly was still depressed.

At the following week's session, Dr. G and Beverly went over her findings, and Dr. G gave her the results. Beverly was never as high-spirited as she was now, as she knew a name for what was wrong with her. Dr. G prescribed some new medication and said he would probably have to adjust it for a while, until he got it to make Beverly feel right. That was just what he did, and Beverly started feeling like her old self again.

It was late 2011, and Beverly had spent most of her time being sick and had not had time to make any friends other than Rose. She did not like the hot desert weather; her plants all died, and she replaced them with cacti. Beverly struggled to keep anything alive. Having plants was her only hobby, and that was just nearly impossible in the desert. Beverly started to miss home, and home was Florida. She had not spoken to her sister, Diana, in years; maybe now would be a good time to rekindle that relationship. Beverly gave it some thought and decided to just make a call to Mexico Beach, Florida, where her sister lived to see how Diana was getting along.

It had been quite a while, in fact years since Beverly and Diana kept in touch. You would think after two sisters find each other they would be so ecstatic that they would be on the phone every day after what happened in the lives of these extraordinary women. Beverly had two divorces, lived through two DUIs, lost her job, moved from place to place, and ended up in California. Not to mention all the psychiatric care she needed along the way. Whereas Diana lived in the Panhandle for thirty years, was married for forty-eight years, had the same job for thirty-some years, and also was in therapy many times.

Their lives went in two completely different directions. Realistically, it would be safe to say Beverly had the more dysfunctional life, and Diana was much more stable. Beverly and Diana, two completely opposites, their lives together were difficult at times; therefore, there were gaps in their relationship. Beverly was single since 1989. Diana had been married since she was nineteen. They had some similarities but were very different. Being so far apart made it even more challenging. However, it was not that they had forgotten each other; their lives went in different directions for some time, but each always thought of the other.

However, there was one idea they were in sync with; that was they never forgot the day they were taken away from that little shack. Afterward, when they rode in that big white car and they were separated, they clinched their little hands together.

As they grew up, both of them wanted to know why their parents give them away. Were they bad girls? Why did they get sent away from foster homes? Who did they look like? Maybe their mother was looking for them. Beverly and Diana would see girls on the street and wonder if that could that be their sister. "Who had brown eyes? Who do we look like, Mom or Dad?" These were mutual questions that Beverly and Diana had discussed when they were together and wanted the answers to. They both had the longing desire to find the answers to these questions. Beverly had nightmares most of her life. Diana suffered with panic attacks as did Beverly. There was a deep need for them to pursue the resolutions to their questions about their biological family.

CHAPTER 5

Beverly had been thinking a lot about Diana and where they left off in their journey to get the answers to questions that had haunted them for many years. Beverly made several calls to Diana to get the relationship rejuvenated so that they could call Marsha, this time to get their complete files on their adoption. As Beverly made another attempt to get in touch with Diana, she had no idea what they were going to open themselves up to or even how to do it, but they had the determination to get things done. Finally, as Diana and Beverly spoke, they enjoyed catching up on the many things that had happened since they had seen each other. They talked about why Diana had pulled away from Beverly some years back, which was always a mystery to Beverly. Diana blamed Beverly's mother, Margaret, for keeping them apart. Beverly explained it was not Diana that she was keeping her from, but Arlene. Margaret was afraid Diana was going to talk Beverly into seeing Arlene and Beverly would get hurt from the heartbreak her mother could cause her. Diana never shared that information to understand Beverly's mother's thinking about why she was unhappy about their being together. Beverly had not communicated those feelings to Diana, and this was where the conflict between them had been for many years. They were able to talk it out now and saw how much time had been lost because of a devastating misunderstanding.

Beverly explained that she had signed up for the program Ancestry.com and was hoping to find some of their relatives that way. Diana was quite surprised that Beverly was still even thinking about their childhood. Beverly told her, "We need to get this information about our adoption once and for all." Diana agreed with that, but how? Beverly told Diana she had been thinking about Marsha. Diana, of course, remembered Marsha from 1982, but where would she be now? Beverly explained to Diana, "Why, wouldn't she be at the Welfare Board in Bel Air, Maryland?" Diana really thought Beverly had been affected by the 120 degree sun out in California. She wondered why Beverly thought she would still be working there. Beverly thought it would be worth the effort to call, even though Diana thought she was nuts!

The next day, Beverly got the number from an old folder she still had from 1982. She called and asked for Marsha George, which was her name but it had changed to Marsha Whitfill, as she had married. They were then able to tell Beverly that "yes, she still worked there," much to her delight. Beverly asked if it would be possible to get her cell number, as she had some important information about her adoption that needed to get to her right away. The lady on the other end just gave her the cell number. Beverly got off the phone with every emotion one could have, mostly amazement that she could get a cell phone number that easy. The next step was to call Diana and tell her first. She was delighted but, at the same time, thought it to be unbelievable that she was still there and they gave out her cell number. Beverly was now going to call the cell and make arrangements to get their full adoption reports. That was to include their parents' report, each of their reports of what happened in 1953.

Beverly called the cell number, and she recognized Marsha's voice on the other end. However, when she gave her name, Marsha did not remember her. Beverly reminded her that Marsha had helped her and Diana, her sister, in 1982 locate each other by a letter that they sent, in the same month, same year. Marsha could not quite put it together right then, but she mentioned she was on vacation and when she got back in May, she would get what information they were looking for. Beverly acknowledged that they always wanted their adoption records. Marsha let Beverly know she would be glad to work on getting that information for them when she got back. Before they hung up, she said, "You will hear from me in May."

Beverly was bubbly with excitement because she had talked to Marsha, even though she did not seem to remember her, which was a disappointment. But it was thirty years, and it was a step toward Diana and her getting the answers they had always wanted. She called Diana to tell her she spoke with Marsha, and giggling, Diana said she wanted to know everything they talked about, and "When are we getting the paperwork?"

Beverly told her to hold on a minute. "First, she did not recognize their names and situation, and second, she is on vacation in Hawaii and won't be back until May."

Diana went crazy. "May? How can we wait that long?"

Beverly informed her, "We have waited over fifty years now." Diana and Beverly now had to start thinking about what they were going to ask Marsha. They both also needed to be prepared for some of the information that may be in those documents. Some of it may be hard to swallow. They were adults, but this could bring you to a childlike state very quickly when you go back over your life and especially such a tragic one. Beverly and Diana both agreed they were prepared for the worst and the best.

Hours passed, and Beverly got a call on her phone, a number she did not recognize at first, and then the voice was very clear; it was Marsha. She called back to say after she thought about it she remembered them quite well. Beverly wanted to give her a big hug. She felt so much comfort with Marsha as she had helped her through such a bad time. They chatted about how both the girls were doing. Marsha asked, "What happened with the relationship with Diana and Arlene?" Beverly, unfortunately, had to tell her that it ended badly. Marsha was worried that might happen as she knew Diana's sensitive nature and wanted to know how she was getting along. Marsha asked, "So you want all your files from your adoption? That would mean any files on your mother and father from the social workers. In addition, there may be files that would pertain to you both taken from the home, your foster care, and finally your adoption."

Beverly let Marsha know that they wanted to know if the haunting questions that they had in their minds were true. What happened on that frightful day they were picked up? How many foster homes, and why were they separated just to name a few. Marsha was sure all that confidential information would be in there, but she wondered, "Are these girls sure they are comfortable getting to read the words of their parents, as their intentions toward them are made clear?"

Marsha was willing to give Beverly her e-mail and was eager for her and Diana to use it to share any feelings they might have going forward in this journey. "That's just like Marsha, always enthusiastic in getting things going, and she's on vacation." Of course, Beverly and Diana were more than excited since Beverly talked to Marsha. In fact, they were on the phone daily, talking about what they were going to find out, what questions they wanted to ask. Both girls had no idea what was going to be in those documents, but one thing was for sure—it was their life, and the answers they needed after all these years.

The first phone call Beverly got in the first part of May was from Marsha, and she had located their parents' file. She wanted to let Beverly know that it was over hundred pages, and she would be reading it. She said that as she reads it, she sees names she will have to block out. Beverly right away let her know, "We will e-mail all the names, so you don't have to block them out because we know them."

Marsha was surprised when they e-mailed every name in the paperwork, and she replied, "You're right. There is no need to block out names." Marsha was going to read a few pages and then call each of them and discuss it with them before going forward. She related to them that it would be like spoon-feeding a baby. Beverly and Diana thought that was an interesting way of putting it, but she must have her reasons.

A few days went by, and Beverly and Diana got an interesting e-mail from Marsha. She asked them to reflect back and give her their impression of the last memories they had before the authorities were notified to pick them up. Beverly and Diana talked about that day quite extensively, remembering back to 1953 when their parents would leave them home alone quite often. The girls never forgot the fighting, drinking, swearing, and moving from place to place. Beverly and Diana knew it was home but never felt content. Then came the most difficult week of their lives. Obviously, things had escalated between their parents to their point that they just abandoned them completely.

Beverly and Diana recalled taking responsibility of getting milk for the baby from the bar next door. One would stay with the baby while the other got the milk. Food had become so scarce that they had to go to garbage cans to find what food they could. The baby Joseph cried all the time, and the girls did the best they could, changing his diapers and rocking him. These little girls were four and seven and were beyond their years with the kind of responsibility they had on their small but tough shoulders. It was at this time that Diana remembered back that "James was sick all the time with asthma, and Katie, our aunt, took him to live with her." That is why Beverly always recalled three children in the little shack by the railroad tracks. Days and days went by and no one came home. Both girls were frightened at night being all alone. They wondered when Mommy and Daddy would come back to get them.

Eventually, a neighbor started to realize that the three children were left alone because they noticed them coming around looking for food. Thus they called the authorities. Beverly remembered the man and woman in the blue suits and gold buttons came to the door and took them out to the car. Diana and Beverly both were crying and resisting, saying that their Mommy was coming back for them. Beverly recalled having dreams about the man pulling her arm to get her in the car, and she would wake up crying, for years, not knowing if she made it up or not.

The next thing they let Marsha know was that they remembered also being sent to Welfare and foster homes, and then thankfully, they were adopted. Beverly and Diana also remembered other drunk times with their father that may or may not be in the paperwork. "One we both recall is he came home real drunk and angry. The baby Joseph was crying for some milk. He did not want to hear that, so he picked him up and threw him against the wall, and he fell on the bed." Diana was hysterical, crying, and Willy went over to console her, and she pushed him away. "We both were scared and crying, not knowing what he might do."

Marsha wrote back, acknowledging that, Diana and Beverly certainly called to mind many tragic memories with such detail. "Now as I go over the parental documents, I will have in mind these memories that I can compare with what is documented by the social worker. One thing is for sure, there will not be many adoptees that can get a play by play description of what happened in their life for approximately three years." Marsha further explained, "Some of it may be hurtful, and you may find yourself having sad days." But Marsha let Beverly and Diana know that she will be there to hold their hands all the way. The girls knew she would as she has shown nothing but compassion and kindness since they met.

Marsha read the pages of documents that the social worker, Mrs. Belle, so carefully recorded of her conversations with Mr. Willy Clark and Mrs. Arlene Clark around April 1953. She first met Mr. Clark when he came in the office complaining about the whereabouts of his wife and his children. He told Mrs. Belle that she had gone to Virginia to her father's, and he had gone after her. Mrs. Belle explained, "That is why the children are here in the custody of the Welfare." She explained they would both have to come in and sign some paperwork. Mr. and Mrs. Clark made arrangements to come in and go before the judge. Mr. Clark agreed to pay twenty-five dollars toward the care of the children but would not sign off for their adoption.

Mrs. Belle kept in constant contact with Mrs. Clark as to her plans for the children. She was working as a waitress, only making fifteen dollars a week and staying with her sister. She had no transportation and was confused as to what to do concerning the children. Mrs. Clark's family did not want her to return to Mr. Clark, but she thought maybe she should for the good of the children. She worried herself about how she could work this out and keep her children. Maybe she could go to North Carolina with her sister Katie and make a home for them. She also had asked her father in Virginia if she could bring the children to Galax, Virginia, to live with his family.

Now, at the same time, Mr. Clark would stop by to talk to Mrs. Belle and ask about the children and if he could go and visit. Many times he would smell of alcohol, so they knew that the stories they heard about his drinking were probably true. When the first payment came due, Mrs. Clark went by when he got his paycheck, made him cash it, and mailed it. Mr. Clark made a time to go see Beverly and Diana for his first visit on Sunday at the Loper's. Mrs. Belle reported back that Beverly was very happy to see him, and Diana was not as excited to see him.

Mr. Clark did show great concern for Diana's ear problem. Mrs. Belle got all the information from him and Mrs. Clark and had Diana checked by their doctor. It seems that this was an ongoing problem that had lingered on, and no one really took the time to get it taken care of. Mrs. Belle called John Hopkins and made an appointment to take her there as her ear was so bad she had comments made about it from schoolmates. It was a long process, but finally it was resolved as much as it could be.

However, Mrs. Belle continued to try to see Mrs. Clark to see if she had made a decision whether she could take the children with her or if she could take Diana as she seemed especially fond of her. It seemed she was getting hit from all sides as to what to do, and she just wasn't ready to give up on her children. Mr. Clark was not paying and always had an excuse for not doing so. He went from job to job. In fact, Mrs. Clark was thinking about going back with him, and then he left the only job on the farm where he controlled his drinking, so she decided against her decision. Mrs. Belle once again had Mr. Clark taken back to court for nonpayment. The judge ordered him to pay, and Mr. Clark said he would out of his next check. He came to the office and told Mrs. Belle he could not pay that week because he had a TV payment due.

Marsha continued to read the file, but she could see what she was going to share with Beverly and Diana was the fact that they could not get things together. The children were in foster care and had been living with different relatives at many different times, which was a lot of moving around in their short little lives. But now Mr. Clark could not hold down a job, and Mrs. Clark was trying to find a way to care for the children on her small salary. Neither of them wanted to give up their rights to give the children up for adoption. However, Mr. Clark found his TV more important to pay for than his children.

Mrs. Clark was becoming increasingly confused about deciding what to do as the months went by. She told Mrs. Belle that as a child she was dragged around and she did not want to do that to her own children. She understood the importance of having a good home and security. Mrs. Clark felt if it had to be someone else that could give them that security and care, then that would be more important to her. Mrs. Clark mentioned that she would go back with Mr. Clark, but she feared the same situation would arise and that would not be best for the children. Mrs. Belle agreed that they had been moved around among relatives, "and now they are placed where they are happy and doing well, and the next step needs to be a permanent one."

Mrs. Belle spoke with Mr. Clark about him wanting to get back with Mrs. Clark and if they could intervene on his behalf. She explained that they worked on behalf of the children. Mrs. Belle explained, "Children should be in a happy, peaceful home where their parents give them a sense of security, which is essential." She explained to Mr. Clark that they had pretty bad times in their home, and he agreed. Mrs. Belle mentioned that alcohol seemed to be the problem, and he wanted to know why she would think that was the problem when Mrs. Clark was running around on him with soldiers. Mrs. Belle remembered the times he came to the office, smelling of alcohol, although nicely dressed.

Mrs. Clark was diligent in trying to get a better job that paid her more money and also enable her to move to a two-room apartment. However, it was becoming clearer that she could not care for three small children on her income and manage the housing situation. Mr. Clark would stop by and see Mrs. Belle and talk of getting a housekeeper to take care of the children while he worked. Mrs. Belle explained, "First of all, only Mrs. Clark can take them according to the judge. Besides, how can you pay a housekeeper and not us?"

While all this was going on for months and months, Beverly and Diana seemed to be doing fine in the Loper foster home. However, Diana kept asking if Mrs. Clark was going back to Mr. Clark so that they could have a family again. Diana did not understand the problems of them getting back together. She, however, longed for her family to be as one again, even knowing about the drinking, fighting, and moving around. Mrs. Belle knew this weighed heavy on Mrs. Clark's decision to let the children go, especially Diana, as she seemed to be her favorite.

Mrs. Clark called Mrs. Belle to speak to her as she had a very upsetting experience and wanted to come to see her at the office. She came to the office on Monday to talk to Mrs. Belle to explain that she had seen Beverly and a little brown-haired boy come in the diner. She and Beverly were both shocked. She didn't inquire about where Beverly was staying or if she could visit at this time.

Mrs. Clark explained that Mr. Simpson came over to the diner to ask if she was Beverly's mother. She was familiar with him as he had a business next door, and he came into the diner quite often. Mr. Simpson acknowledged how fond of Beverly the family was and that they would like to adopt her; when she was ready to make that decision, would she let him be the first to know? Mrs. Clark called Mrs. Belle to let her know of the meeting with Mr. Simpson from next door and his intention to adopt Beverly. Mrs. Belle let her know that it was not done that way; the adoption would have to go through the Welfare Department. At this time, Mrs. Belle inquired once again if Mrs. Clark had made a decision on the future of the children or not as it had been more than a year since they had been under their care. Mrs. Clark still felt adoption was the last thing she wanted to do.

After a while, Mrs. Clark felt as though Mrs. Belle was nagging for an answer. Mrs. Belle tried to explain that she needed to make a plan for these children. They realized it was difficult mentally and physically. Mrs. Clark agreed that letting the children be adopted seemed the only way out. Mrs. Belle explained that she had Joseph for so little time that it might not be so difficult for either of them, and she agreed. She also agreed she could give Beverly up but not to her cousin Mr. Hallons, as something had gone wrong there. She also commented at this time that she just could not let Diana be adopted but maybe the other children, because Diana was her favorite.

Mrs. Clark asked for a visit with Diana and Joseph before she made a final decision. It was Christmas time and she took Diana a bride doll and Joseph a rubber toy. She said Joseph cried the whole time she held him, and she felt Diana looked happy and very well. Mrs. Belle asked her if her decision about the children had changed since this visit. She felt she would never go back with her husband, and the children need a chance at regular homes. "Joseph doesn't understand, and there is no attachment. Beverly's personality is just like her father's, and she probably will not be bothered by being adopted." This explained Mrs. Clark's obvious lack of interest in Beverly. However, she still felt Diana was so soft and thin that it would be too hard on her to make such a big change this time in her life. Mrs. Belle told her she understood her fears, but she would go ahead with the plans as Diana needed security in her life as much as the others.

At this time, Mr. Clark was still refusing to sign off for the children to be adopted. Mrs. Belle tried to explain to him that the children were asking if they were going to have a permanent home. Beverly was asking what would happen to her if her foster mother doesn't want her anymore. Diana was still wondering if her mother and father were getting back together after all this time. Mrs. Belle let Mr. Clark know that they should accept the grief themselves and let their children have permanent homes. Mr. Clark was concerned about what people would think about him if he gave his children up for adoption and what his children would think of him. Mrs. Belle explained, "Joseph will never remember, Beverly certainly seems to take things easily, and Diana may need some careful talking to over a period of time."

Still months went by with Mr. Clark coming in to say he had a plan for the two girls and that he would not sign off on the adoption. Then Mrs. Clark was still hoping to find a way to at least keep Diana and said that she would sign for the other two. However, a warrant had been put out for Mr. Clark for nonpayment to the state, so he called the office and made an appointment to come in and see Mrs. Belle.

Mr. Clark came to see Mrs. Belle; he suggested that he take the two girls to live with his uncle that lived in Bel Air. Then he suggested that he was now staying at the Beta Hotel and he could take Diana and have someone watch her while he worked. Mrs. Belle appreciated that he was making every effort to get the children except making no effort to pay anything where the children were concerned. How did he expect to take care of them when he could not pay twenty-five dollars for them? At this point, Mrs. Belle asked Mr. Clark to sign the release papers on the condition he could ask his uncle and get back with Mrs. Belle. He never returned to the office or called.

Mrs. Belle called Mrs. Clark to the office as she needed some information on the children. She needed to know if the children had their immunization shots. At this time, Mrs. Clark mentioned she had seen Beverly several times, and she would walk away from her and get mad. Mrs. Belle explained, "That is a normal reaction as she is happy and secure in her new home. She probably fears you will interfere with her present life, and remember, she has not forgotten the past unstable life." Mrs. Clark said she understood. Mrs. Belle explained that Mr. Clark had signed the release for the children and wanted to know if she was ready to make her final plans. Mrs. Clark was extremely surprised that he signed.

Mrs. Clark hesitated and felt that she knew it would eventually come to this as she had no way of supporting the children. She agreed to sign, however with the exception of letting Diana visit with her family one more time. Mrs. Belle explained that it was best not to renew family ties at this time as Diana was going to be adopted. She asked Mrs. Clark if one more visit with relatives was more important than a happy permanent home. Mrs. Clark agreed and signed the release forms that day.

Marsha had volumes of material to share with Beverly and Diana. She knew some delicate subjects had come up, spoken both by their mother and father. Marsha would have to go ever so protectively while sharing these facts with them. Marsha knew each of their personalities and knew how they would react. She decided to e-mail a small amount of information, get their feelings, and then have a phone call with each of them.

Marsha first enlightened Beverly and Diana how long a process it was for their parents to even get to the point of signing a release for their adoption. She clarified that their mother for months was trying to make a decision as to how she could make a home for us. She was making little money and had no transportation and no home. Marsha described how this process went on over a two-year period. She and their father went back and forth, trying in their own way to make a decision. Marsha justified their actions by saying they just did not have the " where with all."

Both Beverly and Diana were thrilled to hear for the first time that their parents did try to come back and make an effort to get them back, even though they abandoned them. Beverly, especially, was embarrassed that she had blamed their mother for leaving them home alone, but she had not known that her mother had tried to get her back. Not only that, but as Diana thought, "There was the constant struggle which Arlene had within herself whether to keep us or give us the opportunity she herself never had."

Marsha could see the impression just that much information had made on them. She explained that "when we received the documents, there is much more lengthy description of how many times they met with Mr. and Mrs. Clark over the years." She told Beverly and Diana, "You will notice quite a discussion about payment for your care while you were in foster care. You will notice it was quite a dialogue over Mr. Clark paying twenty-five dollars a pay period. As you will see, over the whole period you were under foster care, he made one payment." Marsha relayed to Beverly and Diana that "he moved around from job to job and hotel, farmhouse, and relatives. Mr. Clark was not able to make a home for you, although he made an effort, even giving up his TV payment when asked by the court."

Beverly and Diana began to feel hurt by the fact that it was more important for their father to have a TV than pay for their care. However, as adults they could see with the amount of education and his alcohol problems that it was understandable, not excusable. As Marsha shared these ideas with them, they had mixed feelings. Beverly began to feel like she understood where her drinking problems got their start. On the other hand, Diana, being older and disliking alcohol so much, she could see why that would be. All things for the girls were starting to come together, some in a good way and some hurt a little.

Marsha explained further how their mother even had thoughts of returning to their father for the sake of the children. But after much thought, she knew he would be the same as before and not provide. The girls more and more could see their mother put much more effort into trying to make a home for them than they had ever thought. Even if they got nothing else out of these documents, this was the best information they learned. Beverly felt like she could forgive her mother as she had been full of hate before for her mother, and she knew that was not the Christian way to feel; whereas, Diana always had good feelings for her mother, and this validated them even more.

As Marsha read through the information, she continued to see where Diana brought up to the social worker that she wanted to get the family back together. When Arlene visited, she would tell Diana she will be picking her up the next time, but she did not. Once again Diana asked if her mother and father will get back together so she could have a family. Marsha tried to explain to the girls, "Although this may hurt, you can see the sense of longing for your family, no matter what kind of circumstances you were living in at the time, the desire to be with family remains strong." Even after all these years, Diana could remember asking to get the family back together. Whereas Beverly said she mostly recalled worrying about not being taken back, and she wanted the security of not being removed from the home.

Marsha had asked Beverly if she remembered going to the diner with the little boy named Peter. Beverly definitely recalled that Arlene gave them candy and gum. Mr. Simpson, who was Peter's father, asked her where she got that, and right away she told him it was her drunken mommy. Marsha was shocked at how much a four-year-old could recall. But Beverly had these memories running through her mind, and was waiting for someone to validate them for years, and now the time had come. Beverly was able to share how much of a load this took off her shoulders—she had not made up these stories as everyone said she had.

After a few more e-mails and phone calls, Marsha was almost ready to send the documents to Beverly and Diana to read for themselves. They both were able to express their feelings and were coming along fine with some of the new information Marsha was feeding them. Marsha let them know she was a phone call away if they needed her or had any questions at any time.

Marsha could see that after their mother visited Diana and Joseph at Christmas time, brought her a bride doll and Joseph a rubber toy, and held Joseph while he cried, things seemed to change. She saw that

Diana was happy, and Joseph really did not know her. When she got to see Mrs. Belle, she discussed this—how she knew this would eventually happen and that the children needed a secure permanent home. She did not speak about Beverly, so you could see the obvious lack of interest in her. Mrs. Clark still felt Diana was so soft and thin that it would be too hard for her but not the others. Mrs. Belle let her know she understood how she felt but now was the time to take the step to give the children, including Diana, the security in their lives. So Mrs. Clark signed the release at this time.

Marsha told them, "Beverly and Diana, you both have been afforded a great opportunity. Now you can look back and think of what your life could have been. Now you have been validated with what really happened in your life." Marsha helped them to appreciate how adoption had made a real difference in their lives and how thankful they should be that their parents finally came to the conclusion that they did not have the "where with all."

CHAPTER 6

Once again, Marsha prepared Beverly for her files concerning the time of her abandonment in 1953, going to Welfare, foster care, and then adoption. Beverly would learn new things about her personality and how it developed even as a small child. Marsha would share with Beverly things that were documented about her fifty-six years ago by a social worker Mrs. Belle. It was amazing how completely she documented virtually the everyday life of Beverly.

Marsha went on to explain to Beverly that she needed her to share some of the "effects of your life after the Welfare picked you up." Also, Marsha wanted to know how she felt from then until she was adopted, what she remembered, things that Marsha should look for so that she would be able to help Beverly process them more easily. Beverly was eager to share what she recalled to see if that was what was documented or if she had dreamed it up as everyone had always told her.

As Beverly thought back, the first place she recalled staying was the family members, Mr. and Mrs. Hallons, and for some reason her mother did not want her going back there. Beverly hoped this paperwork could help solve the questions in her mind as to the occasions, where, and who molested her. She remembered only vaguely the different men who would touch her and that it happened several times. Beverly recalled a man taking her on a porch, behind a wringer washer, and touching her like you are not supposed to do. She recants how she cried; the man got a switch from the bushes and switched her for making a fuss. Her first memories were of the Loper home with Diana and only staying there a short period of time as they had problems living there. She recalled she had bathroom problems and got lots of spankings at the Loper home. Therefore, Beverly thought Diana got mad thinking it was her fault they got sent away. Beverly felt she wet her pants because of something disturbing that was happening to her. To make matters worse, Mrs. Loper requested quite abruptly that both Beverly and Diana be moved immediately. At first Diana was to be taken to Aunt Jenny's and Beverly was to live where Joseph was living. "However, we know this is not what happened and still do not know why there was such a change in arrangements." Beverly remembered a car accident with her father and having glass picked out of her hair. She also recalled her father taking her to the bar next door, called the Casa Mia, to dance on wooden tables, in a pretty dress, while men would flip quarters on the table so her father could buy beer.

Mrs. Belle's description of Beverly was a chubby, blonde child with happy smile and dancing eyes. She seemed friendly, happy, and had no worries or concerns about anything. Her first foster home was with the Lopers, and Diana was there also. Here is where problems began that had not been an issue before for Beverly. Mrs. Loper reported to Mrs. Belle that Beverly ate so much she had a stomachache, and she was giving her milk of magnesia. Also she was wetting her pants, and Mrs. Loper was quite annoyed. Mrs. Belle recommended that she feed Beverly smaller snacks between meals. Also, Mrs. Belle had checked with Mrs. Clark, and Beverly never had a problem with toilet training for quite some time. Mrs. Loper continued to say that Beverly was unusually stubborn, wanted her own way, and was spoiled. "She does not seem to react to any form of punishment."

As the month went on, Mrs. Belle made another visit to see Beverly, and now Mrs. Loper was complaining that she was reverting to baby habits. She had tried spanking, made her sit on the toilet for hours, and made her wash her panties to shame her, but nothing worked. In addition, she did not play well with the other children. In fact, she had noticed that she played by herself on the swing and talked to imaginary people. Mrs. Loper believed this child was stubborn and spoiled, and she could not continue to keep her and wanted both girls moved.

At the next visit, Mrs. Belle went out in the yard to explain to Beverly that she was going to move her to a different home as Mrs. Loper had five children of her own and she could not manage her and

Diana also. Oddly enough, Beverly did not appear upset or concerned but seemed rather pleased at the attention she was getting and the idea of going to a different home.

From the paperwork it was unclear exactly what happened but there was just a mention that Beverly was supposed to be split from Diana as she was going with relatives. Marsha knew this was the most hurtful part of their journey. What happened all those years ago that they were separated? After this, it was mentioned that the relatives could not take Diana because of sickness, so they took her to the farm with Joseph, and Beverly to Mrs. Volts. Beverly and Diana remembered that day very vividly like it was yesterday, when they were torn apart. No one would ever be able to explain what happened or why they made the decision they did as they read it fifty years later. One thing was for sure—Beverly and Diana were robbed of a childhood together and no one could replace that for them. However, they never forgot each other. Their quest to find one another landed them here today and finally together.

Mrs. Volt learned that Beverly had a toilet training problem to watch for, which was evident at the Loper home. Other than that Mrs. Volt was told "she gets along with other children fine." Beverly was told she could call Mrs. Volt "Aunt Pat," and that in a week, Mrs. Belle would be back to see how Beverly was doing in her new home.

Mrs. Belle learned on her next visit how much of a big help Beverly was with the other children, according to Mrs. Volt. She was most polite, and she had no mistakes with going to the bathroom. Mrs. Volt commented that Beverly fit in beautifully and she would like to keep her indefinitely. In fact, Beverly had asked Mrs. Volt to call Mrs. Belle and ask her to let Mrs. Volt keep her forever. She felt so secure. Mrs. Belle was happy to tell Beverly that she could stay. Mrs. Volt did say she had an issue with Beverly telling tall tales to the neighbor kids. Mrs. Volt told Beverly how important it is to tell the truth. Beverly was telling how her parents were drinking and fighting and that she was even made to drink herself by her father when he was drinking. This was very embarrassing, and Mrs. Volt was unaware if this information were true stories from Beverly's home life or could she be making it up. Mrs. Belle spent some time with Beverly, explaining that it wasn't nice to tell stories like that around to other children in the neighborhood. Beverly acknowledged that she understood; however, she responded that she was telling the truth.

At the next visit, Mrs. Belle found Mrs. Volt was having an issue with Beverly leaving the yard and not coming when she called. She punished her by putting her to bed without getting ice cream. When Mrs. Belle asked Beverly why she did not answer when she was called, she said that she just didn't want to come home.

In addition, another problem had arisen. Mrs. Volt was quite concerned that Beverly spoke a lot about sex since she came from the Loper home; she seemed to have much more knowledge and information than a four-year-old should know. Obviously, Mrs. Belle was quite concerned and felt the need to address this with Beverly. However, Mrs. Volt was very happy to have Beverly; she loved her daughter Rebecca and watched for her to come from school every day. Mrs. Volt did say that Beverly worried that if she was bad, she would be sent back and taken away from her home. She felt someone had threatened her with this before, as she kept bringing it up.

A month went by before Mrs. Belle visited Beverly, and Mrs. Volt let her know that Beverly would be spending some time with her sister, Margaret, as she was going to work at the bakery. Mrs. Margaret Simpson found Beverly unusually bright and made a great deal over her. She took her on trips and bought her toys and a new tricycle. However, since she had been going to the Simpsons to be babysat, now she took it upon herself to go across Route 40, with Mac trucks and cars going down that highway, to visit them on her own. Mrs. Volt had spanked her and it did no good, but taking privileges and treats impressed her considerably. Mrs. Volt explained that Mr. and Mrs. Simpson would like to adopt Beverly and said that she was very fond of them.

Unfortunately, while Mrs. Volt was visiting her sister, Beverly went next door to the diner with Peter, their little boy, and saw her mother. She came back with the candy and gum her mother had given her. Mrs. Volt asked where she got that, and Beverly told her she got it from her drunken mother. Beverly announced very firmly that she did not want to go back to live with her because of all the fighting and drinking, "so don't make me go back to her."

At the next visit to Mrs. Volts, Mr. Simpson stopped by to see Mrs. Belle. He wanted to let her know how eager they were to adopt Beverly and that they could offer her a good secure future home. Mr. Simpson even let her know they were buying a house large enough so Beverly could have her own room. Mrs. Belle explained that not only had Mrs. Clark not signed any release form, but nor had Mr. Clark. Mr. Simpson was not aware there was a Mr. Clark as he observed Mrs. Clark going out with men from the diner. In addition, they would have to go through the Welfare agency as well. Beverly came in and was definitely affectionate toward Mr. Simpson. They talked to Beverly a little about her sister Diana and Joseph, her brother; she was pleased to hear about them.

When Mrs. Belle visited again, Beverly was waiting for her restlessly as it was rainy and she could not be outside. Another worker was there, so Mrs. Volt explained to Beverly that she was not here for her. Beverly exclaimed that she had been moved around and around and around! Mrs. Belle laughed and told Beverly that she wasn't moved that much. She was quick to correct Mrs. Belle and named all the places she had lived by name. Mrs. Belle was shocked that she had such a good memory and was proficient with names as she had been. Then she asked for "Ickey," but Mrs. Belle had not seen him for a long time. This was her brother James that lived with her aunt Katie; she was asking how he was doing. Mrs. Belle also talked with Beverly about Diana and Joseph, how he had begun to talk. Beverly seemed to enjoy hearing about her family, especially asking about "Ickey." At the same time, Mrs. Volt was starting to understand the names of all the people Beverly would bring up and who they were. Mrs. Volt also spoke about Beverly needing a glass of water at night and sleeping with her mouth open. Mrs. Belle indicated that "this is probably because she will need her tonsils and adenoids out soon." She also spoke of the same issue with the stomachache problem from overeating at the Lopers' home. Mrs. Belle recommended smaller meals and said, "Don't let her stuff herself."

After a few months, Mrs. Belle brought Mrs. Mearst as Beverly's new worker to meet her so she could adjust to seeing her, rather than

Mrs. Belle. Mrs. Mearst found Beverly a very nice-looking child with blonde hair and large blue eyes. She acted very sophisticated for her age, was quite polite, intelligent, and seemed to be well adjusted. She was inclined to exaggerate or tell lies but did not do this viciously, but in fun. Beverly had not adjusted happily in the Lopers' home. She did not play well with the other children and played by herself. She also had a problem with toilet training. However, in the Volts' home, she had neither problem. Beverly had a problem with exaggerated stories about her family and the Lopers' home. She also ran off to Mrs. Volt's sister's home without permission, which was dangerous. Beverly seemed happy in this home; she was affectionate and outgoing and did not demand a lot of attention, but seemed to be generous and relaxed.

Mrs. Mearst came for a visit only to find another child in the home bothering Beverly, telling her, "This isn't her real mother." However, Beverly did not seem too affected; she was easily managed, well behaved, and an easygoing child. Mrs. Volt wanted Beverly to show Mrs. Mearst her new clothes for her trip to Florida. She was very proud of all her dresses; she showed them and neatly put them back in her suitcase.

At the next visit, Beverly was unhappy that she was not getting enough attention and that she was being scolded too much. This could have been because Mrs. Volt had to pay more time to some of the other children. However, Beverly ran to the door to always be the first to tell everything she had heard. She told Mrs. Mearst that they got a new car and new beds, bed spreads, pillows, etc. She liked to tell things before Mrs. Volt got a chance, therefore to tease her. Beverly was very protective of her things; she didn't want the other children to take them, and she wanted her things nice. She was a very precocious child but seemed happy and well adjusted in the Volts' home.

Mrs. Mearst next visit with Beverly was interesting because "when we were talking, Beverly brought up her sister Diana. She asked if we could arrange a visit with Mrs. Belle and Diana." Mrs. Mearst asked her who was Diana to see if she remembered her as her sister, but didn't mention the word "sister." Beverly mentioned they had always been together, played together, but never used the word sister. Mrs. Mearst asked again, if she meant she was a good friend. Beverly told her, "She was a friend." Mrs. Mearst thought from the discussion that Beverly did not remember Diana as her sister, so she must have heard someone talking about Diana visiting her. Mrs. Mearst made no attempt to make arrangements for these two sisters to have a visitation because Beverly did not call her "sister," only a friend at the age of four.

Mrs. Volt had to take one of the other children for an examination, and Beverly went along; all dressed up, she looked very nice and was excited about the trip to Baltimore. She was very helpful with the other children; she listened very attentively and apparently had a good memory, as she later could repeat what she learned. She behaved very ladylike, although with the other children, Beverly was inclined to be a little bossy. However, her helpfulness with the children overcame that objection. She was somewhat used to getting her own way. Beverly seemed still inclined to tell tall tales about how she had nothing to eat all day or was put to bed with no supper—all of this, she thought, was funny apparently. If you asked Beverly about it, she would deny it or say she way teasing you. Apparently, she loved the attention, so she made up stories.

At the next visit, Mrs. Volt asked if we could move all the children except Beverly, as she had a nervous condition. She felt Beverly was old enough to take care of herself and was not any trouble. Beverly seemed a little mixed up as she thought Rebecca, Mrs. Volt's daughter, was being moved also. Mrs. Volt was trying to explain that her real mommy could not take care of her, and Beverly spoke up and told her that was her drinking mother Arlene Clark. Mrs. Mearst cautioned Mrs. Volt against spoiling Beverly, now that the other children had gone. She would have to think of the time when Beverly would be leaving and did not want Beverly to be unhappy in her new home.

About a month later, Mrs. Volt called to say that Mrs. Clark followed them down the street, got out of the car, and came over to Beverly. Mrs. Clark asked Beverly if she knew who she was, and Beverly said she did not know her. She asked again, and she said, "Arlene," and told her to leave her alone. Beverly did not want anything to do with her and would not go to her. Mrs. Clark asked if Mrs. Volt was her foster mother, and Mrs. Volt did not care to answer. Beverly clearly got upset, started crying, and expressed clearly that she did not want to go with Arlene. Mrs. Clark was very provoked, but Beverly remained the most upset by the whole encounter.

The next visit was to get Beverly vaccinated. Beverly came running to Mrs. Mearst, all smiles and eager to go. On the way over, they talked and Mrs. Mearst noticed how Beverly could count, knew colors, could print her name, and seemed to have a large vocabulary. She could identify most animals and foods and was very well behaved. She was not shy or afraid and was polite. After her shot, the doctor was teasing her, asking if she had ancestors, and Beverly told him, no, she did not. On the way back, Mrs. Mearst asked Beverly if she remembered her father, and she said she did and her mother. "Can you tell me their names?" She gave the names, "Willy and Arlene."

Mrs. Mearst then asked if she liked her father. She said that she did not because he was bad. But Mrs. Mearst thought that he was very fond of Beverly and was always very good to her. Beverly then told her that he was good to her but not to Arlene. Then they talked about Diana and Joseph to see if Beverly remembered them. She remembered them. She remembered Diana and "Ickey" but did not remember Joseph.

Beverly remained in the Volt home for at least year or more. Mrs. Volt reported her to be "alert and learns quickly." She actually was ready for school that fall, but was not able to start because of her birth date. She adjusted nicely and was well behaved. Actually, she was a great help to Mrs. Volt when she had the children, but she was looking forward to having her independence when they were removed from the home. She seemed to be getting along by herself and not missing them too much. She remained fond of Rebecca and spent a lot of time with her. She loved going places and seeing people and had a very outgoing personality. However, she was slightly spoiled and was inclined to exaggerate or make up stories; then again she had been known to use her stories to get attention and tease adults. Beverly continued to be well behaved.

They took Beverly for her psychological exam today. On the ride down in the car she was fairly quiet. Although, during her exam she acted quite silly, and instead of answering the questions, she would say she didn't know. Mrs. Volt expressed that she did this when people complimented her. However, she was sure she got credit for the questions. Mrs. Mearst explained to Beverly that she would have a new worker from now on, and she did not seem upset.

Mrs. Volt brought her sister Mrs. Simpson into the office to meet Mrs. Case about Beverly. Mrs. Simpson was asking to adopt her, telling Mrs. Case she felt she fit into their home, and they all were crazy about her. Mrs. Case told Mrs. Simpson at the Welfare Office that they knew her family background and felt this would not be good for an adoption placement. "We can't make a child completely forget their own, and unfortunately, she will not forget her past altogether. Also, her family lives in the same neighborhood and could later have some contact with the family." Mrs. Simpson did not feel as though that would make any difference. She felt that they were prepared for all of this. Mrs. Simpson asked if they had a release for Beverly yet, and they let her know that they were working on the plans for Beverly.

Once again, the new worker, Mrs. Case, visited Beverly and found her to be a tall, exceptionally pretty child with ash-blonde hair and blue eyes. She had a new green dress and appeared to be very clothes-conscious. She was a very precocious child, enjoyed playing hostess, showing Mrs. Case around the trailer, and was content to listen to the grown-up conversations. Then she started talking about her doll she got for Christmas and all the details about her playmates. Mrs. Case asked Beverly if she would like to take a ride the next time she came for a visit, and she accepted with alacrity, stating she will also dress up her doll to take her along.

Several months later, Mrs. Case mentioned to Beverly she was sorry she did not pick her up for the ride she had promised, and Beverly smiled pleasantly and did not seem to mind. She seemed to be a very pretty child and was again dressed in an expensive-looking cotton dress. Mrs. Volt said she was working at the bakery, and at these times her sister Margaret was caring for Beverly. They realized in retrospect that it was her sister watching Beverly more often and they did not clarify this. However, Beverly seemed a very poised, precocious child and was pleasant and apparently obedient. Although at times she seems spoiled, she was not obnoxiously so. Beverly showed off her new doll and the new dress she had gotten for it. Mrs. Volt was anxious as to when they would be moving Beverly. Mrs. Case told her, "Probably by the summer, therefore she would need to prepare Beverly for her new home." Mrs. Volt expressed difficulty doing so as she had her so long and felt like her own child. Mrs. Case understood how she felt but knew she would want the best for Beverly.

In the summer, Mrs. Case visited Mrs. Volt to see Beverly and found she had grown taller. She was attractively dressed in a very pretty pink cotton dress with a stiffened petticoat attached. On every occasion when Mrs. Case had seen Beverly, she was always beautifully and expensively clothed and appeared very clothes-conscious herself. She would smooth her skirts as she sat down and was very careful not to mess her dresses. She was very happy when Mrs. Case made a fuss over her new dresses. It was Mrs. Case's impression that Beverly was a very feminine "sugar-and-spice"-type of child. She also was wearing a child's pink pearl necklace and bracelet, which, Mrs. Volt informed Mrs. Case, was a gift from Aunt Margaret. Then Beverly brought a professional picture that Mrs. Simpson had taken of Beverly and her two sons to show Mrs. Case. Mrs. Volt explained that Beverly and their youngest child, Warren, showed quite a resemblance to one another. Mrs. Case explained that perhaps the similarity was in the coloring.

It was at this time Mrs. Case suggested that Beverly go for a ride, and she agreed with eagerness that she was pleased to go. Before Mrs. Case left, she explained to Mrs. Volt that she was going to talk to Beverly about adoption, and when she brought her home she may be upset. Mrs. Case further told Mrs. Volt that she would need to frequently talk about adoption to Beverly to get her prepared for her move to a permanent home. Mrs. Volt emphatically stated that Beverly would be upset about leaving the Simpson home and not so much her home. Mrs. Case was very surprised at this, and Mrs. Volt went on to explain that Beverly had been playing with Mrs. Simpsons' two sons. Mrs. Case further stated that she would need to help Beverly understand and accept this move even more, speaking in glowing terms about adoption. Mrs. Volt agreed to help Beverly know how wonderful it would be for her.

On the drive, Mrs. Case found Beverly very relaxed and chatty when asked what the things she liked to do were. She mentioned skating, playing with Warren, the younger Simpson son, and playing with her doll. She was very observant, pointing out places she had been to and animals she knew. After a while, Mrs. Case asked Beverly if she had ever heard of adoption and what she thought it was. Beverly explained, "It was when people took you to live with them, and you became their little girl." She expounded on this by telling Mrs. Case she would have a family of her own. Mrs. Case wondered if Beverly would like her to find Beverly a home with a mommy and daddy, and a little boy she could have as a brother. Beverly right away stated to Mrs. Case that she already had a brother, and his name was Peter Simpson. Mrs. Case explained that he was just a friend and had acted like a brother, but was not like what she would have when she were adopted.

After being quiet for quite some time, Beverly began to express that she wanted to stay right where she was! Mrs. Case asked where she meant, and she explained with her mommy and quickly changed her expression to Aunt Margaret and Daddy. Then several times she referred to Mr. Simpson as Daddy and Mrs. Simpson as Mommy. As it was arranged, they drove Beverly to the Simpsons' residence, and she exclaimed that this was where she lived. Obviously, it was a real question in Beverly's mind as to where she lived—with Mrs. Volt or Mrs. Simpson.

At the same time, Mrs. Case had arranged for Mr. and Mrs. Jones to visit Beverly as a possible adoptive child for them. They were eager and very pleased, excited at the thought of having a chance to visit with her. However, things came to a stop as the department received a copy of a petition from Mr. and Mrs. Simpson, requesting adoption of Beverly Clark and an enjoinment preventing the agency from removing her from their care until the case was heard.

However, the Welfare Department was not done yet. When they read over the petition's Section Five, it said that the best interest was not to remove Beverly and put her in a strange home; they challenged that with another petition to Judge Clay just a month later. Nonetheless, Judge Clay felt that Mr. and Mrs. Simpson had handled this deviously, not giving the Welfare proper consideration. In as much he felt after going over the petitions and the Simpsons were examined by Attorney Henry Charles, it was in the best interest of the child to remain in the Simpson home. The case was closed on 11-30-1955, and the adoption was final on March 5, 1956.

Marsha explained that she had come to understand some of what Beverly had questioned over the years about what happened at the foster care home, thereby helping her to see the answers. It was quite clear that Beverly did not have a toilet training problem before she entered the Loper home. Marsha felt it was a combination of just being removed from your family home and other factors, and also it seemed as though more was going on there as well. Beverly was having potty problems and stomachaches and was unusually stubborn, and basically, Mrs. Loper could not seem to find any punishment for her. And yet Mrs. Volt had none of those problems; in fact, it was the opposite. Beverly spoke very openly about sex for a four-year-old; she did not wet her pants, and she did tell about things that she heard were going on in the household. Marsha agreed with Beverly that she might have found the answer to her questions about being molested.

Regarding the two girls being split up, it was unclear as to why, other than Mrs. Belle could not take Diana to Mrs. Clark's sister due to her sickness, so they took her to Mr. and Mrs. Famos with Joseph and Beverly to Mrs. Volt. However, this did not answer the question as to why there did not seem to be any discussion between the social workers or anybody about keeping Beverly and Diana together. Marsha realized this was the most heartbreaking part of this journey for Beverly as well as Diana. It was hard to express to Beverly that "this is one part you will have to live with, and you may never know why." Marsha expounded on that by saying, "Look what you have now by finding each other as you have. Some children never have that experience."

Marsha noticed that Beverly had a happy-go-lucky attitude, and as the worker put it, she did not seem to let things bother her. She was quite aware of things going on around her. Marsha saw that when Beverly was staying at the Volts', she was very independent and would go to see friends across a highway when she was told not to go. It was at this time that

Beverly saw her mother in a diner with Peter, now her adopted brother; she identified her as her "drinking mother." Marsha could see that Beverly was very aware that her parents drank, even though the social worker told her she told tall tales. Beverly knew she was not making these things up; she remembered the life they had endured. Marsha reminded Beverly of Mr. Simpson going over to the diner to see her mother, Arlene, to ask her to let him adopt Beverly. "Obviously, even though she said she was not ready, this was the beginning of Mr. and Mrs. Simpson going directly to your mother and around the Welfare Department."

Another trait that Marsha noticed and which Beverly mentioned was that she liked to kid a lot. According to Mrs. Mearst, "Beverly did exaggerate and tell tall tales, but it seems it was all in fun many times. Obviously as Beverly feels this is her way of covering true feelings and hurt that she may have felt at the time." Also, Marsha noticed that once again Beverly would have an occasion to see her mother, Arlene, and get upset and cry to Mrs. Volt saying she did not want to go back with her. Even though Arlene seemed provoked by this, Beverly certainly made her feelings clear to everyone involved where she wanted to live. As Marsha went on to say, "It is not unusual for adoptees to feel like this when they have lived through the trauma that Beverly had just been exposed to so recently. Beverly remembers how afraid she felt when she would see her mother, thinking after she got to a good home, she was going to have to go back to the home life she remembers."

As Marsha read on she saw where the subject of Diana came up again, and the social worker, Mrs. Mearst, ignored Beverly's plea to have a visitation with Diana. This time Beverly even asked her to talk to Mrs. Belle, the previous worker, to set up a visitation, but because she did not refer to her as her sister but only as a friend, they seemed to ignore Beverly's plea. Beverly once again let Marsha know that this was just not acceptable when a four-year-old asked to see her sister, because they had always been together but not called her sister, just by name, and that should have been enough. Beverly reminded Marsha, "This is what makes Diana and her hurt so deeply." Marsha thought, "Reading this again will forever cement it in Beverly's heart that they did not try in any way to keep us together." Marsha admonished that "letting it go will be your closure."

Further, Mrs. Mearst took Beverly for a ride. Marsha noticed that once again she questioned Beverly about who her mother and father were and tried to see if Beverly was able to give their full names. She went on to ask her about her brothers and sister. At first she named the children at the foster home, and then Beverly went on to say "Diana" and "Ickey." Marsha was sharing with Beverly that she did not forget Diana although she may have not remembered the word "sister" as she had been moved around with quite a few children. Beverly explained to Marsha when she went through this paperwork, "The fact that she asked about Diana and they did nothing is what will stick with me all her life." However, since Marsha helped find Diana and Beverly and put them together, the pain had become an ache. Beverly felt that these social workers are gone from this earth, "and we are still here wondering why they paid no attention to the pleas we both made to see each other and to be kept together."

It wasn't long before Marsha explained after this that Mrs. Simpson went to the Welfare Office and expressed her feelings about wanting to adopt Beverly. The office worker at the time explained to her that they understood their interest, but because they lived too near the family, it would be difficult for Beverly. Mrs. Simpson explained that that did not bother them; however, they let her know they did not even have a release for Beverly yet. Marsha let Beverly know that they were putting them off as they were not going through the proper channels for adopting children. At this time they were already, without Mrs. Volt's knowledge, working on another family for Beverly. Beverly remembered there was a controversy over her adoption when it came time to adopt her, and it almost did not happen with the Simpsons.

Marsha went on to say, "There is quite a bit in your paperwork about that as the Welfare was convinced they did not know you were spending so much time at the Simpsons. But that seems not to be the case as one time after a visit with Beverly, they returned you to the Simpson home." Mrs. Volt on two occasions told them her sister Margaret was babysitting Beverly while she worked late. Beverly explained that she felt the whole thing got out of hand, and she stayed over there so much, got so attached to their family, and finally when they realized it, it was too late. However, it does feel tragic to Beverly now thinking she might have been taken from the home she felt secure and happy in, just because the Simpson family was not following procedures.

Marsha pointed out to Beverly that even though she had a third social worker, Mrs. Case, she seemed to handle it with ease. However, when it came time for Mrs. Volt to start telling Beverly she was going to be adopted, of course she did not want to be the one to break the news. Marsha could see why this was going to be difficult, as her sister was planning on adopting Beverly and they had something in the works that Mrs. Case knew nothing about. "Beverly, you will see they already had another family, Mr. and Mrs. Jones, set up that had a little boy, ready to go through the adoption process.

However, the Welfare got a petition to keep Beverly in the Simpson home right before they could remove you to take you to the Jones' home." Therefore, the attorney for the Welfare sent another petition asking Judge Clay to rescind this petition as "they had made a home for Beverly that was not a strange home," as they put it in the petition. Beverly felt very strange to think her life could have been totally different if that Judge had ruled a different way. Beverly began to think of her children and grandchild, Angelina.

Her whole entire family and friends would not be the same, and Beverly began to struggle with this vulnerable feeling. Marsha told her, "Beverly, you are now living in reality, and you must put these challenges behind you and look how remarkable your life has turned out through all this adversity." Beverly agreed that she had come to learn she has had opportunities that she never would have had with her biological family; while she no longer blamed them, she was able to appreciate the life they were able to allow her to enjoy.

At this point, Marsha felt she could send Beverly's paperwork on to her and that she was fully prepared to read the contents. She felt Beverly was able to answer some of the lingering questions on her mind about when she was molested and who it might have been; she now can find some comfort that it was spoken about and she did not make it up, as she was led to believe. Beverly would also be very delighted to know her new parents were diligent in getting an attorney and fighting the courts to keep her in their home as they felt this was the best for her. She and Diana may never get a straight answer as to why they did not try to keep them together, but the joyfulness they shared now and the closure they will be able to have with writing this book will be forever. Marsha wanted Beverly to feel comfortable calling or e-mailing her if she had any thoughts or feelings as she read about her life from 1953 to 1956 when she was adopted.

CHAPTER 7

It again began with Marsha finally receiving the documents on Diana late, as her paperwork came from St. Mary's County in Maryland. Diana had been adopted from St. Mary's County; however, she had the same worker as did Beverly, so that was quite unusual. As Marsha began to go through the document, she was quite overcome by the difference in children when she began to read about Diana. Therefore, she felt she would need to get Diana's frame of mind about what was contained in these documents before she shared them with her. Marsha asked Diana to try and give her an overall view of what she recalled after they were taken from the Welfare.

Diana remembered wanting her family back together and wondering where they were. She recalled asking about her family as she held on to Beverly's hand closely. Diana had fears all her grown life as to why they were not placed together. Even though they both spoke about each other, there did not seem to be any effort to keep them in the same family. That fact had torn Diana apart for years, and she still struggled with the pain. Could Marsha find the answer, because it was dreadful to both Diana and Beverly? Maybe Marsha could let the boogey man out of the closet. Also, as time went on, Diana knew the workers did not try to make arrangements for Diana to have any visitation "even though we both asked." Diana wanted some answers and was hoping to find them in these documents, as Marsha read them and when she got them to help her solve the mysteries of "why."

Mrs. Belle described Diana as a slender little girl with medium-brown hair, brown eyes, and a sprinkling of freckles. "She has a serious and sensitive nature and seems to have an unusual ability to tell about her relatives, family birth dates, and addresses pertinent to her case." Mrs. Belle also noticed that she had a badly infected ear. "After talking with her for a few moments, you could see she is quite frightened," so Mrs. Belle decided to discuss a new home for her. Diana did not ask any question but paid close attention.

At Mrs. Belle's first visit to Diana's new foster home, the Lopers expressed she was very happy to see her and wanted a big hug. Almost immediately she began to ask about her family, especially wanting to know how they were, and she obviously was homesick for her mother. It was at this time that Mrs. Belle reminded Diana about her appointment to get her ear checked at John Hopkins. She was a little nervous and worried about their visit.

A few days later, it was Diana's visit to the hospital, and she seemed fine; however, once again she asked about how her family was doing. Mrs. Belle explained how foster care worked and the reason Diana was in foster care. Diana seemed to understand but still craved any knowledge or bit of information she could get on her mother or father. Diana would have to come back to John Hopkins as they had only X-rayed to find a polyp that would need to be removed. She did not seem concerned about an operation. A month went by, and the treatment was changed again to begin silver nitrate treatments instead of an operation.

Mrs. Clark made a visit to see Diana at Mrs. Lopers' and was very concerned that she must find a way to get the children back before they got too attached to someone else. She was well aware that Diana was anxious to get the family back together, and that influenced her considerably. Mrs. Belle noticed that Diana was obviously her favorite.

Mrs. Belle had already gotten permission from Mrs. Clark and was picking Diana up to go to John Hopkins Clinic for a treatment, when Diana exclaimed she had another visit from her mother. She was very pleased by this visit and seemed very content. Once again, Diana began to talk about her hopes for the future of getting the whole family back together, which seemed to always be on her mind. "When we arrived back at the Lopers', she let Mrs. Belle know that she had spoken to Mrs. Clark, and she still had made no plans for taking the children back." Mrs. Loper explained that if this was so, she would like the children removed as soon as possible, and her complaint was with Beverly.

On the way to the hospital, Diana inquired again about her family wanting any information about them. She also wanted Mrs. Belle to know she was attending Bible school and really enjoyed it. Diana was excited over her bag of coloring and comic books. Mrs. Belle discussed the operation and stay in the hospital. Diana remarked that her mother would be taking her home from the hospital. Mrs. Belle had to remind Diana that she would pick her up and take her home. Diana explained that she meant after her ear was better, her mother was going to come and get her. Unfortunately, Mrs. Belle had to explain that Mrs. Clark had not made arrangements for Diana as yet, so she could not expect to go with her very soon.

Mrs. Belle picked Diana up from the hospital, and the nurses expressed how well behaved Diana was while at the hospital. They arrived at the Lopers' home, and Beverly was happy to see her sister. As soon as Mrs. Belle gave instructions on how to take care of Diana's ear, Mrs. Loper asked that Mrs. Belle remove the children by August 1. She remarked that it was not working out with her children home from school. She complained not only about Beverly but also that Diana got into things more than one might expect. Mrs. Loper suggested that Diana not be with children that are family members. Mrs. Belle agreed and explained she would do her best to find them another home.

While Diana was healing and was being kept quiet after the operation, she did get a visitor. Mr. Clark came by to visit to see how she was doing after the operation. When he got to see Diana, he cried; however, Diana did not respond like she did when she saw her mother. Diana asked her father when he was going to get back with their mother. Mr. Clark explained that he was ready to, but he was waiting for their mother. He went on to tell Diana that he had a big house now and he had to do his own cooking and clothes. Obviously, if he had to be by himself, he could not take the children to a home like this with no one to care for them.

Mrs. Belle stopped by for a visit and found Diana very quiet and subdued for the first part of her visit. She explained that she was all right, but then she began to chat away about her father's visit. After giving Mrs. Belle all the details of what he talked to her about, she appeared not to have much feeling about the subject. Diana knew it was Mrs. Loper's birthday and wondered if she was still going to be there to celebrate as she had been told they were going to be moved soon.

As the visit with Mrs. Belle went on, Mrs. Belle expressed to Diana that Mrs. Loper had all she could handle with her own five children. At first she seemed to accept this, but apparently Mrs. Belle could see that was a problem with Diana. When Mrs. Belle inquired as to the problem, she found that Diana had blamed Beverly for them having to be moved and was mad at her for a week, not even speaking to her. Mrs. Belle let Diana know that she should not be angry with Beverly, as it was not her fault. Mrs. Belle assured Diana that they had a nice home they would be moving them to; she just was not sure when it would be.

On Mrs. Belle's next visit to take Diana for her checkup, Diana was happy to get her ear looked at by a different doctor that she liked. He checked it thoroughly and cleaned out particles and said it looked in good condition. The doctor expressed how the adenoid area had completely healed and did not think she would need any more treatment. However, Diana would need a six-month reexamination at the clinic. This was good news for Diana as she had so many problems with this ear, and finally they had gotten to the bottom of the issue. After Mrs. Belle arrived back at the Loper home, she wanted to talk to Mrs. Belle about Diana's visit from her father. Mrs. Loper enlightened Mrs. Belle that Diana had held back and was unwilling to show him any affection. Diana told him that he didn't even love her. Mr. Clark tried to reassure her that he did, but was not very convincing as she did not believe him. "You could see it in her eyes." Mrs. Loper went on to say that he smelled of liquor and she felt that may have been the reason Diana did not want to go near him. Over the time she had had Diana, she got her to stop biting her nails, but after his visit, she went right back to biting them.

Mrs. Belle asked Mrs. Loper, "What seems to be the issue you are having with Diana?" Mrs. Loper felt that Diana was a very troublesome child, as she had gotten into everything in her home. "She seems to get into the older children's things, takes them out of their drawers and puts them in different places. Without anyone knowing it, Diana seems to poke into every drawer and cupboard in the house. She has also become a nuisance to the older girls. When they are reading, she turns the pages further on just to annoy them. This interrupts my children, and I do not want to discipline her for these actions." Mrs. Loper felt she was someone else's child, so she did not discipline Diana. Mrs. Belle assured her they would expect her to discipline her "the same as you would your own."

They talked a little about moving the girls on August 15 "as we had a home that could take them both, therefore keeping the girls together. However, Mrs. Loper let me know that would not be acceptable as she wanted them removed by August 1." Mrs. Belle said then she would need to make other plans as the other home with Mrs. Cox was not available until the fifteenth. This did not seem to matter to Mrs. Loper as she had plans for August 1, which she was not willing to change.

Mrs. Belle inquired of Mrs. Clark if she could help in the interim for the two weeks for the girls because of the immediate need to remove the children from Mrs. Loper's. Mrs. Clark thought she could make arrangements for Diana to go to her sister Jenny, and she would let her know. So the arrangements were made to take Diana to Aunt Jenny and Beverly to where her brother Joseph was staying at the Famos residence.

A few days later, Mrs. Clark called to say that her sister's child had the mumps. "Would that be a problem bringing Diana there?" Mrs. Belle felt she should call the doctor because of all the problems and the recent operation on Diana's ear. She called, and the doctor informed Mrs. Belle it would not be a good idea to take Diana, just having had surgery, around sick children. Mrs. Belle called back to let Mrs. Clark know that she was going to take Diana out to the farm where Joseph was living as she felt Diana would be happy seeing him. Mrs. Clark agreed that it would be good for Diana.

Mrs. Belle arrived at the Loper home to pick up the children, and they were all ready. Clothes and toys were all packed, and they were watching for Mrs. Belle on the porch. Everyone was very happy and friendly in saying their good-byes. Diana seemed perfectly willing and happy to be moved at this time. Mrs. Loper told Diana that she would see her at Aunt Jenny's home for a visit. Mrs. Belle let her know that

Diana would not be going there because her child had the mumps, and Diana could not go there because of doctors' orders. Diana seemed to understand the conversation and took the whole thing in stride. It was at this time that Mrs. Belle clarified that Diana was moving to be with Joseph instead, as she knew she would be anxious to hear. Diana was happy that she would see Joseph on the Famos farm. However, right away she wanted to know where her sister Beverly was going to be. "As we dropped Beverly off at the Volt home, even though she had expressed such interest, Diana left without the least sign of strain. As we drove on, we talked about the Famos home and how much she would love being with their family." Also, Mrs. Belle mentioned that she should respect other people's property and not go through their things as she had done at the Lopers'. Mrs. Belle put into plain words that it was not right going through dresser drawers and cupboards, and it made everyone annoyed and unhappy. Diana agreed and said it would not happen again.

As they approached the farm, Diana could see Joseph in the yard, and she began smiling. "You could just see the joy as her face just lit up with excitement. Almost immediately Diana was playing with the children very easily and naturally. Diana especially showed so much joy over seeing her baby brother as it was family that meant so much to her."

A few days went by, and Mrs. Famos called Mrs. Belle to let her know that Diana was very happy, and they were very fond of her too. She described a difference in Joseph and how much he enjoyed playing with his sister. However, Mrs. Famos wanted to report that Diana had a sore place on her leg halfway between the groin and knee mostly in the evening. Diana said she had it before, and Mrs. Loper rubbed something that burned on it. After discussing it with Mrs. Famos, they decided it might be a strained muscle, improper shoes, or psychological. Mrs. Famos agreed to put sturdier shoes on her and also rub her leg to see if it relieved it or if they needed a doctor's visit.

Mrs. Belle arrived for her visit a few days later, and Diana came running to the car for a hug. She was very happy, and the family seemed very fond of her also. Mrs. Famos even asked about the possibility of keeping Diana, although the only drawback was all the ironing. Mrs. Famos knew they were getting more children in for care; however, Mrs.

Belle expounded that she would use the other foster homes for those children.

Mrs. Belle also went on to say that "even though we had Diana and Beverly together, we felt it would be just as well for Diana and Joseph to be together, especially since Diana enjoys it so much." Mrs. Famos asked that Mrs. Belle think this matter over and she would talk to Mr. Famos about keeping Diana, "then let us know what you decide." They talked a little about Diana's leg, and Mrs. Famos expressed to her that she only put the sturdy shoes on one day, and then let her go barefooted entirely. Then one day, Mrs. Famos inquired of Diana if her leg really hurt or was she just in need of some loving. Diana smiled up at Mrs. Famos and said she guessed she needed love. Mrs. Famos went on to tell her that she would find plenty of loving in this home; then Diana exclaimed she probably would not have a sore leg anymore.

Mrs. Famos came to the office a week later to say she wanted to keep Diana but feared she was too much in competition with another little boy named Lonnie. She really felt that although she wanted to keep her, it might be better to give her up. Mrs. Belle agreed about the competition and made it clear that she would go forward with the plans to only leave her there for a visit. On the other hand, it would take a couple of weeks to make arrangements, and Mrs. Famos agreed there was no hurry.

Three days went by, and Mrs. Famos phoned Mrs. Belle to say she wanted to reverse her decision of giving Diana up because of competition. She went on to say she spoke with both Diana and Lonnie about different problems with them and seemed to work them out. Also, she spoke with Mr. Famos about an agreement concerning showing affection to these children; together they would be able to keep both children contented. Mrs. Belle let her know she had not made any plans for Diana, so happily, no harm had been done, and she could reverse her decision. However, Mrs. Belle said, "If you run into this problem again on a long-term basis, we will be glad to remove Diana at a later date because of this competition problem." Mrs. Famos felt sure she could handle this situation, and that everything would go along nicely from now on.

Mrs. Belle made the next visit to see Diana and found her to be a bit shy and concerned as to why Mrs. Belle was coming to visit her and if she had brought some news about her family. Almost immediately Mrs. Belle changed the conversation to how she liked being at the farm and would she enjoy staying there. Diana responded with a positive answer that she wanted to stay and that she liked it there. Mrs. Belle went on to tell her that the Famos family was very happy with her and wanted her to be part of the family and stay indefinitely. "Also, as your sister Beverly is doing so well where she is, we wanted you to know that she is fine too." Diana was happy but seemed to have a concerned look on her face as she tried to process all the information Mrs. Belle was sharing. After a quiet moment went by, she told Mrs. Belle she was going to Sunday school regularly and that she had been to a carnival the other night. They then got onto the subject of her new school, and Mrs. Belle found that she anticipated this with considerable pleasure. The conversation seemed to divert her attention from the subject she always wanted to know about, which was her sister Beverly.

The little Famos child Sally Mae came to ask if Diana could stay a little longer as they enjoyed playing together. Mrs. Belle immediately assured her that until Diana's mother made arrangements to take Diana and Joseph, she would be staying right in their home. Both girls had seemed to worry about this, and Mrs. Famos shared with them not to worry and just enjoy each other's company. However, the children were on edge, not knowing at which time they may be asked to leave, and it was hard on the foster children as well as the family children.

Diana seemed to fit fine in the Famos household and was getting along with the family. She even asked Mrs. Famos again, as one might understand, if she was part of the family now that she had been there a while. Mrs. Famos reassured her again that at least for the present she was part of the family. Diana seemed to accept that coming from someone she had grown to love, as family meant everything to her. Now it was time to register Diana in school. This became a tough decision as when she was with her family she had been moved from school to school, and they were unable to find her records. Mrs. Belle felt it might be difficult for her to start second grade. On the other hand, why hold her back in first grade.

On her first encounter with school, she was sent home with an earache. Mrs. Belle explained all the issues they had with her operation and treatment with her ear, so it was not unusual for her to have an ear problem right away. Although she did not have a fever or a cold, they felt it was not necessary to call the doctor. At church the next day Diana seemed fine as after church there was a party, and within an hour her earache was gone. Mrs. Famos felt as though she needed the extra attention. Diana was the type of child that needed all the cuddling she could get from Mrs. Famos, and she was willing to give it to her. The next school day Diana had no problem going to school with cotton in her ear and a scarf on her head as a precaution.

Mrs. Famos met with Diana's teacher to see how she was doing in school as she knew that second grade was a challenge for her. The teacher felt that children that are not with their biological parents anyway are put in a lower group usually; however, with her help, she could move Diana up, and "she will be able to do second grade work." The teacher was giving her extra assignments and gave of her own time to help her. Mrs. Belle wondered if this was putting too much strain on Diana; however, Mrs. Famos said she had not seen any signs of that. "Diana does not worry about her schoolwork."

Another activity came up for Diana, and that was to join the Brownie Scouts. Mrs. Famos expressed that Diana had shown no interest in the program as yet. Mrs. Famos further let Mrs. Belle know that "Diana is rather fragile and immature for her age, not very strong physically, so she may not be able to take on any other project other than her school activities." Mrs. Belle felt that "we should not hold Diana back from these activities if she has the desire to do them. At the same time, we don't want to put unnecessary strain on her so that she cannot complete her homework." Mrs. Famos expressed that if it was early in the evening, she might be able to attend, so "we will discuss it with her to get her feelings on joining to see if she has an interest." After a week went by, Diana had another issue with her ear and was taken to the doctor to find a secondary infection and was given Adriamycin capsules. The doctor saw here after a week and said she did not need to wear a scarf; however, he would see her again in two weeks. Mrs. Famos offered the information to the doctor that Diana just does not have any stamina.

The doctor suggested that they put her on a multivitamin, and he would check her again in two weeks. Part of Diana's issues seemed to come from the desire to not make mistakes in school. Her teacher expressed that she was so stressed when she made a mistake and brought that stress home, making Mrs. Famos feel that second grade was too much for her.

Mrs. Famos had called the office to let them know that Diana had learned from school about the Brownie troop and was very interested in joining. It was going to cost $1.00 to join for the registration, and then Diana would need the handbook and uniform. Mrs. Belle suggested that she call their other division that handled that as they had funds for children who needed assistance. She said, "I understand they have uniforms available at their division," and Mrs. Famos was happy to hear that as Diana seemed to be growing so fast that the allotment for dresses, was not quite sufficient at their Brownie troop. Also, Mrs. Famos inquired and found the meetings were right after school, and she felt this would not interfere with Diana tiring out too much. Mrs. Famos was happy to know there was assistance for this program for the children as Diana was excited to go.

Another situation came up concerning Diana, so Mrs. Famos called the Welfare Office to consult Mrs. Webb as to whether it would be acceptable to cut Diana's hair. She explained that it had grown quite long; however, it was stringy and untidy, which made it difficult to work with. Mrs. Belle felt that there should not be any concern cutting it to her shoulders. Then Mrs. Famos mentioned that Diana did not like parting her hair in the middle as had always been done, and she would like something different. Mrs. Belle felt that Diana was old enough to make her own choice, and it was very nice that she wanted to change her hair to suit what she liked. Mrs. Famos was also concerned about Christmas coming up and not being able to shower Diana with enough gifts as some of the other children. She was speaking in particular of Lonnie, as his mother always brought an enormous amount of gifts, and although Mrs. Famos was able to provide some for Diana, she wondered if her mother would bring her gifts too. Mrs. Belle did not know if Mrs. Clark had planned on this; however, she hoped that Mrs. Clark made the effort as it would mean a lot to Diana. At this time, Mrs. Belle asked how Diana was doing, and Mrs. Famos remarked that she seemed happy and was not worrying so much, although she still was asking for her mother.

It was now getting close to Christmas. "At my visit to see Diana, she rushed and hugged me at the door. She was getting taller, and her face was getting rounder." But the first thing Mrs. Belle noticed was that adorable new haircut, even thinking that it could be a little shorter. Mrs. Belle asked Diana how school was coming along, and Diana was not very enthusiastic about it. She just said, "It was all right."

However, she bounced back with how delighted with Brownies she was and also that she went to a birthday party, receiving many party favors. Diana didn't stop there; she went on to say at school they were having a Christmas program and she had a part in it, she was proud to say. Mrs. Belle was quite impressed with her excitement over her activities.

After considerable conversation, Diana leaned over to Mrs. Belle and told her she had something to tell her that no one else could hear in the family. Mrs. Famos took all the children to the kitchen. She first inquired about her mother and father. Mrs. Belle told Diana she had not seen her father in quite some time. Diana exclaimed that she thought he worked on the Osborne farm, so Mrs. Belle let Diana know that he left there, and they had not been in touch with him since then. "However, we have seen your mother, and she looks the same. She lives in Aberdeen and is still working at the diner." It was at this time Mrs. Belle felt it necessary to tell Diana that it did not look like her parents were getting back together for a very long time.

Nevertheless, Mrs. Belle clarified whether Diana still felt happy living in the Famos home, and she agreed. Once again her attention turned to her sister Beverly; she wanted to know about her also. Mrs. Belle reminded her that she lived in Aberdeen with a nice family and told Diana a little about the family. Diana then turned her attention back to the possibility of her mother coming to visit her and as to the reason why she had not been to see her, for in her mind, the other little boy, Lonnie, got visits from his mother regularly.

Mrs. Belle further went on to explain to Diana that her aunt and uncle in Aberdeen had moved out of the county, and her uncle in Havre de Grace had sold his car. Therefore, it was difficult for her mother to get a ride out to see her way out on the farm as Lonnie's mother did. Diana spoke up and exclaimed that they would be going home soon. Mrs. Belle had to tell her, "Just because she has a way to visit him, it does not mean he is leaving soon." Diana seemed to be able to accept this, but at the same time you could see she wished her mother would visit more and how much she will not give up the hope of the family getting back together.

Diana went into the kitchen to play with the other children. Later that evening, Diana spoke to Mrs. Famos and expressed that there was one other place she would like to be, and that was with her own mommy and daddy, other than their home here.

Mrs. Famos asked her if she knew why she was not with her parents. Diana seemed to have a question about that, and Mrs. Famos thought she should explain. She first explained that there had been considerable trouble in her home, and she and her brothers and sister had to be taken from the home.

Mrs. Famos had pointed out that "quarrelling does not go on in a happy home such as ours. Therefore, we are providing a home where you can find happiness." The next morning, Diana came downstairs and exclaimed that she just wasn't thinking about it anymore.

As the days went on, Mr. Famos became fonder of Diana, so much so that he felt she could do no wrong. In fact, everyone who came in contact with her became fond of her, including a woman at their church. She had inquired if the children were up for adoption as she was interested in both of them. Mrs. Famos responded that at this time they were just in foster care. Mrs. Famos was also fond of Diana and was thinking ahead about the doll she was getting her for Christmas and all the new clothes, as she had grown out of so many things. Mrs. Belle called in answer to Diana's pleas to see her mother and explained further to Mrs. Famos that the parents were separated long before the children were picked up and also that Mrs. Clark was quite young to have four children at such a young age. Mrs. Belle felt this information would help Mrs. Famos understand the situation and the small possibility of her parents getting back together. Therefore, she could help Diana wherever possible in regards to her constant need for her family getting back together.

Mrs. Clark visited with Mrs. Belle to discuss the possibility of their placing Diana for adoption. She was not happy and very reluctant as she felt she was closest to Diana of all the children and "because she is the eldest, it would do her the most harm." Mrs. Belle let Mrs. Clark know that she would need to be the one to explain in person to Diana that she could not provide a good home for her and that Mrs. Clark needs to let Diana be adopted. Mrs. Clark found this to be extremely difficult to do and did not know how she could even do it. However she wanted permission to take a doll to Diana for Christmas, "so we talked it over and got directions for her to the farm."

Diana was all dressed up in her new green taffeta dress for church and school much to her delight; it seemed to give her new joy in life. She had a part to sing in the school program, in the chorus, and when she arrived home from school, she had something important to tell Mrs. Famos. Diana said she had been thinking about it and this was the happiest she had been in her whole life. Mrs. Famos asked her why she would say that, and she said, "There is no drinking, cussing, and everything is pleasant." So she was very happy. This seemed to be a culmination of considerable thought and questioning over the past weeks.

It was now getting close to Christmas, and Mrs. Clark phoned to say she was having trouble finding transportation to get her gift to Diana. Mrs. Belle offered to pick it up and deliver it for her; however, she wanted to be able to take it to her and present her gift to her. In the meantime, Mrs. Clark phoned Diana to let her know she would be coming with a gift as soon as she could. Mrs. Belle was curious how Diana reacted to that phone conversation, hoping that it did not upset Diana, not knowing if Mrs. Clark would even come to see her. Mrs. Famos explained that Diana was not at all upset or even seemed bothered by the call at all. She was more interested in all the wrappings, gifts, and festivities going on in the Famos home. Diana expressed that she did not have any of this in their home last year, so it was a very happy occasion for her.

It was about few days later that Mrs. Clark came to see Diana with a large bride doll as a gift; she was so happy to see her mother, and Mrs. Clark cried a bit over Diana. On the other hand, Diana appeared happy to see her mother, but did not cry or show special excitement over it. Even after her mother left, she did not have much to say about her mother's visit. Mrs. Famos could see the progress Diana was making both with her happiness in their home and with not being so competitive with Lonnie. Also her schoolwork had greatly improved and she was doing much neater work.

Mrs. Belle stopped by for a visit, and Diana was still in school, so in speaking with Mrs. Famos, she found that Mr. Clark had called for a visit with Diana and Joseph. In as much as he had no transportation, he spoke on the phone with Diana very briefly. After ending the conversation, Diana said she could not hear him or understand what he was saying. Diana was noticeably uninterested in talking with her father and went about playing with the other children; she did not want to speak about the conversation.

Mrs. Famos went on to say that Diana was very cheerful about all the Christmas parties and local programs. Mrs. Belle then asked if she had any problem with Lonnie's mother bringing him a lot of gifts. Mrs. Famos explained that Diana was so caught up in all her activities and attention she received that there was no problem. In fact, Mrs. Famos had noticed that since Mrs. Clark's visit, she had not mentioned a word about her mother, and she had not had one of her lonesome depressed spells.

It really seemed as though they had reached a turning point with Diana; she had come to accept foster care at last. The door swung open, and Diana rushed in to show her doll from her mother and her Brownie Scout dress; she was very excited to see Mrs. Belle. Right away, Mrs. Belle addressed the fact her mother had visited and wanted to know how Diana felt about her visit. Diana let her know it was just okay, and she seemed disinterested in the subject. However, Mrs. Belle went on further to ask if her mother let her know that she had no plans to take her, but must leave her in foster care, and Diana agreed. Again Diana showed very little interest in her mother or even talked about her; she only said at this time she was very happy where she was anyway.

After this visit, Mrs. Belle made a point to see Mrs. Clark to go over her intention after visiting Diana. As they talked, Mrs. Clark said that she felt Diana was happy, looked well, and was content in the Famos home. However, she could not bring herself to give Diana up, as she may be able the other children. She felt Diana was soft and timid and will find adoption too difficult. She was most fond of this child and was anxious to hold on to her. Mrs. Clark went on to say her sister Jenny was buying a new home in Aberdeen, where she could take Diana and make a home for her.

She felt her sister had always been most fond of Diana also, so she wanted to take her there, rather than send her to a strange home. Mrs. Belle explained, "At this time it would be necessary for all the children to be tested to be adopted, so we will include Diana, even though you have not decided at this point." Mrs. Clark conceded that would be a good idea.

At Mrs. Belle's next call to check on Diana, Mrs. Famos reported that Diana was drinking so much milk that they were going to have to designate a special cow for her very own use. Mrs. Belle laughed and let her know that "we would still expect that she eat a balanced meal with meat and vegetables." Mrs. Famos assured her that "if she doesn't clean her plate first, she does not get more milk, and that seems to have solved the problem." Also, she wanted to report that Diana had done much better on her school report card, although she still was a little slow in reading.

Mrs. Famos went on to say that Mrs. Clark had called the house several times, trying to set up a time to bring her other sister, Katie, that had Diana's other brother, James, to visit Diana. They called back and forth to first get Diana out of school, which was not proper procedure;

then they called another time to say they were coming, but never arrived. Mrs. Belle, of course, was concerned how Diana fared with all this back and forth going on, and Mrs. Famos recounted that Diana did not seem to care if she came or not.

Mrs. Famos explained that Diana finally pronounced she was happy living here in this home. Diana went on to say that although she thought of her family a lot, she no longer wanted to talk much about them. Mrs. Famos was happy that she was able to express her feelings about not being so concerned and that her mother was going to come after her wherever she was living. Mrs. Belle felt like she was gaining the security a child needs to have to be placed for adoption.

The Hearing Clinic called to say Diana was in need of radium treatments beginning in April. Mrs. Famos had phoned Mrs. Belle to say she would need a new coat and some new dresses for Diana before she went to John Hopkins for her treatments. Mrs. Famos let her know her ear was still itching and that the teacher spoke of an odor coming from the ear. At the same time, she wanted to report that Diana had asked if Beverly could come to live with her at the Famos home. Mrs. Famos reminded her that Beverly had a very nice home she already lived in and was very happy. To Mrs. Famos's surprise, she then asked about her parents and if anyone had heard from them. She explained to Diana that her mother does not have a home to bring her to; therefore, she needs to stay there, and Diana acknowledged she understood.

On the way to John Hopkins, Mrs. Belle explained to Diana about the treatment to put her at ease so she did not feel apprehensive. "As we rode on in the car, Diana approached the subject of her parents, and we discussed how various members of her family were getting along." Mrs. Belle once again clarified with Diana the fact that her mother and father were so unhappy together that they were not going to be able to get together to make a home again.

Diana seemed somewhat able to accept this answer without too much difficulty. They had a long wait; therefore Diana read a book to Mrs. Belle, and she was quite impressed how much she had improved in her reading. Finally, she had her radium treatment, and the doctor was happy with her progress. The doctor said she could have the treatments done locally from now on and into the future. On the way home, Mrs. Belle tried to talk further about Diana's mother and father, but found she was most unwilling to talk about their relationship. So Mrs. Belle asked Diana if she saw Beverly, "what she should know about you?" Diana expressed, "Tell her I am fine and happy where I am."

Although Diana spoke right up and told Mrs. Belle that, she exclaimed how Mrs. Belle could see Beverly but Diana could not? And she felt that was not fair. Mrs. Belle went on to tell her that she doesn't see Beverly much either.

Mrs. Belle felt there was some distress over moving either child at this time, as it would do terrible damage to either one. She felt it may not be possible to permanently place Diana at this time. However, Mrs. Belle thought, "We can move forward in placing Joseph in a permanent home." Mrs. Belle anticipated a great deal of difficulty with Mrs. Famos moving either child as Diana was quite attached to her brother Joseph.

We arranged to pick Diana up from school for a ride to get better acquainted. Diana was happily speaking about her day at school and about the upcoming May Day activities. After talking casually for a while, Mrs. Belle asked Diana if she had heard about any plans for Joseph. Her cheerfulness faded as Diana began to retreat a bit into herself; she looked up at Mrs. Belle very seriously with those big brown eyes and nodded in affirmation.

Mrs. Belle went on to ask Diana if she knew what adoption was and if she thought it would be a wonderful thing for Joseph. Mrs. Belle continued on, "He would have a mommy and daddy that loved him and a permanent home with a family which has always wanted a little boy, just like Joseph, but have never been able to have one.

They have all this love to give, and it would be a wonderful thing for Joseph to be their little boy. Even though Joseph has Mr. and Mrs. Famos now, he would have a mommy and daddy and a home of his own forever." Diana was quiet, but at times Mrs. Belle felt she was discussing this subject with an adult. Diana was so intelligent. Diana sternly shook her head and let Mrs. Belle know it was all right. A few seconds went by, and Diana asked Mrs. Belle if she had any children of her own. She replied she did not. Diana looked expressionless.

The ride became quite quiet for a while; then Mrs. Belle remarked that she may find a wonderful mother and father that she could have for her very own. Diana snapped her head around rather quickly and turned those fearful big brown eyes upon Mrs. Belle. Mrs. Belle could feel her tension, so she went on to say she would not do this unless Diana wanted this and it would make her happy. Again the ride got quiet as Diana was thinking and taking all this information to heart. Diana spoke right up, "I have a sister named Beverly, you know!" Mrs. Belle acknowledged that she was her worker also and that they were trying to find a nice adoptive home for her also. She then questioned Diana about Beverly to see what she remembered about her sister or even other members of her family. Diana recalled that Beverly had thin hair like hers, but that was all. She remembered her mother saw her at Christmas but not since then. Mrs. Belle reported that she had not seen either her mother or father in quite some time; they felt it was time to find them a happy home, and their parents felt that way too. Mrs. Belle clarified, "Your family wants all of you children to have a wonderful home because they cannot provide one. Therefore, we will not be seeing them again." As once again they sat in silence, Mrs. Belle ask Diana what her thoughts were for her future. Diana replied she did not know for sure, but one thing she did know, she was going to be a mother and raise her children right, not anything like her mother. Mrs. Belle commended Diana on her dreams for the future and said she knew Diana will be a good mother someday. She also hoped that she could arrange with Beverly's worker a visitation someday soon. Mrs. Belle tried to explain how the system worked, as her sister Beverly had a different worker; however, by the look on Diana's face, she was only concerned about arrangements to see Beverly. As they reached the Famos residence, Diana was happy to see she had a new coat and some skirts waiting for her to try on. This seemed to make things all better for the present time.

Mrs. Famos called to Mrs. Belle to say she had upset Diana by talking to her about moving her. She felt she should not have been discussing or suggesting anything about a move at this point as "she is very happy here." Mrs. Famos reassured her she was taking her for her treatment, and Diana exclaimed she would go as long as there was no discussion about her family. In the meantime, Mr. Clark called and talked to Diana rather incoherently; he sounded as though he had been drinking. He threatened he was taking the Welfare to court as they would not let him see the children. Diana was unable to understand him, so Mrs. Famos told her he probably just had a bad cold.

While taking Diana for her test, Mrs. Belle talked with her about Brownie camp and Bible School Day camp. Diana seemed quite thrilled to be going with the other children, even being away from home. While they waited, Diana read a story, and Mrs. Belle was definitely impressed with her progress in reading. When she was done reading she looked up at Mrs. Belle to tell her that Mr. Clark had called to see her and said the Welfare would not let him. Mrs. Belle explained that was not true. He was mistaken. Mrs. Belle felt sure he just did not have a ride. However, Mrs. Belle was wondering if after she spoke with him, did she want to see him, and Diana acknowledged that she did. During the ride home, Mrs. Belle talked with Mrs. Famos about the possibility of placing Diana for adoption. Mrs. Famos definitely had questions as to whether Diana, at her age, could accept adoption or not. "First of all, she is very attached to Joseph, and splitting them up would be tragic at this point in her life."

Mrs. Belle expressed that they would give it consideration; however, they had been thinking it over for months and preparing for it. Mrs. Belle tried to show Mrs. Famos that it would be better at her age now to have a permanent home than to be in foster care as an older child. Mrs. Famos relayed an incident in school that had upset Diana where kids were being made fun of because they were foster kids. Mrs. Belle felt her mother should be the one to speak to her about being adopted. Mrs. Famos did not agree with that. She felt someone else could prepare Diana much better, someone who was very gentle and could talk sympathetically. Mrs. Belle agreed and assured her, "We will do our best to make sure Diana gets the proper attention she needs going forward." Mrs. Belle let Mrs. Famos know that she would no longer be working with the agency and will need to say good-bye to the children at the end of the month.

"On my last visit, Diana was very pleasant and polite. She was quite tanned and looked very healthy. Diana began with great excitement to tell me about her Brownie Day camp. Diana was very proud of her Indian dress and her headband with her Indian name Brown Eyes on it. She was even more thrilled that soon she would be going to Bible School camp." Mrs. Belle asked to see her last report card as she knew she had struggled to keep up in second grade because of all the moving around she had done. The teacher commented that "Diana is careful and neat but still has a problem with reading and arithmetic." However, she was promoted to third grade, which seemed to put a smile on Diana's face. It was at this time that Mrs. Belle needed to inform Diana that she would be leaving the agency. Diana seemed to be very disturbed but was not able to get the words she wanted to speak to come out, so there was just silence.

For her first visit, Mrs. Mearst went to the Famos farm to see Diana and Joseph. Diana was very charming and friendly. Her hair was cut in an attractive Dutch boy haircut with bangs, which showed her well-formed features that would develop into a beautiful young girl. A sprinkling of freckles across her nose and under her eyes gave her a wholesome pixie appearance. Diana began, without any hesitation, telling about her school day and how she got her booster shot, finally ending with how much she liked school. She brought out her Christmas book that you could see she had taken a lot of pride in, as she kept it neat and clean. Diana began to read from her book with such expression that Mrs. Mearst was quite impressed and praised her for her ability to read so well. At the same time, Joseph reached over and tore one of the pages out of her book. Although you could see she was unhappy, she just smiled and went on to say, "Mommy will glue it, so it is okay."

"As my visit went on, Diana played with Joseph, dressed him up, hugged on him, kissed him, and cuddled him constantly. It is quite obvious it would be most tragic to separate the two of them. Diana held my hand and followed me to the door and invited me back again."

It was a final appointment for Diana's ear treatment, and Mrs. Mearst felt it would be a good time to see how she was feeling about her parents. When she mentioned if she missed visiting her mother and father, Diana shrugged her shoulders and looked out the window, but was very quiet. "We drove a while as she was rather pensive and not saying a word. Then she began to speak with all authority, explaining that when she has children, they will speak nice language, have good manners, and get good grades." Diana went on further to express how they would be normal children, and she would never, never let them be adopted. Mrs. Mearst felt she spoke with great feeling, and she stated that she certainly hoped she did grow up and have a nice happy family. She went on to say, "When you have a happy family life in childhood, usually you make a happy family yourself." Diana shook her head as though she agreed and showed she was a child with much depth of feeling.

After they arrived at the Famos home, Mrs. Mearst spoke with Mrs. Famos about preparing the children for adoption. At first Mrs. Famos was positively against preparing Diana for this move. She felt Joseph would take the move easily, as he would forget being there rather quickly as many of the other children had in the past. However, Diana was going to be more difficult to prepare because of her sensitive nature, and they had such an attachment to her more than any of the others. Mrs. Mearst acknowledged that this was a difficult process for many foster parents, and she would not be criticized if she could not perform the task. However, the alternative would be to send Diana to a different foster family that would be able to prepare her for adoption procedure. Mrs. Famos was aghast at the thought of moving her for the possibility of hurting Diana's sensitive nature anymore. Mrs. Mearst further explained that "if Diana is worked with properly, she will not be deprived of her opportunity of accepting adoption and having the happy family she deserves." Mrs. Famos agreed to do her best to prepare Diana, but went on to ask if both Diana and Joseph could be placed in a home together as she felt if not, Diana would have a breakdown. Mrs. Mearst expressed that "of course they would try to keep them together," but she could not guarantee a placement when there was an older child involved. Usually, older children seemed to do well when there was a clean cut with the old home; they accept the new home more readily. However, this might not necessarily be true in Diana's case.

Later that summer, Mrs. Clark's sister, Jenny, called the Welfare to ask if Diana could come to her home for the summer for a visit. Mrs.

Mearst explained that they were planning to place Diana in an adoptive home as soon as possible, and a visit with family would surely upset her and delay their plans. Jenny expressed her excitement for Diana to get a home of her own and that she would finally be settled. She asked Mrs. Mearst if she would tell Diana how wonderful she thought it was that she was getting a nice family and that she had called and asked about her. Mrs. Mearst agreed she would certainly do just that.

Diana was on the porch when Mrs. Mearst came for a routine visit. She saw Mrs. Mearst and seemed shy and a bit nervous. Mrs. Famos let Mrs. Mearst know she had been discussing adoption with Diana, and when she saw her, it may have caused some anticipation on Diana's part at first. However, Mrs. Famos explained that she felt Diana was accepting all the discussions much better than she anticipated and was happy with the results so far. It was still very obvious that Diana's attachment for Joseph was very deep as she was constantly making over Joseph, showing how much care and love she had for him. Again they spoke about cutting Diana's hair before she went with her new family, and Mrs. Mearst thought it would look nice in the Dutch boy haircut she had previously. Mrs. Mearst let the children know she would take them on a short ride the next time she came to see them.

Three weeks later, Mrs. Mearst arrived for her ride with Diana and Joseph. Diana was all dressed up in a pretty cotton dress and was in high spirits, chatting constantly as they got in the car. As they drove down the road, Joseph was pointing out all kinds of objects to Diana, and she was just giggling and expressing how cute he is all the time. She went on to ask Mrs. Mearst if she could take her favorite bride doll, a gift from her mother, to her new mommy's and daddy's home. Mrs. Mearst explained that normally children leave all the toys at the foster home and get fresh new things at their new home. "However, when you meet them, you may ask if it is all right." Diana was so enthusiastic and excited she exclaimed that it would only be three more weeks. She was bursting with joy and was eager to talk about her new home. Diana then asked about her dollhouse, could she take that also? Again Mrs. Mearst explained she would have to ask her new mother when the time came. Diana, being inquisitive, spotted a turtle on the road, so we had to stop and back up as she was very excited about her discovery.

Mrs. Mearst had one more visit before Diana would be visiting her prospective family. Diana had her new Dutch boy haircut and was very pleased when everyone made over her new attractive style. She was still eager to know about her new family and asked Mrs. Mearst if she could tell her anything about her new mother and father. Unfortunately, Mrs. Mearst had not met them herself yet, so she could not provide any information for Diana as yet. She then asked how much longer it would be before she moved to her new home as she was getting anxious. Mrs. Mearst explained that they did not have an exact date yet but would be able to tell her on the next visit, which would be September. This answer seemed to satisfy Diana for the moment.

For the next few weeks, Mrs. Famos brought the children to the Welfare Office to play in the playroom while she was out of sight to get them adjusted to being left alone. Diana would get books and read happily, and Joseph would play with a Ferris wheel. The last week Mrs. Mearst let Mrs. Famos know they had a prospective family in mind that lived in the next county, and they were making arrangements in two weeks for a visit. Therefore, before bringing them, she would need to take Diana to the doctor for a final checkup. "Also, if there are any special needs the children have, please write them down so that I can give them to the new parents." Right away Mrs. Famos remarked how much Diana needs affection. Also Mrs. Famos was concerned about Diana's ear and the fact that "she is afraid of her head under water, and in fact, so is Joseph." She said she was not real sure why, but they were both so afraid she felt something somewhere must have happened. So she always proceeded with caution.

At the next visit, Mrs. Mearst picked Diana up for her final checkup with the doctor. As they rode in the car, Mrs. Mearst mentioned to her that she would probably have to start school where she was before she went to live with her new family. Diana explained that Mrs. Famos had already told her, and she was happy that she would see her classmates and teachers again before she left. Diana was quiet for a while, and then she began to read out loud. It had become obvious how proficient she was in her reading. When they reached the doctor, Diana did not have any fear in her examination. The only suggestion he made was to have her take penicillin when she had a cold. Mrs. Mearst then asked Diana if she wanted to tell the doctor her news. Diana very glowingly said that she was going to be adopted! The doctor expressed how wonderful that was for Diana to have a family of her own.

The big day finally came to bring Diana to the office to meet Mr. and Mrs. Lawson. Diana was singing all the way in the car; she was so excited and cheerful that she was getting a new mommy and daddy. Her spirits were high like you had never seen from her. She included Joseph by asking him who was he going to see today, and he even replied, "My new mommy and daddy," and then he giggled. It was gratifying for Mrs. Mearst to see such joyfulness from these children after what especially Diana had been through. She asked again if she could have her favorite doll, and Mrs. Mearst told her to ask her new mother. The children were taken to the playroom, where they had spent many days, so they were familiar, and then the Lawsons were brought in. Diana acknowledged them and introduced herself while Joseph eyed them very seriously. Diana began to play to cover up her embarrassment as they began to make over her. Mr. Lawson asked her to show him some toys, and she right away relaxed; they all loosened up, the social worker left the room, and everything went fine. After quite a while, Mrs. Mearst came back to take Mr. and Mrs. Lawson in private to talk, where it was decided that their wish was to take them home the following morning.

After meeting her new parents, Diana was beaming and was obviously very happy on the way home. Joseph seemed a little detached from Mrs. Famos—more than usual, as she tried to hug him while he pulled away. Mrs. Mearst let her know that the connection with the new family went beautifully. She told Mrs. Famos that she would pick the children up in the morning, "So please have their things ready by all means so that we do not have any delays. Say all your good-byes before we arrive." Mrs. Famos expressed that she would have them ready on time.

The next morning, Mrs. Mearst met Diana, who was all dressed up and eager to go and just beaming. However, Mrs. Famos immediately started crying. She took Joseph to the front yard to take his picture while he was very unhappy and did not want his picture taken. Mrs. Famos had a total breakdown and was totally uncontrollable. Diana took Joseph, who was not crying, to the barn to get Mr. Famos; he was carrying Joseph and had Diana by the hand, who now was crying. Mrs. Famos scarcely noticed Diana as all her attention was on Joseph, leaving Diana without a good-bye. Mr. Famos brought the children to the car and said how wonderful it was to have the children with them and that they were going to have a nice new home. As Mrs. Mearst drove down the long driveway, Diana cried all the way; however, she had been there a long time, and it was hard to leave the people like the Famos' that were so nice. Diana rather quickly dried her tears just to respond to Mrs. Mearst that was not why she was crying. She went on to tell her that Mrs. Famos was going to miss Joseph a lot, and that was why Mrs. Famos was so upset. Mrs. Mearst went on to say to Diana that they were going to miss her a lot too, but Mr. and Mrs. Famos were happy that Diana and Joseph were getting a new permanent home where they could call it their own. Mrs. Mearst could see Diana was more concerned by the lack of interest in Mrs. Famos's attention to Diana rather than her making such a scene over Joseph. However, as they rode along, the tears dried up, and once again the happy singing began about having a new mommy and daddy of their very own.

Diana and Joseph cheerfully went into the playroom that was very familiar to them and waited for Mr. and Mrs. Lawson to arrive. As they entered the room, you could see Diana's face beaming with delight. She was ready for this new adventure. She walked out of the room very eagerly, holding Mr. Lawson's hand, and Joseph holding Mrs. Lawson's. Diana was skipping along to the car and Joseph was laughing as they opened the car door. Without any hesitation, all four got in the front seat as they drove away, all obviously very content and happy as they waved good-bye for the last time.

As Marsha read through Diana's file she certainly could see why Diana felt the way she did about wanting to get the family back together. Her file brought out the numerous times she asked about her parents as to whether they were doing all right, when she would get to see them, and if they would get back together. Marsha felt this was devastating to a small child that was old enough to remember her family and still had the desire to be together, no matter how bad the circumstances had been. All she knew was she wanted a home with her family. Everyone tried to console her, but she still went back to the same question about wanting her mother. Even though she was questioned about her father, she felt if he stayed on the farm, he would be a good boy, and then they could get back together. Marsha felt heartbroken to see the sadness Diana felt then and had carried all these years as she questioned wanting that family unit. The second challenge Diana displayed was about her sister Beverly. She had a great yearning to visit her, and she craved any information about her, although it seemed no one took her pleas seriously. Consequently, she carried this burden of finding her sister all her life and hoped that someday she would find her. Marsha knew she would need to discuss these two subjects with her and get her state of mind before she sent this document to her so that she would feel comfortable to discuss it with her if she needed Marsha.

Marsha phoned Diana, and they had a nice chat; Marsha let her know that reading her paperwork was very enlightening. Marsha explained, "Many of your feelings are documented as you explained them. First, your desire to be with your family is quite extensively spoken of in the paperwork. You may find it hurtful as to how many times you asked and did not get much satisfaction from the social worker. There were even times where they tried to get you to cut those feeling off, getting you ready for your new family."

This process is difficult for any child, but for a sensitive child like Diana, it is even more challenging. Marsha continued, "I know you will have times of sadness. Therefore, you may need to stop and call me or e-mail." Also, the burning desire to visit Beverly was quite evident, and yet Diana was told that Beverly was happy in the home she was in. Marsha, unfortunately, had to tell Diana, "You may never get an answer as to why they did not try to keep you together as it is not clear. Although that is the question both of you have suffered with, unfortunately it may never be answered."

Marsha went on to explain that much of the document gives you a daily and weekly documentation of what went on in Diana's life as she was in two foster homes. Although it was, at times, a struggle for Diana, she was a happy child that took interest in her school activities and was very attentive to her brother, Joseph. She was a sensitive child with great feeling as to what family meant to her. As Marsha sent off these documents, she knew there would be grateful days and sad ones, and most of all, Diana could hopefully realize some closure that she has longed for so many years.

Finally, both Beverly and Diana got their documents about their childhood, starting in 1953, when they were picked up and taken to the Welfare Department. Little did they know there was such documentation of their lives recorded for them to read fifty-six years later! All these social workers had passed away, not knowing that all their hard work of taking down all the things they did and said, then typing them out, and keeping the records would be there for Diana and Beverly after their passing. Diana and Beverly wished that they could thank them for being so thorough so that they were able to see how their personalities had developed. The workers jotted down sometimes phrases that were said. When Beverly read them, she could just see herself saying that. Diana also could feel the feelings she had at different times when the social worker would question her. They felt as if they were right back in those homes sometimes, although the intense nature of the information was not always favorable.

Both girls were grateful for the opportunity to read the documents to see if they could get answers to questions that had haunted them for years. Beverly remembered many things, but she could not put the pieces together as no one was willing to sit down and tell her what had happened. Therefore, she had to investigate on her own. The horrible truth about who had molested her had damaged her for life. She hoped the documents could give her answers. And they did give her some.

Most of all the distress over why Diana and she were separated was what she was hoping they would find. They both were adjusting to the fact that they would never know why the social workers did not work more diligently to keep the sisters together. Diana and Beverly read their documents for days and days and continued to read them to make sure not to miss one crumb of their life.

The phone calls began as Beverly was still living in California with her son Scott. First, Diana would call as she came across something in her paperwork. They both had copies of each other's papers; they both would be in disbelief that the social worker took them to the first home and they had problems there. Right away they could see what the problem was and why Mrs. Loper wanted them out of there. But what really made them break down was that if the foster mother had waited two more weeks, the social worker had a place for them to go together. Diana and Beverly had the hardest time getting past that point.

There it was in plain sight. Beverly and Diana were devastated to know that was their chance to have a life together. They knew they must go forward and be strong to get beyond this tragic mistake, but they felt powerless like they were left high and dry. Days went by, and there were more calls and more crying as they dug through the tragedies they had encountered. Beverly and Diana tried to see the good in the last foster homes as they were treated well, however, the lingering desire to just have a visit was there, and no one would listen to their pleas.

They did their best to read through the documents without being so inconsolable that they did not have to call Marsha every day. However, she was there for them as their confidant as they needed her. She would always be their cherished friend.

The documents from their parents gave them many new names and places; therefore, they began to look up those places on maps. Then Beverly and Diana used Ancestry to look up family names to find the history first on their father and mother. As they began to receive more information, Beverly sent away for their father's birth certificate. Diana got their father's military record. From that point on, they kept adding to the list: death certificates and obituaries including those of grandparents and aunts and uncles. Things started to snowball for both Beverly and Diana; they began to realize what a big family and the history and heritage there was to learn about their natural family. Beverly and Diana were talking one day, and during the conversation, Beverly suddenly asked, "Why don't we go back to where it all started, take a trip for a month and see where our ancestors came from?"

Diana said, "That would be fun! How would we do it? You are in California." Beverly responded that she would fly to Mexico Beach and rent a car, and they could leave from there for their journey.

First, there was a great discussion about thinking through about where they would go and what place they would be looking for first. Beverly called Diana to say, "We should take down notes of towns, streets, places, homes, and landmarks we want to visit so that we are not backtracking." Diana had a friend in North Carolina they could stay with, and it just so happened that their mother's family were from Yadkinville, North Carolina, so that was a good start. Beverly expressed to Diana, "Get as much down on paper as to where we want to go and take all the paperwork on our family that we have so that when we get to Maryland, we can look up our cousins." Diana did not live in Aberdeen, like Beverly did until she was sixteen; therefore Beverly remembered the area well. Beverly got out the atlas and started marking their journey as she would be the driver. Now things were starting to get exciting, and with all the heartache they had just endured in reading and reliving their childhood, this journey would be helpful for closure.

Beverly was thrilled the day was here when Patty, her daughter-in-law, and Angelina took her to the airport for her journey to find the missing pieces to her natural family; good or bad, she wanted to know. They said their good-byes. Beverly had three pieces of luggage to check at the desk, so she didn't have to carry anything as it was a long flight. As it was, one flight was delayed, and Beverly missed the next flight; therefore, she had to wait.

That was a two-hour delay; after all was said and done, she got to Panama city airport at 10:00 p.m. Tired and not very happy, Beverly got the rental car and started down the road to Mexico Beach. Beverly called Diana for directions as she had never been to that airport. As she was giving her directions to turn on Route 22, Diana said, "You know about coming through that long stretch by Tyndall Air Force Base." The words barely got out of Diana's mouth when Beverly saw a flashing light behind her to pull over. As Beverly pulled over, she told Diana she knew what she was going to tell her. The policeman asked Beverly for her driver's license and registration; he asked if she knew why she was being pulled over, and of course she did not.

The officer explained that the speed limit was forty-five, and she was going sixty. That was a $250.00 fine. Beverly respectfully explained that she just came from California and was not familiar with the car she was driving or the road she was driving on. Beverly went on to tell her story of her adventure and journey to find her family roots; he smiled and kindly let her go this time. That was Beverly's first break of the journey.

Beverly and Diana were so enthusiastic about their journey that there was no waiting. They were up and ready to say good-bye to Vito first thing in the morning. They had the RAV 4 packed full with luggage, water, laptops, paperwork, blankets, pillows, boots, rain gear, maps, cameras, etc. Beverly explained if they were to buy anything they would have a hard time finding a place for it in the SUV. They had one stop, and that was Dunkin' Donuts for a half-cut tea for Diana, coffee with cream and sugar for Beverly, and two chocolate cake doughnuts that was a ritual every morning. They were so overwhelmed first to be together as sisters to see how well they would get along and be able to get to know each other in a deeper way. On this journey, Beverly and Diana had that as their goal to bond as sisters, something that was so tragically torn from them so many years ago.

Vito gave them some instructions on taking some back roads, and it was a nice change as they would be spending most of the day on the highway getting around Atlanta before rush hour, as they would be staying with Diana's daughter Lynne. As Beverly drove down the road, she knew now was her opportunity to really get to know more about Diana. She always found it difficult to get her to talk, but she was going to make an effort to change that on this trip.

Diana had expressed that she wanted to catch up on the times they lost when they were young and would have gone places as girls and laughed and carried on as teenagers. Both of them had planned to make this a trip one where they would bond and one they would never forget. In fact, on this trip Beverly and Diana discussed writing about their story when they got home.

They both wanted to pursue their dream of sharing their struggles over the years with others who might have the same unfortunate story, thereby assisting others as well as obviously themselves on the road to recovery and closure. They knew they would spend hours talking about this and every night writing their activities down in a journal so that when they were ready to write they could recall the good times.

They did stop at a Wendy's for a salad and a half-cut tea; they became addicted to the tea, although they usually enjoyed MacDonald's better. Both were ninety-nine cents so that made them happy. On their ride again, Beverly did carry on most of the conversation as she was the outgoing one. Diana did her share when the conversation came around to horticulture as she knew the name of every plant alive; just ask her. The timing was perfect as they missed the traffic, got around Atlanta, and headed for Woodstock. Of course, Diana the grandmother was getting anxious to see the boys, Gianni and Paul. They pulled in the drive to Lynne's lovely two-story home around 5:00 p.m., when the door swung open, and Gianni came out like a bolt of lightning with Paul not far behind. Beverly loved her hugs from her nephews too, but when boys aged five and three get going, it is difficult to turn them off.

Lynne had gone to her favorite restaurant and picked up fish tacos, and what a spread they had. Diana mentioned to Lynne all the new and exciting ideas they had for the future, including writing the book. Lynne was delighted to hear about the project and that they were going to do it together. Lynne was wondering how that was going to come about, so Beverly spoke up and dropped the biggest surprise, even for Diana. Beverly was thrilled to say she had been contemplating moving back to Florida. She went on to say to further that for her commitment to writing this book with Diana, she would need to be available. Diana, shocked of course, was concerned about her son Scott, Patty, and Angelina. Beverly's frame of mind was that they had their life out there, she was not happy with the hot weather, and she just did not feel complete. Naturally, Diana was thrilled to hear this and kept questioning if Beverly really meant this for sure. Beverly expressed she had prayed about it and given it a lot of thought, and it felt absolutely right.

They played a little with the boys and then made the beds up and crashed so that they could leave early for North Carolina in the morning.

It was the second day of their journey November 1, 2012. They left early to hit the Dunkin' Donuts on the corner they noticed coming in and got their usual. The day was about 45 degrees, so it was a little chilly compared to Florida; however, as they drove up the back roads to Highway 40, they could see where they missed the trees changing about two weeks earlier. Some still had brilliant colors, so all was not lost. Beverly and Diana started cheerfully talking about who they were going to look up in North Carolina from their mother's side of the family. The excitement was beginning to grow the more they discussed just which grandmother's grave they might find or if they could find the house that their mother lived in as a child. Sometimes, it was overwhelming to think after all these years that they were going to walk in the same town their mother called home. Diana always wanted a snack, so out came the crackers, carrots, water, and of course gum, which they had plenty. The next thing they took note of was the price of gas. What a difference from Florida. It was $3.50 a gallon when they left, so they were expecting to save some money on gas as they went up through the states. Sure enough, the first stop was $3.09 a gallon; they wished they had some way to carry gas at that price!

Beverly thought that traveling with Diana was just great; they got along beautifully and talked a lot just like sisters should, although they did seem to gravel, argue, and blame each other a lot. However, in the end they loved each other and never had one disagreement so far. It was quite a full day, but they arrived in Kernersville, North Carolina, around 5:00 p.m. to Diana's friends Louise and Jon Sanderson. Their home was a lovely brick home on a hill loaded with trees in the backyard and a large circle drive. As you enter the home, it was magnificently decorated with antiques, beautiful hardwood floors, and center kitchen and bar area; then Louise directed them to the huge staircase with wood rails to the guest room. She had the bed made with eight-hundred-count sheets and handmade quilted coverlet for the bed. The bathroom was laid out with matching towels, hand-stitched shower curtain, handmade soaps, and basketful of toiletries for them to choose from. It was like walking into a room that could have been out of *Gone with the Wind*. They felt like queens!

Louise was a very talented woman; she played the cello since she was twelve years old until she was fifty, where she played with the Atlanta Symphony Orchestra. Jon, her husband, had a PhD in music and also was a director at the Atlanta Symphony Orchestra. They spent hours listening with reference to their excursions through countries abroad. What a glamorous experience in life they had lived, and Diana and Beverly were able to live it through their eyes. Culture like this you can only hope to come across hopefully once in your lifetime. Diana and Beverly were filled with extreme joy as they said goodnight and went to their room, wondering how their next day could top this one.

It was November 2, 2012, and the lovely friends insisted on taking Beverly and Diana to breakfast before they started out on their journey for the day. The housemaid Anya went along with them to help with Mr. Sanderson as he was up in years. She was a lovely person from the islands and a very good cook for the Sandersons, although they loved to go out to eat. After a rather large breakfast that Beverly and Diana were not accustomed to, they rode back to their home to get their things to start on the road to Yadkinville. Right away, Mr. and Mrs. Sanderson wanted to know if they would be back before dark, as they would like to invite them out for dinner. This was just more than the sisters expected; however the Sandersons insisted that they were their guests. Beverly and Diana let them know they would be home by 6:00 p.m. if that was acceptable. Louise told them to be careful and would see them around 6:00 p.m., or the sisters were to call if something held them up from making that time.

Now they were finally on the road to find the very first of their mother's side of the family; their name was Shores. As Beverly drove, Diana's responsibility was always to take care of the map. As the Historical Society and the library were closed, they decided to get a city map to locate some cemeteries and churches. They started down 601 to where David Shores, which would be fourth great-grandfather, should have been buried. Diana yelled, "stop," and pointed to the road sign. Beverly turned around, and both of them could not believe their eyes. There it was, Shore Road. Imagine that!

They pulled over, snapped a picture of Diana pointing to the sign, and continued on down the road, feeling that there must be some family on this road. The road was hilly, and off in the distance, you could see a silo and a large farm on the left side and a small home on the right.

As you can imagine the mailbox on their right said Shore and then the next one by the big farmhouse also said Shore, so they pulled in the yard by the farm. Diana looked at Beverly like "What are you thinking?" Beverly told Diana, "Get out. Let's go to the door." Beverly went to the front door with Diana following slowly behind her.

As Beverly knocked and no one answered, you could see the relief on Diana's face. Then Beverly went around to the side door, and Diana's eyes got big as saucers for she was not usually as forward as Beverly could be. Beverly knocked, and a nice lady, Mrs. Shores, came to the door. They explained that the Shores were their ancestors, and she welcomed them in and told them that the gentlemen in the small house that they passed might know a little more about the family as he was much older. However, the sisters were just excited to be near part of the family that could be their ancestors, and that was enough for them. She told the sisters about the church where many of the Shores had been buried, "so you could visit to see if you recognized any names."

As Diana and Beverly traveled down the road, they noticed the cows grazing in the field, so they knew they still worked the farm. However, the names she gave them were Luther, Jack, and Louis, and they were not familiar to the girls. When they reached the church, there was a huge stone with Shore and several small stones through the graveyard, but they did not see names they could connect with. However, they did notice that it said "Shore" and not "Shores," so they began to wonder what the difference was. "Sometimes there is a family feud and they split, and one adds an S to distinguish from the other" was one of their thoughts. Beverly and Diana were going to check this out at the Historical Society.

Their next stop was Winston-Salem, about an hour's trip because they had address of their grandfather's and great-grandfather's home. As they got into town, they drove around and kept looking at the streets going up and down until finally they came upon the street. So down the street they followed the houses; it was a very long street that seemed to lead into town and that it did right to a parking lot. Obviously the homes had been torn down to build a school and a parking lot. Of course, they are talking about the 1900s, but they still got out and stood in the lot, just to feel like they were there.

When they were headed home, they discussed a lot about the difference in the name, something that was puzzling them. Beverly felt someone would know the story behind this, "We just have to find that person." After a lovely dinner out at a fine restaurant with the Sandersons, they came home exhausted after all the excitement. Diana decided before going to bed to Google David Shores, and up came a document with an article written about his descendant Benjamin Shores, who was a bootlegger. The article was intense and profound, titled "Moonshiners on the Warpath." It read as follows:

Moonshiners on the Warpath

The Landmark Statesville, Iredell Co. NC September 9 1881

A Seizure in Yadkin County—Recapture by an armed force "The Woods just full of them"—The Revenue Officers finally victorious—Ludicrous side scenes.

News having reached this place of the recent seizure of a wagon and mules in Yadkin county, and some blockade brandy, the property of Benjamin Shores, by Deputy Collector J C Sullivan and a small posse, a reporter from The Landmark sought out Mr. Sullivan, yesterday and from him learned the facts in the case, which were as follows:

On Friday evening August 25th, about 4 o'clock, he was on his way to Yadkinville, traveling on the Wilkesboro and Hamptonville road, in the vicinity of Buck Shoal, when he overtook a man by the name of Benjamin Shores, accompanied by one Isaac Shores Jr., driving the wagon, drawn by two mules, in which as he passed by he discovered a barrel, which he suspected contained a quantity of block. Passing on to the house of H M Money, he dismounted, and finding Messrs. Gentry and Myers, of the internal revenue service, summoned them to his aid, and awaited the coming up of the team, hailing the parties, he told them he must search the wagon, and at the same time took hold of the reins of the old mule. At once the parties in the wagon commenced beating the mules with a large stick, upon which the animals reared and started off in a gallop with Mr. Sullivan swinging in midair. Calling lustily for aid, he was joined by Gentry who seized the reins of the other mule, and by hard efforts they succeeded in mastering the situation. They were joined about this time by Myers, whose anxiety (?) to find his shooting iron had materially retarded his progress. The party then searched the wagon, finding a cask containing 23 gallons of good brandy, which had never made the acquaintance of an internal revenue gauge, or a tax-paid stamp.

Finding evidence sufficient to warrant seizure, the wagon and team were conveyed to the house of Mr. Gentry, where arrangements were made to stop overnight. Messrs. Sullivan and Gentry fearing an attempt might be made to wrest the property from them during the night, concluded to keep watch. About 8 or 10 o'clock they were approached by an armed force, numbering some six or seven men, backed by some fifteen or twenty more, secreted in the adjacent thickets. In short, to use the language of the officers, "the woods were full of them". The assailants were armed with axes, rocks and clubs, and in less time than it takes to tell it, they had surrounded the wagon, and just as Deputy Collector Sullivan was in the act of drawing his revolver, he was seized by three of the attacking party, one on each side, while the third stood over him with a stone swearing he would "slit his d—m brains out".

Gentry, who was armed with a double barrel shot gun, presented it at the parties who were maltreating Sullivan, but dared not fire lest his aim should take effect alike on friends and foes. While affairs were at this crisis, others of the party drove off the team, and finally the officers were left without further molestation, the invaders departing in high glee with the property. In the hurry and scramble of leaving they ran the wagon against Gentry's jersey which was standing near, entirely smashing the whole thing to pieces.

The officers immediately collected a small party and started in pursuit, and about 6 or 7 miles from the place found the wagon left in the road, literally full of clubs and stones but minus mules and brandy. The officers then proceeded to Yadkinville, where after some negotiations, carried on through friends, the moonshiners agreed to surrender the mules and reveal the whereabouts of the brandy. They at once stated to secure the brandy which was said to be at old man Hudspeth's. Arriving near the house they met Mr. Hudspeth on his way to the spring nearby, carrying a huge cedar water bucket, they told him they had come after the brandy that was concealed at his house by the Shores; but he said there was none there. Deputy Collector Sullivan dismounting advanced toward Mr. Hudspeth, for the purpose of interrogating him, but the old gentleman, seeming to take the movement as a hostile intention (though it was not so intended) drew his bucket on Sullivan, saying, "Don't you touch me, d—m you!" The noise having reached the house, a swarm of women came to the old man's aid, brandishing brooms, shovels, tongs, axe and had they made a sudden onset, at the moment, there would have been no doubt a regular stampede of the entire force. As matters, however, did not reach a climax, while the old man and the women were parleying with each other, one or two went on to the house where they soon found "block" hid under the bed behind some goods and boxes. After some little delay the brandy was safely secured and the posse quietly moved off, not however, until after they had been generously treated to a number of "cuss words."

Thus ended the skirmish, some parts of which were said to have been intensely ludicrous, and others not quite so much so. The posse at last arrived in Statesville without further adventure, and delivered the property into the hands of the revenue authorities to be disposed of as the law directs.

Now it was November 3, 2012; it was a beautiful brisk morning, and this time they were headed to their old stopping ground, Dunkin' Donuts. They also stopped at Burger King to pick up some egg sandwiches for the Sandersons as they seemed to like those occasionally. The sisters headed back to Shore Road to meet Jack Shore. That was the small house on the right they had missed; they wanted to see him just to see if he knew any of their family. The sisters were especially interested in the difference in the Shore and Shores and thought, "Maybe he would know something about that." As Beverly knocked on the door with timid Diana waiting slightly behind, a rather large grizzly man chewing tobacco welcomed them right in after they introduced themselves. He explained that he had lost his wife, but he would share what he could remember. As he chewed and spit, he began right away to tell the story of the difference in the name. "Wow, that was just what we wanted to know," the girls thought; it was like he was reading their minds. Jack explained that they were all related, but they split off. "Some are in northern and some in southern part of Yadkinville." He directed them to go to the next little town, "where there is a crossroad, you will see a Dollar store. Go to the cashier and ask her where the cemetery is for the Shores. She will know."

Beverly and Diana went on down the road, came to the Dollar store, went in, and began to ask the cashier. A lady in line spoke up and said she knew the Shores. She was very nice and wrote down the name of a lady from her church; the lady's father was a Shores. The directions sent the sisters down the road to a gray house on the left, and Joan and Jim came out to greet them. They were very pleasant, gave their e-mail, and told the sisters about the Mountain View Church and the graveyard where her uncle, Columbus Shores, was buried. Their grandfather's middle name was Columbus, so now they were overjoyed that they had the right Shores. Beverly and Diana giggled like teenagers as they drove around to the graveyard to find many of the Shores buried there.

Happy that they had made progress as they met family, they followed the road around, not really knowing where they were and came upon a small Historical Society that was open on Sunday. The girls stopped in on the chance they may have information on the Shores. As it happened, they met a nice knowledgeable woman named Judy. Beverly and Diana explained what they were doing, and she was quite encouraging about the Shores and suggested that on Monday they meet with a gentleman named Andrew, who knew all the Shores, northern and southern. Beverly looked at Diana with intense jubilation in her eyes. In fact, Judy called Andrew and not only made the arrangements but also gives them the number. Now the sisters were on fire with excitement. What a day the girls had! They had some dinner as they tried to contain their high spirits.

It was quite late when they finished eating and got on the road, but they were full of enthusiasm as they reached the Sandersons'. Beverly and Diana found Louise still up and wanted to talk; it was all they could do to talk one at a time. Louise had to slow them down several times. She could see how happy the sisters were not only to be together, but exploring their past to realize how times had been for their family. They thanked Louise for being there to support them and sharing her lovely home. Now they had a big day planned, so they needed a good night's rest. Diana and Beverly went to their room; Anya had fresh sheets and towels each day, which topped the evening off as something out of the ordinary and unique.

On November 4, 2012, the sisters arose to a chilly day but did not change their routine breakfast at Dunkin' Donuts. They knew they had to meet Andrew in Yadkinville at the library, and he did not seem the type to fool around when you had an appointment. Beverly and Diana walked into the library; although it was small, it was quite buzzing, and of course Andrew spotted them immediately. He was a jovial fellow and eager to help them. They chatted a while, and he brought out a chart showing the land areas that the Shores owned, which was quite extensive. Andrew went on to bring out this large book titled *Fredrick Schor*. He was the patriarch that came across on the Pennsylvania ship, the *Sandwich* on November 30, 1750. He was one of the German pioneers from Switzerland. They first settled in southwest Virginia to farm and work in the lead and silver mines. However, the king's declaration decreed the land must be returned to the Cherokee Indians. "This is when Fred Schor and his family moved to Mill Creek, Surry County, North Carolina, where he finally passed away."

After receiving some history from Andrew, he then shared with them the name of a man, Chester Wooten, who knew all about the Shores. At that point, he proceeded to call him on his cell and told him that he had two women interested in the Shores family. Chester was working on the farm that day but said he would be thrilled to meet the sisters at Bo jangles' the next day to take them to the original Shore farm and distillery. Beverly and Diana agreed immediately to meet him at 8:30 a.m. on November 5, 2012, at Bo jangles' across from the library. Just in case there might be any issues, they took down his cell number along with Andrew's. The sisters thanked Andrew for all his efforts and his time in sharing so much information with them and explained that someday he would be in their book about their journey to find their roots.

Beverly and Diana thought there might be a little time for some shopping in order. Their favorite stores were T J Maxx and Marshalls. They knew there had to be one maybe not in Yadkinville, but they had to go back through Winston-Salem. So they got on the computer and looked them up. After they found the address, Diana put it in her Garmin, and they went right to the door. Beverly and Diana knew that it was dangerous when they arrived at the store. Unfortunately, there was no self-control for either of them as they both bought things they didn't need; after all, they were on vacation. Anyway here is what happened: Beverly and Diana got what you call buyer's remorse. They got the items home, thought about it, said they didn't need that, and at the next stop at one of the stores, they took it back. The girls just had the joy of buying; even though they took it back, they had some pleasure even if it was short lived.

The ride home was full of excitement as they had learned so much about their ancestors and could just feel the salt air on their faces as they came across on that large ship, the *Sandwich*, for weeks and weeks. Louise was waiting at the door. She was very anxious for them to go to dine at one of their favorite restaurants; even Jon was ready. The sisters were pretty tired; however, not to disappoint their hosts after such wonderful hospitality, they smiled and Diana responded just how hungry she had gotten in the last hour. The restaurant was a few miles down the road, and prime rib was their specialty. That meal topped off a wonderful day for them. Beverly and Diana felt so special to have friends so pleasant and accommodating as they followed their dreams.

They woke up on November 5, 2012, anxious to meet Chester Wooten, who was married to a Shores. Now Beverly and Diana started to think here they were in a small town, two women meeting a guy in a pickup at Bojangles' they didn't know, wondering if they had thought this out completely. So far they had met such accommodating people, and all had been hospitable, so they just didn't have any fear. As Beverly and Diana pulled up to Bojangles', they saw an old red single cab pickup with an older gentleman and his dog sitting in the truck. They looked at each other as if to say "that must be him." He got out, opened the door, and asked politely if they minded riding with the dog. Then shaking hands, he confirmed that they were cousins. Beverly and Diana felt immediately at ease, smiled, and explained a little about their journey, what they had already learned, and asked what he could add to their adventures so far. Chester took them out a winding road and then off the beaten path until they came to a small house. There in the back was a tall chimney standing alone. So he told them the story as they got out of the truck, how this was the place where the original Shore family farmhouse stood. All that was left was the chimney, the basement, and a two hundred-year-old hickory tree. He told the story of how his father-in-law would not spend $ 40.00 to repair one side of the house, so it deteriorated. He and his sister were so mad for him not spending the money to fix it, that they bought all the property and fixed up the small farmhouse, which "is still lived in at the front." He then took them way in the back of the property where the old distillery was still there but mostly deteriorated. Beverly and Diana were just thrilled to stand on the spot where their ancestors lived and farmed their land.

Before they left for the car, Chester wanted to tell them one old story that had been handed down for many years. He said he would take them to the old cemetery that belonged to the Shores up on the hill in a remote area that was very hard to find, "but as we go, I will tell you the story." There was John Cooney Shores who had twenty-two children and eight bastard children because the wives refused to have any more children with him. The story went that he supported every one of those children, fed them, clothed them, and educated them. He was a well-known man in those parts; they called him "Cooney." When they got to the cemetery, there they found some of their great-grandparents, David, Rachael, and John Cooney Shores buried on the hill.

Chester was very accommodating and kind to spend time away from his farm to show the sisters around the southern area where the Shores lived. He also let them know that every year in June on the first Sunday, all the Shores from all over get together for a big family reunion and invited them. Beverly and Diana were eager to be able to come to one; however, it might not be this next year as they were working on their book, but maybe the following year. It certainly was a pleasure, and Beverly and Diana thanked him for his hospitality.

It was November 6, 2012, as they packed the car to leave the Sandersons' lovely home. Louise was very specific that they should return on their way home. Beverly and Diana would not think of going through North Carolina without stopping, as Beverly's son Blake and his wife Cindy would be moving to Ecuador, and they would be coming back through to go to a party in Asheville, North Carolina. Their next stop was Galax, Virginia, where their mother was raised and their grandfather worked long hard hours at the saw mill. They had a lot to talk about on the way as they were on information overload. Beverly and Diana were trying to keep folders and spiral notebooks with notes of each family to keep track so that when they got home, they could put it all together.

As Beverly and Diana reached town, it was getting very cold and windy, but the first thing they saw was the Chamber of Commerce. They stopped in and got a map of Galax and asked about a good place for lunch. The lady directed them to the corner barbecue that you could smell as they opened the door coming inside. They drove down and found a place right in front; it was almost like things just fell into place for them. The smell was luscious as you walked in; they ordered two big sandwiches with fries and two large teas. You could feel the Southern atmosphere all around as you sat waiting for your meal. It was the real deal. After Beverly and Diana finished eating, they noticed right across the street was the courthouse, so they decided to check it out.

They found school records on their grandfather Moses and their grandmother Mae. Actually the reason they had a hard time finding her on the Ancestry was because her name was Polly in school. The only way they knew it was her was because it showed her parents' names, and Beverly and Diana knew their names. Also, they were able to get the marriage certificate for their great-grandfather John H. Shores, who was married to Eliza Goodson; however, it named his parents as Giles and Holly, which was not what they had from Ancestery.com. Next, they went to the library and copied more information on the family, and while they were there, they met a gentleman named Jim. They had been trying to find lodging for less than $150.00 a night, and he heard Beverly and Diana talking and offered his cabins for half price. All they had to do was come back at 7:00 p.m. and follow him home. By that time Beverly and Diana were hungry again, so they had something light and picked up some snacks for the cabin. They met Jim at 7:00 p.m. and followed him up the road; it was a somewhat steep winding road with sharp turns, and very dark. Beverly looked at Diana like "how are we going to remember how to get down to town in the morning?" They kept going up, and the temperature kept dropping; it was now 28 degrees.

Finally, they pulled up beside a very nice cabin in the woods. Jim went in and started the fireplace and turned the heat on for them. They started to unpack the car, and it was cold! Beverly and Diana just took enough in for the night. The bedrooms were so cold, you could not sleep in them, so they took all the blankets, and the couch had two recliners in front of the fireplace. So that was where they slept. That certainly was an adventure, but what was to come in the morning? How to get back down to Galax was another thing. Beverly and Diana were way too tired to worry about that now; they watched a little TV and fell asleep with it still on.

On the morning of November 7, 2012, it still was brisk outside, so they put some warm clothes on and spotted a gas station, which they had not seen in the dark coming home. They drove over and asked the lady there for directions back to town. Obviously, it was not the first time she had been asked that question; she got her paper with a little chuckle and wrote down each road for them. They thanked her, and she said she was happy to do it with her Virginia Southern hospitality. Beverly and Diana started down the winding road, and as they were turning around and around they looked at each other, knowing without these instructions they would have never gotten down to Galax.

First they had to find a Dunkin' Donuts and have their usual. They went inside, and of course they shared their story of being separated as sisters and the journey they were on to find their roots. Everyone was always eager to hear their story and wanted to read their book when it came on the shelf. They were always mentioning names of their ancestors to see if anyone knew them and could help them with their history.

After breakfast, they headed back to the library to find out about the Lineberry, Goodson, and the Shores. Jim came over and asked how they slept, and they explained how cold the bedrooms were, so they slept in the living room and were quite warm. He suggested that they go across the street to the nursing home, and there may be some family members still alive that could help with their search. They looked through some files and decided they might do better going to the nursing home. While they were over there asking if there were any families affiliated with their family names, they met a nurse in the hall that heard why they were there, and she came to find them talking to one of the patients. She knew the Goodson family and was familiar with the family graveyard; however, she knew it was by the parkway but could not tell Beverly and Diana how to get there. She was very pleasant and obliging as to let them know how acquainted she was with the graveyard and yet embarrassed that she could not give them directions. Although she did say that it was up a remote road off the parkway. Beverly and Diana thanked her and were glad just to get that much information.

They decided to go on the parkway and give it a try themselves, and it was a magnificent ride. The scenery was just picture-perfect; of course that was not what they were there for, so they had to focus on small roads that led off into the woods. Beverly looked at Diana after trying several roads; even though they had a 4 × 4, it had started to get dark, and they felt it was better to stop for now. As they came off the parkway, they saw a nice-looking restaurant called MaCado's, so they decided to give it a try before going up the mountain. They had a superb Spanish dinner and topped it off with flan for desert. Now they were ready for the jaunt home.

Beverly took her shower first and then came out to find Diana putting the dining chairs under the door knobs of the doors as she said they did not lock. They hardly had to worry way up there with no one around in the mountains. Diana came out of the shower, and Beverly had the beds made up so they could watch some TV. They had some interesting things to chat about their day and think about what to do the next day. Diana mentioned that "Wythe is where the girls' school had been." She thought maybe their mother and her sisters might have attended it after their mother passed away. Beverly suggested that they make that their next stop tomorrow. They were not asleep very long when Beverly woke to find Diana on the porch with a broom. Beverly jumped to her feet to see what she was doing out in the cold. Diana exclaimed that she had heard a noise out there, and she was looking for whatever was on the porch. Beverly asked her if she was crazy to protect herself with a broom from maybe a bear or any animal out there. They came inside but there was no sleeping; Diana kept them up all night hearing noises or intruders.

It was November 8, 2012. After having their breakfast at the usual place, they drove north to Wythe, Virginia. They had looked up the Abingdon School for girls, which was a short distance from Galax. At their grandmother's death after her last child, their mother, and her sisters were young between the ages of fourteen and four. However, Beverly and Diana were only guessing that this might have been the school the girls were sent to, and if they had pictures of the children, they might get to see their mother as a young girl. When they arrived, a very pleasant lady showed Beverly and Diana what pictures they had salvaged as they had a big fire back in the 1940s that destroyed much of their records. It was just optimism on their part to have the possibility of finding a picture by some coincidence. However, the sisters left, heads hanging low, still yearning for that desire to find some small connection to their mother.

As Beverly and Diana drove back to Galax, they were pleased that at least they tried to find the home their mother might have lived in during her teenage years; the sisters noticed as they went down the street the Wythe Genealogical Society for Grayson County and Carroll County. So as they pulled in; two very sweet ladies helped them after hearing their story. They were familiar with the church and graveyard and gave Beverly and Diana directions out to it once again. They wanted so much to see both their grandmothers' gravesites. With their directions, the sisters drove out to the church and went inside to look at the Bible to see if their ancestors' family names were in the open Bible. No one was around, so they could not see if they had an older copy which may have had some of their names, as there were some Goodsons buried in the graveyard.

Beverly and Diana were beginning to think they were not going to find the family gravesite, but they were not giving up yet. As they drove down once again toward the parkway, they passed an old bottled gas company. Beverly backed up and decided to ask if anyone could give them direction to the gravesite. The large garage door was only slightly cracked open, so Beverly pushed it open enough to get inside. Then she went in and shouted to see if anyone was working there. Along came a short stocky older gentleman with a big smile on his face, asking how he could help. Beverly began to pour out her guts as to how many times they had tried to find the cemetery for the Goodson family. He said he could not give them directions. Beverly just hung her head and started to walk away. But he said, "Wait just a minute. Get in your truck, and follow me." Beverly was shocked! He was going to take them right to the cemetery. What a nice thing to do. First of all, as they followed him around the parkway, they could see where they had missed the mile marker; then he turned on this old dirt road and went up through some trees to a large grassy area, and there it was—a beautiful gated graveyard with flowers all marked and well cared for gravesites. They thanked him for his kindness, and he said it was his pleasure. The tears began to flow as they opened the gate and started to look at all the Goodson ancestors. It was such an accomplishment to finally reach their destination.

As they followed further up the road, they came to the Snow Hill Baptist Church built in the late 1800s. And there they found their two grandmothers. That was the biggest delight of the day. They found Mae Lineberry, who was their grandmother on their mother's side; and Eliza Goodson, who was their great-grandmother. Also, they located Eliza's husband John H. Shores, their great-grandfather and their two children. This was family, and they were elated to be able to discover this part of their past. This just topped their day off; now they just needed to find a room for the evening.

As they continued on the parkway, it was a picturesque ride through the countryside, so they decided to try and make it as far as Roanoke, Virginia, by 6:00 p.m., as they did not like driving in the dark. As usual, Diana took care of the map, while Beverly did the driving. They drove along and enjoyed the excitement of their day and how neat it was that they finally were able to stumble across someone to take them to the cemetery. Finally, as they were riding along, Beverly asked Diana to find a road off to the left that would take them to the highway to Roanoke. Diana seemed to be studying the map quite intensely, but Beverly did not hear much from her. She kept on driving, and soon they saw turkeys, and then they saw some deer. The more they drove and the darker it got, the more Diana seemed to be getting upset with Beverly, and she was in charge of the map. Beverly asked her if she had seen a road that turned off the parkway yet that would get them to the highway. Diana gave Beverly a not-so-nice a look and the comment came out as if to say, "Do you want me to make a road?" Things were getting tense in the car; up till now there had not been one disagreement.

Diana made sure to let Beverly know that she better not get to the hotel at 9:00 p.m. Finally, they came upon a sign that went to Roanoke. Diana was not happy; however, they turned off, and Beverly explained,

"It cannot be far." They drove a short distance, and then the first hotel Beverly saw she pulled into and went inside to get a room. Much to Beverly's surprise, the rather large grouchy lady had no room and proceeded to say that "there are no rooms in Roanoke." That was not going to make Diana a happy big sister to deal with, so Beverly decided not to tell her. When she got to the car, Beverly said she decided they would eat first and then find a room if it was okay with Diana.

They both really liked Applebee's. Right down the road there was one, and they pulled in and were seated in the bar area where the TVs are visible from the tables. The place was packed, and this table had just come open, so they grabbed it. Now Diana started asking what happened at the hotel, they stopped at. "You haven't shared with me." As the waiter came to the table right at that moment, they ordered as they knew what they wanted. Diana looked at Beverly and asked again. Beverly then called the manager over to the table and asked if he could help suggest a room for the night. Of course, immediately he exclaimed, "Not in Roanoke!" Now you could see the look on Diana's face. She had fear in her eyes like "what are we going to do?" Looking up at the TV, they could see the game being played, and then they realized, it was Florida State and Virginia Tech. No wonder there were no rooms available with those two playing. The manager came back to their table as he had called further north and found a room for them, which was very accommodating of him. Beverly looked over at Diana and let her know it all worked out. They had a lovely dinner with a hot brownie for desert and then got on their way. They drove back about thirty miles, and the weather was very cold; the hotel was not the nicest. They had to drag their suitcases up two flights of stairs, and to top it off it was 9:00 p.m. Diana was not happy. Beverly was going to have to make it up to her the next day.

It was now November 9, 2012, and they had left Virginia on their way to Aberdeen, Maryland, their original hometown. Before they left, they had to hit a Dunkin' Donuts for their usual. Beverly had to make Diana smile with her chocolate donuts. As a special treat, she had chocolate icing too. They got rolling down the road and then started laughing about Beverly asking Diana to find a road to turn off to Roanoke. Diana just kept laughing because she kept thinking Beverly wanted her to get out and make a road. They had more fun and giggled over that, saying how silly they both could get sometimes, just like as if they were young sisters growing up together.

They stopped and got good directions to get around Washington, and they knew they wanted to be in Aberdeen before dark once again. Everything was fine until they got to DC; the traffic got real slow, and they just crept along. Then the traffic started to move along at a pretty good clip as they got near Baltimore; then the tunnel came along, and it was backed up for hours. Diana does not like the tunnel, so that was going to be frightening for her. Finally, they reached Route 95, and it was still backed up. It was now 3:00 p.m., and the Friday work traffic was letting out. Beverly felt like she was driving in Los Angeles, California; everyone driving fast and in and out of traffic. However, they drove through it all and made it to Aberdeen to the Clarion Hotel at 5:30 p.m. to check in. They had planned to stay seven to ten days, and they said the rate was $139.00 a night, so Beverly gave her AAA card, which brought it to $119.00. Knowing that they might stay longer, Beverly asked to speak to the manager. They gave her the name and said she would be available in the morning. Beverly and Diana felt they would tell the manager their story and that her hotel would be part of their book and see if they could get a greater discount.

Along with their paperwork came a coupon, "buy one dinner get one free," so they took their suit cases to their room, which was very adequate for their stay and went to the restaurant for dinner. They picked the Maryland crab cake dinner, which came with salad, baked potatoes, grilled vegetables, and desert. It was one of their many crab dinners, and it was delicious. Once you have lived in Maryland and had crab from the Chesapeake Bay, you will never forget the taste and always want more. They went to their room full and happy with their first day of crab. They had an enormous day planned for tomorrow and a lot of people to meet. Beverly and Diana were home, and now they were going to explore places they remembered when they were four and seven. What a thrill!

Beverly and Diana got up on November 10, 2012, and went down to the complimentary breakfast. They stopped at the front desk and asked for the manager, who had already left for the day. The girl at the desk said she would call her at home for us; the sisters told her their story and that they would stay longer if she would give them a better price. Kiera was nice enough to give them the name of a place they could get a pedicure to relax from the long trip, and then when they got back she would have an answer. They drove to the place Kiera had recommended and found it to be a very lovely place with nice massage chairs so they both got a pedicure and chatted as they relaxed. It was now about noon, so they headed back to the Clarion, and Kiera still had not talked with the manager. Therefore, when they arrived, she called and woke her up and was kind enough to relay their story, and she gave them a price of $89.00 a night. Beverly and Diana were thrilled with that price, and she offered to lower it if they stayed longer than seven days.

As this was going to be their bum-around day, they decided to go to Bel Air to Applebee's and also do some shopping at TJ Maxx. Diana had not brought any clothes for Sunday church, so they needed to get her a skirt and blouse. It was funny they asked the waitress in Applebee's, "What is a nice store to shop in around here," and she said, "None really, as the only store is Macy's." She let them know that she was from Baltimore City and that is where she did her shopping. Beverly and Diana were not too good for Macy. Therefore, they went to TJ Maxx to find a jacket, skirt, boots, wedge shoes, and some wild-looking hose. These were all things Diana could wear when she got home too.

After they finished their shopping, they went to the grocery store to pick up some laundry detergent and get some quarters, so they could do laundry from the trip so far. Diana spotted some black walnuts that were hard to find, so of course she had to get several bags. Then they made their way to the Clarion and up to their room to sort out their clothes for the next day as they had a drive in the morning for Sunday church. Beverly and Diana both washed and folded several loads of laundry so they would be ready for the rest of the week, as it would be full of adventure meeting the cousins and, best of all, finally having lunch with Marsha.

It was now November 11, 2012, and Beverly and Diana had their breakfast with Margaret and her son Mark, who put them at the same table and got their drinks. They were very accommodating, and Beverly and Diana made friends with them right away. The first place they wanted to go was their first foster home and that was the Lopers'. They could not remember where the old farm was located, so they had found Mr. Loper's son's home, and they drove there to see if he was home. They pulled up in the drive. Beverly went to the door, and no one answered; it was a little discouraging. However, as they backed out of the drive, they noticed a man on a mower across the street and stopped and asked if that was the Loper home, and he said it was. By that time they were confronted by a large pickup truck that pulled up beside them and the driver asked who they were looking for. The man on the mower told them, "They are looking for you, Robert." Surprisingly, he remembered them as foster children, and he asked if he was ever mean to them. Beverly and Diana just laughed. They exchanged numbers so that they could meet up one day while they were here with his two sisters as they were teenagers, and they remembered Beverly and Diana quite well. Robert certainly was overwhelmed that they even were able to locate him.

Beverly and Diana had certainly had a flash from the past, hoping to see the girls, and maybe they would get to see the farmhouse and see the swing that they used to swing on for hours. But for now they had to go back and get ready for Sunday church as it was down in Edgewood, and Beverly was going to see her high school friend that she had not seen since 1967. When they arrived, Beverly said, "There is my friend and her husband, Janet and Barry Andrews." It was exciting after all those years to see her and her two sisters, Kelly and Brenda. Imagine going back in time! These friends had gray hair and grandchildren. The Bible discussion was moving, filled with scriptures, and inspiring for the times they were living in were such perilous times, and fulfilling Bible prophesy. Beverly and Diana were able to enjoy fellowship with the congregation afterward and even met a brother who remembered Beverly when she was just a little girl.

When asked what they would like to have for dinner, of course Diana was the first to say "crab." Janet knew the best place to go was called Joe's, so they all followed her as Diana and Beverly were not very familiar with Edgewood. Beverly had left the area in 1966. They had crab dinner once again, but the highlight of the evening was the mushrooms stuffed with crab. Those were scrumptious! Beverly and Diana will never forget those. They had to say good night, but Janet and Barry invited them to their home for dinner one evening before they left, which was a kind gesture, and they accepted.

As Beverly and Diana drove home once again in the dark, they reflected back on some of the wonderful people they met today and how they have touched their lives then and now.

CHAPTER 8

On November 12, 2012, Diana and Beverly took off happily to the breakfast room to find they had been moved down one table as "The Balloon Man" was sitting where they normally sat. However, their setup was right next to him, and Margaret and Mark introduced Beverly and Diana and wanted them to share their story. As Beverly began to tell the story, Jeff started making Diana and Beverly a balloon of a penguin and a rubber ducky. As they shared their story with others listening in, obviously they became instant friends. Jeff and his wife Laura came in the Clarion to eat all the time, so they let the sisters know when they would meet back to get an update. While Beverly and Diana were giving out the dynamics of their story, Jeff and the waiter Mark found out that they were related. It was just a small world when you get to talking with people, and they talked with everyone around them.

After breakfast, Beverly looked over at Diana and confirmed that they are going to Uncle Benjamin's farmhouse on Poplar Grove Road. Diana, of course, always was questioning Beverly's ability to remember where things were, as she moved away from Aberdeen when she got adopted at nine. Beverly recalled their uncle's farm from four and had lived in the area till she was sixteen. They programmed the Garmin to Poplar Grove Road, and it took them out in the country to Street Maryland, which did not even have a light when Beverly lived there, but now it did. Beverly remembered old Walker's Store and she pointed that out; then she saw a white farmhouse. The problem was it did not have a porch on it, but Beverly was almost sure that was it. Diana asked her what they should do now. One thing was for sure: Beverly was not stopping without finding out if that was the old Clark farm.

As they drove down the road, on the right side, there were small homes. Beverly pulled into the first driveway and said to Diana she would be right back. Beverly went to the door and knocked, but no one was home. She came back to the car, went to the next home, knocked on the door, and waited a few minutes—nobody home. Now to the third home on the block, knock on the door, nobody home. Beverly was beginning to get discouraged, but there were two more houses. Diana admired her tenacity. She asked, "But don't you think you have knocked on enough doors?" Beverly pulled into the drive of the next-to-the-last home and went to the door, and a nice older lady came to the door. Beverly asked if that was Benjamin Clark's farm.

The lady at the door went on to say, "Sure it is the Clark farm. However, he passed several years ago." Beverly asked her if she knew who owned it now, and she said, "Well, of course, his son Tony." Beverly jumped for joy, and Diana's tears started flowing. Beverly gave the lady a big hug, and she did not even know why but was glad to help. They sat in the car for a moment to get themselves together as they were about to meet their cousins. What was that going to be like? Would they even remember the story about them? Maybe they might not want anything to do with them. But one thing was for sure: Beverly looked at Diana with those twinkling eyes to let her know she was right about that being the farm.

Slowly, down the street they went not knowing what to expect but with all the anticipation that they would welcome them just as much as they wanted to be welcomed into their family. Of course, Diana let Beverly go to the door first. Diana was a little timid. Beverly knocked, and a very sweet lady opened the door, smiling widely. The sisters introduced themselves and asked if this was the Clark residence. Very calmly, Beverly tried to tell her the story of why they were there, and the lady said, "Wait, l will get Tony. Come on in and sit down." Beverly immediately spotted the kitchen and remembered her father bringing her over there and putting her on a stool, on the table to pick glass out of her head as they had an accident. The memories brought a lump in her throat and tears to her eyes.

Before long, Tony came through the door and shouted, "Howdy, Cuz!" They all hugged! He remembered the story about what had happened as his father had talked about them, and they had played over there many times but they were small children. But who would think after fifty years they would just show up? Diana and Beverly sat and talked about his family and Uncle Benjamin. Beverly and Diana asked if they knew anything about their grandparents, and they did not. They said it was something that was not discussed. However, he told them about his sisters that were older, and he knew they would love to see them, "and they would definitely remember you. They all still live right around the Street and Darlington area." He was nice to give them their names and phone numbers so they could call and set up a time to meet. He took them over to Shelly's, his sister's, house, so they would know how to get there. It was something they will never forget; it felt like going back in time and living in a moment in life you never got to have. For Beverly and Diana it was hard to describe their feelings because they could have been raised as part of this family and lived right here, therefore never having the opportunities they have had in their lives. It was also frightening as it would have changed their whole life. They said their good-byes and let Tony know they would call to set up a time to get together.

Just as they got in the car, they got a phone call from Shelly asking them about coming over on Saturday so that they could share some pictures. They even said they had a picture of their father. Diana's big brown eyes looked like they were going to pop out of her head, Beverly started shaking her arm, asking what she was saying. Shelly and Diana just kept talking and making the arrangements for Saturday. Finally, when she got off the phone she told Beverly about the picture of their father. Beverly almost ran off the road. Now the girls were getting somewhere. Diana said, "They are asking us what we know about the family because we have been on Ancestry." Beverly expressed to Diana that their next day will be the Historical Society in Bel Air.

It was a cold rainy day on November 13, 2012, and they had a lot to tell Margaret at breakfast about their day. They got to their regular seat, and Beverly was getting her coffee ready when Margaret came over, eager to hear about the excitement of the day before. Diana was quick to tell about how they knocked on doors until they found where their cousins lived. "We met our cousins and have made arrangements to get together on Saturday to look at pictures and share stories about old times." Beverly jumped right in on the conversation and expressed with great delight that "we are getting a picture of our father." Margaret was so pleased for them; she felt like she was living this dream right along with them.

Beverly called Uncle Bob and talked to his wife, Lula, about having dinner later in the evening. She told them that the Saks's outlet was having a big sale, and they should go to check out the specials. Of course, every woman likes a good sale, so down to Saks they went. It was packed and there was a long line, and you had to get a number and wait out in the cold and rain until your number was called. Beverly and Diana were not sure if it was worth the wait, but all the ladies around were insistent about getting name brands for 50 percent to 75 percent off the marked-down price. Actually they waited two hours before they walked in to three large rooms full of people and clothes in large piles almost stacked to the ceiling. There were some on racks but very few. Beverly went over to a pile to look through the clothing, and a lady jerked the pants right out of her hands and let her know that was her pile to just try on. Therefore, you could only look at what was on the racks. It was unbelievable! They waited two hours for this messed-up arrangement. There was no organization to anything, no one to assist you, and patrons were standing right in the middle of the floor, trying on clothes. It was a madhouse. Later, they found that customers were buying to resale the clothing on eBay, not for their personal use. Beverly and Diana had wasted enough of their day at this store.

They called Aunt Lula and told her the fiasco they had just encountered at Saks, and she was sorry they wasted their time. She asked them to come by the house, and they would order some crab and have Beverly's cousin from her adopted family over to visit. Beverly was excited for Diana to meet her family as this was her dad's brother, Uncle Bob. After they arrived, Lula let them know that they didn't deliver anymore, so Beverly's cousin, Carol, suggested that they drive to Winter's Run for crabs down on Route. 7. So they got Uncle Bob in the car and they followed them toward Edgewood. Lula went on a back road that Beverly was again not familiar with, so she was trying to keep up with her and stay close. The night before Beverly had asked Diana if she would remind her in the morning to get gas. Actually, they both forgot. After quite a while, not knowing how much farther they had to go, Beverly looked down with a shocked look on her face as if to say "We better stop soon." Beverly tried to call Lula to tell her she needed gas, but to no avail. She would not pick up her phone. At the next red light, Beverly saw a gas station on the left, and she hopped out of the car, ran to Lula ahead of her, and said she needed to get gas. "Just pull up ahead and wait." Beverly had to make a right turn then make another left at the light, come back, and make another left and then a right into the station.

As she pulled in, she felt the car float and the pedal release as there was no gas. However, the first pump had a cover on it as it was empty, so Beverly kept rolling until she came to a stop at the next pump, where she was able to get gas. She looked over at Diana and let her know then that they just rolled in without gas. Diana was visibly shaken at the moment as Beverly pumped the gas.

After filling the car and getting back on the road, they could relax a little, but that was a close call. It wasn't very long before they arrived at the Winters Run, and Carol was already standing out front. Beverly gave her a big hug and couldn't recall the last time she had seen her, but if she had to guess, it might have been sometime after college.

Now Carol was a grown woman with children. They helped Uncle Bob out of the car; now that he was in his nineties, he had slowed down a bit. They got a big table, and the waitress asked if they were having crabs. Lula said, "Yes, bring us two dozen large crab." Beverly looked up at the price on the wall, and they were $65.00 a dozen. She thought that seemed a bit expensive. However, they had all the fries, coleslaw, hushpuppies and shrimp cocktails with that also.

First they came to the table and covered it with brown paper, and every inch was covered. It was about an hour's wait, and then out came these huge buckets of steaming crab with the smell of old bay seasoning following the waitress as she came to the table. Beverly and Diana both could not believe the immense size of each crab. Uncle Bob said, "Beverly, you wanted crab, now dig in, and let's see how many you can eat." Diana and Beverly were determined to eat crab every day if they could to get their fill, because there is nothing like Maryland crab.

They took some pictures to remember the great adventure with Uncle Bob, knowing it might be the last, and they wanted to hold on to the good times. Beverly asked Carol to let her follow her back to Aberdeen as it was dark, and she did not see well in the dark. Carol took them on the highway, where it was much easier to follow the road signs. Beverly and Diana were full to capacity, and all they wanted to do was lie down and relax. Beverly's cough was coming back, so they would have to stop and get some cough syrup at Walgreens, or there would be no sleeping for her.

When they arrived to their room, there were their nice warm beds; this was the third bottle of cough syrup, and Beverly was not feeling so good. Diana right away got on the computer as she was determined to find more of the Clark family, and she was not going to stop, not even on the trip. During the night, Beverly kept coughing, so Diana had to keep getting up to give her a cough drop so she could let it dissolve in her mouth and sleep. Who would get up all night and do that but your loving sister that you found after fifty-six years? That's who.

It was now November 14, 2012. They had their breakfast as usual and gave a report to Margaret. Briefly they explained that they would probably go to the Historical Society for the day and look up their families. At the Historical Society, they met some nice people that showed them some books on different families and how you look up your ancestors. The first item they came across was the coat of arms for the Morris family, which was their father's mother's family. Then they were able to locate the obituaries for William W. Morris and also for their father's brother Ray. They informed the sisters that "the genealogical group meets on Thursday and we have a gentleman that heads it up that can be extremely helpful in finding your ancestors, if you would like to return when he is available." Beverly and Diana informed them they would be back first thing in the morning.

However, there was a guy reading a paper sitting across from Beverly and Diana that was friendly, so they asked if he knew if Ray Osborne farm was still around. They remembered the farm because their father worked there, and they had lived there. Also they remembered as small children—especially Diana had memories—that their daddy was a good boy when they lived on the farm because he did not drink. The fellow replied immediately that sure he knew the farm. It was just up the road, but there was only the farmhouse left. Beverly and Diana did not care; they had to see it as it had fifty-year-old memories.

They started down Main Street to Osborne Parkway and made a right. It was all different with a Wendy's on the left, and behind was an apartment complex. However, they turned right, as the gentleman had said they would see a big rock and to turn there to the right. Beverly and Diana stopped to take a picture of this enormous rock with the name Osborne engraved on it and 1914 underneath the name. Then they followed the long driveway up to the large two-story farmhouse.

As they got to the house, they both began to tear up as they remembered their father working there. Of course, the big barns were gone as they had apartments built behind the old farm. As they stepped on the porch, they remembered quite well riding their trikes on that very porch as little girls. Then they went around the side. Diana said, "Beverly, look through the window. Are the stairs right in the middle of the house?" And yes, they were. Diana and Beverly remembered going up those stairs to their bedrooms each night.

As they stood there, going back in time, they thought about what life would have been if they had stayed with the family. However, as they continued on this journey, they without a doubt realized what a wonderful opportunity they were given by their adoptive families.

Again they had an eventful day, and now Beverly and Diana were invited to Janet and Barry's home for dinner. They had to stop at the hotel to change their clothes and freshen up for dinner. Then they set the Garmin for Janet's address, and within an hour, they were at their front door. They have a lovely small home, and Janet served salad and a shrimp dish, which was scrumptious.

She brought out some old picture as far back as high school, and they laughed about the crazy things they used to do. Janet used to live with her granny, and they used to try and sneak out, but granny was sharp and would catch them in the act. Beverly now keeps in touch with Janet by e-mail, which she had not done for years. They had a wonderful dinner and even better company. They put the Garmin on and got right back to the Clarion with no problems. Beverly and Diana had to get a good night's rest as they were going back to the Historical Society and meet with the genealogist, which would prove to be very enlightening.

It was November 15, 2012, and they were meeting with the genealogist at the Historical Society; they were hopeful this was going to be a memorable day. Before they got on the way, Beverly and Diana had their breakfast and could not go without letting Margaret and Mark know of any progress they had made. They were always excited for the sisters and also were sharing their story with others, so they had to get the latest news.

Beverly and Diana had done a lot of research to mostly find information on their father and mother. Beverly had written by e-mail to someone in Bel Air to help her find documents on her father's military records, which was most helpful in getting other records. His name was Henry C. Peden Jr. As they arrived, immediately a very nice gentleman walked up and asked if he could assist them. They sat at the table and tried to give him a brief synopsis of their story and asked him to start with their grandparents. He right away went into action. He went from file to file, and he gave them some books to look through and made some suggestions. After several hours, he came over to them and acknowledged that he was not giving up but that it was lunchtime, and they were having lunch brought in. He asked if they would like to go down to a café and be back in an hour to continue. He said he had a disc at home, which he would get and bring back as he felt it had some information they may be looking to copy.

Beverly and Diana walked down the street to a café and had a sandwich; needless to say it was a crab cake plate and was delicious. After enjoying that, they walked back to the Historical Society and met with the gentleman they were working with before. He was so eager to show them that he had found their grandmother. He had her death certificate, and she had died in 1940, which answered the question as to why their cousins did not know her, as she died before any of them were born. They were so happy with him. Then they asked about their grandfather; he said, "Let me look at one more place." They were sitting very calmly, and he came over and squatted down between them and exclaimed that he wanted to show them something he had never seen before. Beverly looked down at him and asked him, "By the way, what is your name?" He replied that his name was Henry Peden. Beverly and Diana could not believe their ears. Here this was the man Beverly was e-mailing from California that had helped her get documents to find their father. First they all had a good laugh over that, then back to business. Mr. Peden had found the beginning of an application, in 1919, for a marriage certificate for their grandmother and grandfather. There were only four questions answered, and then it was not completed and not filed. Therefore, they were not married before their father was born; in fact, she would have been pregnant as she stood there getting the license. Mr. Peden explained that back in those days, it was shameful and it was up to the court whether to give the license or not. Now whether that was the reason they had no knowledge. However they did know that their grandparents got married in 1920. At least Mr. Peden made their day as they found out about their grandmother and why none of the family seemed to know her.

On the way home, they spotted a restaurant called Micks; it looked nice, so they thought they would try it for dinner as they did not have plans. It was a very nautical-type setting and tablecloths, so you might say it was a little upscale. Diana and Beverly gazed at the menu, although there was no reason other than to see different ways to prepare crab. Diana spotted crab-stuffed potatoes along with crab cakes, so they both had the same dish. Diana talked about the crab-stuffed potatoes all the way home until Beverly was ready to scream. They had a long fulfilled day and had accomplished more than expected, which made them cheerful and ready for the next day of their journey.

It was a great morning on November 16, 2012, as they had been invited to the farm where Diana lived along with their youngest brother. That was the second foster home Diana was in, and she loved Mr. and

Mrs. Famos very much. Their son still lived on the farm, although it had been completely restored. Diana was extremely emotional and ready to visit the last home she lived in before her adoption. They had to visit their friends down in the restaurant to give a quick update to Margaret so she could share with all the others that were following their story. Joyfully, they drove out to the farm over the hills and past Diana's school she attended as a child. She began to tear up as they approached the long driveway to the Famos's home. Beverly drove slowly in as Diana could hardly keep her composure. She looked to their left and saw the enormous tree that had grown so high since they played under it some fifty years ago. Then she glanced to the right and could see the barn where Mr. Famos would get the big red tractor out and take turns with each of the children riding down the big hills, where the hay was kept.

She now had tears streaming down her eyes as Beverly reached over to hug her with compassion, knowing these were memories which were wonderful and intense at the same time. Beverly could feel her happiness as she trembled in her arms ever so slightly. As they came to the back door, a beautiful woman came out with a lovely inviting smile. Diana was first out of the car and into Dr. and Mrs. Famos's arms.

Beverly was also welcomed equally as she came into their warm but meticulous home. The lavishly restored kitchen with tile and wood floors was absolutely magnificent. It was a pleasure to meet the son and his wife of the family that were so accommodating to so many foster children. Dr. Famos's sister, Clarisa, who enjoyed playing with Diana as a child, lived just up the street and was joining them with pictures when Diana came to live there.

As they were talking, she came in and was just overwhelmed to see Diana sitting there after all these years. What a homecoming for Clarisa and Diana. They hugged and laughed about the tadpoles and going down to the creek when they were told not to, but took the punishment instead. All the memories of fifty-six years came back just like it was yesterday to them.

Diana looked at the pictures, and she could not believe she was so chubby. While in other pictures, she was just a little bit of a girl. Beverly and Diana shared with them the purpose of their journey to find their roots and to help get some closure from some of the complications of their early beginnings. Diana had wonderful memories here at their home; however not all their memories were as great. And yet they had met some impressive people that meant something to their lives and were having a splendid time getting to bond as sisters, rather than crying over what was taken from them.

Their visit could have gone on through lunch; however, they already had plans for lunch. Diana said to Dr. Famos and Mrs. Famos once again how happy and loving their home had been and what a good basis it gave her to grow up and have a happy home herself.

Their lunch date was a very special one as it was with Marsha at the Tower restaurant in Bel Air. Beverly and Diana were tremendously excited for this meeting as they had talked since 1982 but of course, had never met Marsha. This would be a first for all three of them. They arrived first and got some drinks and had to tell the waitress why they were there and who they were meeting. Once they told their story, everyone wanted to know when the book would come out. Little did Beverly and Diana know that it really does take a good year to write and do all the research to get a book ready to send it off for editing. They were both getting giggly, waiting for Marsha to arrive, and were acting like a couple of schoolgirls.

As they were acting silly, in walked a very nicely dressed woman, and they knew it was her. Both of them jumped to their feet to greet Marsha. It was the highlight of their trip. Nothing could have made them happier than to meet the person that put them together first in 1982. Then years passed, and again in 2012 they connected with her for her help to find closure in their lives from all the years of pain and suffering, wondering who you are, where did you come from, why did your mother give you away, and most of all, why were you split up? These questions only caused grief, heartache, alcoholism, divorce, mental issues, and self-esteem issues, and now it was time to finally face them and get closure. Beverly and Diana went to the wisest, most compassionate, empathetic, kindhearted, considerate, thoughtful, and hardworking person they knew to help them on their journey, and that was Marsha.

Undoubtedly, it was the greatest conversation they had yet, sitting with their friend and confidant, having lunch; it was surreal. They shared the pictures from the Famos's farm, and she remembered sending children out there for foster care. Beverly and Diana shared with Marsha about all their travels thus far and what they had discovered. How they had met cousins that they had never met and who were shocked when Beverly and Diana showed up at their doorstep. Also, they had found the children from the first foster home they were in and had met all three of them, and they are going to have breakfast with them later in the week. Beverly and Diana explained the documents they discovered with Mr. Peden's help at the Historical Society about their grandmother, how she died in 1940, and that is why none of the cousins knew her. So they were able to solve a mystery while they were here even for them. As they were about to depart, Marsha wanted to share one more piece of good news with them. Beverly and Diana's ears perked up and could not wait, but looked at each other hoping it was what they thought it was going to be! Marsha explained that recently some of the laws had changed, and she could now petition the courts for a copy of their birth certificates from their biological parents. "Now it may take until January for me to get them, so you may have to remind me." Beverly and Diana were ecstatic and eager to tell the world that they were getting their birth certificates. That meant the world to them. Marsha didn't have to worry about them reminding her; she knew they would be on the phone or e-mail all the time with her. That was the best news, and she kept it to the end—that stinker!

There was not much more you could say to Beverly and Diana to make them any more high-spirited right now. They felt like they got the world in the palm of their hands. The sky was blue, sun was shining, and it was all for them. However, they were meeting one of Beverly's best friends from high school for a snack around dinner. So of course, they had time after a three-hour lunch, so to their favorite store they went, this time to Marshalls. They looked around. Diana went in one direction and Beverly in another, and they always managed to find something. Beverly happened to be on the jeans isle and found the neatest soft gray jeans Diana's size. Diana fell in love with them and tried them on, and they fit great. So they paid for them and headed back to the Clarion to change before they met Beverly's friend Kathern.

Beverly's friend wanted to meet at Pat's Pizza for chicken wings on Route 40. They arrived and waited a little while, as Kathern was late coming back from Baltimore. Beverly was excited to see her, although she had seen her in 2007 at the class reunion. But they had some catching up to do on how her craft business was doing, her ex-husband, and her new house. They had a nice time but left early as they were tired after a full day. Beverly was happy to see her friend Kathern as they said good-bye.

Beverly and Diana certainly had a full and contented day; however, Diana suggested that before they got to the Clarion they should stop in for the $1.00 brownie bite they advertised at Applebee's. Beverly agreed that it would be a good idea. As they pulled up to go in, Beverly remarked to Diana how well the new jeans fit her and how comfortable they looked. Diana agreed and said she would love to get another pair. Little did they know that they were going through the emergency door; anyway, they grabbed a waitress, and she said, "It is okay, would you like a booth?" Beverly and Diana explained, "We don't need a menu. We know what we want. We will have two brownie bites." Also, Beverly wanted coffee and Diana wanted half-cut tea.

As they are waiting, they were discussing how great their day had been, and to top it off, they would be getting their birth certificates from their biological parents. Beverly reminded Diana that her son Scott always teased her that she was going to find out that "her birthday is not really January 1." Diana couldn't understand why he would say that. Beverly expressed that "he thinks someone made up January 1." Beverly knew he was kidding, but she just had to show him once and for all.

About that time their brownies came and they were just a bite, but it was just enough to take care of the desire for something sweet. The waitress dropped off the bill, and Beverly picked up the bill to take a look. Beverly started to laugh. Diana asked her, "What are you finding so funny about the bill?" Now Beverly continued to laugh. When you are tired and something hits you as funny, you can't stop laughing, and it becomes contagious. Diana too started laughing. Beverly asked the waitress to come over to the table. She could barely get out what she wanted to tell her, because she was laughing so hard. Finally, Beverly pointed out on the bill. "We are paying $1.00 for the brownie and $2.49 for a drink, and we have to leave a tip. This defeats the purpose of the $1.00 brownie." However they paid the bill and left a tip and continued laughing for being so foolish to pay that much for a drink and a brownie.

Beverly headed for the car as it had really gotten cold; she looked back and saw Diana was bent over by the door. Beverly wondered if something was wrong with her. Diana looked up at Beverly, and she was laughing so hard, it was unbelievable. Not only that but she had lost control of her bladder on her new jeans, which was making her laugh even more. Now Beverly joined in the laughter in the middle of Applebee's parking lot in the freezing cold. These were light gray Michael Khor jeans. How could she! Finally, Diana made it to the car, and Beverly put some paper down for her to sit on. They drove across to the Clarion. Beverly parked the car and told Diana that she was not walking in with her with wet pants all the way down her legs.

Before Beverly knew it, Diana was gone; she got to the elevator, and no Diana; she arrived at the room, and there she was, and they both had a good laugh after a wonderful, fulfilled day.

This day was special to write about in the journal, especially meeting Marsha. Beverly and Diana will always cherish that day as Marsha is the glue that put Beverly and Diana together.

It was now November 17, 2012, and how could they top yesterday? First, they went down to breakfast as they had a lot to talk about. There were some new people that had heard about their story from Margaret and Mark, so they had an audience. Diana decided she was going to have a biscuit and gravy, and Beverly went all out and had eggs, bacon, and sausage. They were happy to share the new things they learned, and everyone had goose pimples as they listened to their story.

Beverly and Diana thought they might find out about their grandfather as he had some connection with the Aberdeen Proving Ground at the Library. They asked the lady at the library if she had any knowledge of any records of civilians that worked there around

1919. Her name was Mrs. Smart, and she explained that she did not. However, her husband happened to be the historian for the APG, and his name was Jeff Smart. She was kind enough to call him, and he was not available. He gave them his number and said he may be able to help. We called Jeff and he was kind enough to look at the records from 1900 to 1920 and found no record of our grandfather working there.

Beverly thought that she would ride by the two homes her family that adopted her lived in when she was in Aberdeen. One home which she lived in first in 1956 was on Webb Street. Beverly drove up to the home and went up and knocked on the door. A lady opened the door and invited Beverly in, and she told the lady who she was and that she had lived there years ago. Beverly chatted for a few moments and had one request, which was, could she see her room? The kind lady pointed down the hallway saying, "Go ahead." Beverly slowly walked to the end of the hall, looked to the left, and there was her small, but the first happy place she felt safe. As the tears welled up in her eyes, only good memories came to her heart as this was her real start in life. Beverly thanked the lady; she was very kind, and they parted.

Diana looked at Beverly, knowing she was very emotional at that moment. Beverly expressed how it felt to visit her room that meant so much to her at such a tragic time in her life. She recalled how much she developed from a scared little girl, worried that someone was coming to get her. Beverly remembered hiding food under her bed, afraid still of not getting enough to eat from her previous life. But most of all, as she grew up, these things got better until she realized that adoption was for keeps. Diana was happy Beverly got to experience the time in her home.

Their next stop was the last home they lived in before they moved to Florida in 1966; it was located on Ferndale Road. It was a beautiful two-story brick home with a stream running beside it with white birch trees lining the stream. They had a huge yard and a back alley way behind the house. When Beverly pulled up, she saw the two trees her mother had planted by the front walkway to the front door. They were about four feet tall when they lived there, and now they towered above the house. Beverly went to the door and knocked, but no one was home. However, that was fine. Beverly had such good memories there also:

riding her bike down the alley and sledding down Mr. Lindsey's hill when it snowed were her happy times.

After leaving there, Beverly and Diana wanted to go to Havre-de-Grace to see if the home where their grandmother lived on Otsego Street was still there since 1940. Beverly thought this was a long shot, but "that area still has a lot of old homes and it may still be there." Diana explained to Beverly that if it was there, she was taking a picture. They had the Garmin, and they had the address from the Obituary as the last address, so they had accurate information. Beverly and Diana could not believe their eyes; there was an old apartment building with maybe four units. Amazing! Their grandmother lived right there and walked on this sidewalk that Beverly and Diana were walking on, cherishing every moment.

For Beverly and Diana to ride to Havre-de-Grace it felt nostalgic, knowing that their family lived there and worked there. It made them feel part of what would have been theirs if things had worked out. They next followed the street down until they came to Stokes Street, on which their grandmother lived in 1930 with their father and their two uncles. However, as they came to that street, they saw that one side had been torn down and there was a parking lot. And yet they knew they were standing in the area where their father played as a child, and that was enough for Beverly and Diana.

It was time for lunch. Someone along the way had recommended the Olive Tree for crab cakes, so of course, Beverly and Diana had to try it as they headed back to Aberdeen. After dinner, they were meeting the cousins around 6:00 p.m., out in Street, so they were prepared for an eventful evening with them. The waitress came to the table and recommended without a doubt the crab cake dinner, so they went along with that. After having their salad, which was very nice and had a lovely house dressing, along came the biggest plate of crab cakes they had seen yet. It smelled lightly of old bay, had drawn butter and large pieces of crab, and what was holding it together was not breading but just meat. It was amazing and wonderful. Beverly felt this was the most luscious meal by far they had eaten. Diana thought there was no way they could top this dinner, and maybe they would come back one more time.

Beverly and Diana set the Garmin for Shelly's house, and they found their way very easily. Tony had stopped by but did not stay, so they got to say good-bye to him. After that, they went inside and met Shelly's husband, her daughter, and her husband. Everyone was very pleasant and hospitable, accepting them as part of the family, even though they really never grew up with the family. About that time Jean came in, and they all hugged, and you could see who the talker in the family happened to be. Beverly and Diana started out by sharing how they met and how they found their parents, including Uncle Benjamin. In fact, they had spoken to him back in 1982 when they first met each other. Beverly shared what they had done on their trip so far and the things they had discovered. Diana asked if they remembered them staying with them at the farm when they were kids. Jean spoke up and expressed how Beverly used to run around and hide under the table. They were teenagers, and Beverly and Diana were still young, but they said, "When our parents died, we don't know what happened to all the pictures." So they were not very much help in filling in some of the blanks about their grandfather. However, to their surprise, they had a picture of their father in the Philippines, holding a bunch of bananas on the beach. Beverly and Diana were so delighted to have a picture of him. They had a picture of their mother, but neither of them knew what he looked like. He was tall and slender and had thick black hair. Beverly was especially surprised as her younger son was over six feet, slender, with black hair, and everyone always wondered who he took after as his father was five foot nine and Beverly was five foot six. Beverly and Diana felt once again that they had a special night that they will always remember with family that could have been under different circumstances.

On the way home, Diana began to talk about the great experiences they had in their lives. Beverly also agreed that they had wonderful opportunities in their lives that they may never have had if they were not adopted. All the family were very respectable people and lived in the same area that they were raised; however Beverly and Diana appreciated being given the chance to travel and see many parts of the world.

On the way back to the Clarion, Diana decided she wanted a brownie bite again, so Beverly pulled in to the Applebee's, which was right by the Clarion. They both laughed as they approached the door and went in to be seated. The waitress came to the table, and Beverly ordered two brownie bites and two waters. Diana just smiled as they talked about their day and how special it was to have a picture of their father. Now they could get it enlarged and make two copies. After eating and paying the bill, they were satisfied not only with the brownie but also with the bill. Diana, especially, had a good laugh but not too much of a laugh this time. As they chatted away about what they were going to do the next day, they pushed the button for the elevator to open, stepped in, and kept talking; however, they did not push the button to go to the second floor. Beverly was talking again about how fortunate they were both to find good families and then to find each other. Diana started laughing out loud, and Beverly looked at her like "Hey, this is a serious conversation." Then Beverly started laughing because Diana was laughing, and before long, they both realized they were just standing in the elevator and talking. "We better get to the room before we lose control of our bladders and have another embarrassing situation," said Diana. Beverly expressed that "this is becoming a way too often occurrence."

In the room, they lay on the beds just to relax from their busy day and to think over their plans for tomorrow. Beverly had one person on her mind but was apprehensive about bringing her up to Diana. Diana had met Aunt Katie; that was the one that kept their other brother. She and their mother did not get along so good. They really didn't know the whole story behind their problems, but they did know that they were centered on their brother James. Diana had asked her if they could stop by and see her, and her reply was negative. Beverly did not like that answer and was not willing to come all the way from California to Maryland and not meet Aunt Katie. At one time, she met Diana and shared pictures of herself and Diana and Beverly on a farm. "Aunt Katie took us places when we were babies, so why would she not want to see us?" Beverly asked Diana, "If we drove two hours to Linkwood, which is very small town, would you remember the street she lived on?" Diana just could not remember. They looked it up on the computer, phone book, and Spokeo to no avail; there was no address. They had her phone number, but if they called, she would just tell them not to come. Diana felt that "we should not bother her." Beverly was angry that she would not welcome her sister's children when she raised their natural brother. She said, "This is an important part of our trip as she knows things that will fill in blanks for us, so we need to see her." Beverly and Diana could not agree whether to go or not; therefore, they decided to sleep on it and in the morning make the decision.

Both girls went to bed happy but had one thing on their minds, Katie.

It was Sunday, November 18, 2012, a special day, as Beverly and Diana were waking up with a big decision to make, and that was the first thing on their minds. They got ready for breakfast and did not have too much to say as they dressed. However, Diana expressed that she did not like the idea of just driving to Aunt Katie's unannounced. Beverly spoke up, "It is better than calling to give her the opportunity to say we cannot come to see her." The sisters did not change their routine a bit; down to breakfast they went, welcomed by Margaret, to their same table. Beverly had scrambled eggs and bacon and freshly brewed coffee. Diana went for the biscuit and gravy again with her half-cut tea. Margaret came over for an update, so they explained how special it was to get a picture of their father. Actually that was the highlight of the day for them. Beverly told Margaret, "We have a dilemma. You can help us make a decision on how you would handle the situation." Beverly went on to give her the details, then asking what would she do, "call or show up." Margaret readily expressed her feelings to just "show up!"

Off they were to Linkwood with the Garmin at least getting them to the town which did not have a "stop" light, only a blinking light. Beverly was happy to go and was chatting away while Diana was a bit nervous, worried what Aunt Katie might say to them. Even more so, Diana had to remember where she lived when they got to town. Beverly figured that Aunt Katie's husband was a reverend in town before he passed away. "Surely someone would remember him?" she thought. Beverly was not afraid to knock on doors to ask people if they knew someone she was looking to find. Diana was also afraid to go through the tunnel again, so first they had to get through that situation. Beverly explained to Diana, "She would have to enjoy seeing how we turned out as grown women, would you not think?" As they began to get closer, Beverly began to recall the bridge and remembered this was the way to Ocean City, Maryland. Beverly said, "We can go to the beach if she doesn't invite us in or is not home." As they were driving, Lula called to invite them for dinner with Uncle Bob again. She was going to the opera, but their cousin Oliver was going to be there to go with them. Beverly said, "We probably will not be back until 4:00 p.m." Lula said, "That is fine." Beverly could feel the determination like a burning fire in her stomach, the closer they got to Linkwood.

As they came to the blinking light, they saw a road to the left with barricades, and on the right was a small gas station and store. Beverly went in to the store to ask the owner if they knew Katie and the reverend. The store-owner said he had been there thirty years and did not know of them. "However," he said, "You could ask some of my patrons as they come in if they know them." Beverly asked one young man, and he looked puzzled and had no help for her. Beverly went to the car and told Diana what had happened and explained, "We should drive down the road and see if you recognize any of the streets from being there before." As they drove slowly down the road, Diana looked around, but nothing jumped out at her. Beverly kept asking, "Does anything look familiar?" Diana snapped back that she was there fifteen years ago! Beverly chuckled and said she was just kidding, but before they knew it, there was another small town. They thought there was nothing to do but turn around and go back. As they were driving back, they noticed that the houses were very sparse, so it had to be one of these. Diana, for some reason, suggested that "we go to the right around the barricades down that street." There were two houses on the right, and as they were driving past those to turn around, they passed a man on a John Deere tractor. When the sisters came back to his house, they asked him if he knew the reverend and Katie, and he said, "Sure! They live right next door. See her red car in the driveway." You could have knocked them over with a feather!

Beverly and Diana had things work out for the best like this on their journey, and they smiled every time another reality came together. Beverly pulled into the yard and noticed the door was open and a lady was standing in the doorway, doing something at the top of the screen. Diana was about two steps behind Beverly. Of course, they recognized the lady dressed nicely in jeans and pretty shirt as Aunt Katie. She looked up at them standing there and proceeded to go right back to what she was doing with the screen door. Diana spoke first and said her name and then introduced Beverly as her sister. She did nothing, not even look away from the door. It was like they were frozen in time, standing there. Who was going to make the first move? Maybe she was so nervous that they found her, she just could not speak. Beverly spoke next to ask if she could help her with the door. At that moment, Aunt Katie spoke sharply, "Now is not a good time," and shut the solid door, and there the sisters stood! Beverly was feeling angry and hurt that no matter what happened between families, it was not their fault. Diana stood as still as a statue. It was like time stood still, waiting, as they were not going to move. Beverly felt like she was going to get in if she had to kick the door down. Slowly, the garage door started to rise, and when it got to the top, Aunt Katie motioned for them to come on into the house. The house was very clean and neat. She was not kind, but she invited them to sit down in the living room.

Diana, desiring to make peace, said to Aunt Katie, "We are not here to tell stories about our mother. The past is the past. We know what happened to us as children. We have forgiven our parents and know that they had hard times. In fact, we are very happy we had the opportunities we have had with the families that adopted us and gave us wonderful happy homes. However, those few years we will never forget, and it has stuck with us all our lives. We have scars from the situations our parents put us through, and now we are on this journey to finally have closure in our lives. One of the worst things that we will never really get closure completely on is why they separated Beverly and me. We came to see you to help fill any gaps that you can for us. Also to share stories about you and our mother as young girls and what kind of things you liked to do." When Diana met her mother, she was unable to convey those things to her. Beverly wanted Aunt Katie to know that "we are not digging up dirt, just want to know about happy times."

Aunt Katie began to talk about Arlene having a rough life but said that "she brought it on herself." You could tell she was bitter toward Arlene but did not give a reason. About their childhood she said that they were poor and did not have a very eventful life. However, she was quick to point out that of all the sisters their mother was the one that was a floozy. She said, "She drank and ran around." Beverly and Diana looked at each other, thinking, "What a thing to tell her two grown daughters." They were beginning to think Aunt Katie was jealous or had a grudge toward their mother. Then she began to tell them about their mother's death. She had called Diana when she passed away in 2007, but they did not know if she was cremated or buried. Aunt Katie in her crude way exclaimed that "she was chopped up donated her body to science." It was an appalling conversation, and at this point the sisters felt once again that Katie spoke disrespectfully of their mother, no matter what kind of life she had lived.

Beverly asked if she would share any pictures that she had of them. Reluctantly, she got the box out and began to go through it, finally coming to this cute baby girl she said was Beverly. She offered to make a copy and send it to Beverly. Also, she had a nice picture of all four sisters. She offered to make a copy and send to them.

Aunt Katie continued to look through pictures and came across some girl that looked like a girl in pin-up poses, and that was her sister Mae. Beverly sure thought that it was odd for a sister to send pictures like that of yourself in your fifties to your sister. Aunt Katie then told them about Mae having three husbands and living in California and also giving up her child. She continued to say how "drinking seems to run in the family, not only your mother, Arlene, but also Jenny and Columbus, your grandfather." She got about halfway through the box and looked at them with a question of what did they know about their mother's other children. Diana spoke about that as Arlene had told her about two. Aunt Katie questioned, "Is that all she told you? Arlene did not tell you there were more?" They both looked at each other, and of course, they wanted to know if there were any more. Aunt Katie just snickered like a little kid would and let them know there were more, but she was not talking about it anymore. Beverly thought to herself, "She has no right saying things about our mother. She has passed on, and if she wanted us to know, she would have told Diana."

Aunt Katie went on to speak of her own children in unkind words saying that her daughter wasn't very nice. The only nice kind words she had were for their brother James. She showed them his military photos and said how handsome he was in them. It was obvious he was her pride and joy. She even said that she encouraged him to see Beverly and Diana, but he made the choice not to keep in contact. After seeing her and realizing how she felt about their mother and how she had acted toward them, it was hard to believe. Beverly and Diana both felt that she was angry and jealous that Arlene never let her adopt James as she let all the rest of them be adopted. Diana thought, "She is spiteful and carries a grudge against Arlene and did until she died." Aunt Katie explained to them how she took James to their father's funeral in 1966 out of respect and turned right around when they asked what he was like and called him "stupid." After that comment, Beverly and Diana had heard all they needed to hear from this woman. They were respectful and thankful that she was hospitable. Unfortunately, she in no way treated them as though they were nearly as good as their brother James.

They got on the road, however, and reached Uncle Bob's too late for dinner, so they visited with Beverly's cousin Oliver, Carol, and Lula from her adopted family. Oliver was very interested in hearing about all the exciting adventures they had on this journey. As a young boy, he did not even know a lot about my adoption. "My brothers never talked about it, so neither did my cousins." Beverly shared with him about the book they were writing and the research that they were doing before they start. "This project will be at least a year or more to accomplish what we want to fulfill our hopes and dreams," she explained. Oliver was very proud and anxious to get a copy to see their accomplishments and learn more about his cousin.

Diana was quiet as they left Uncle Bob's, and Beverly was satisfied to let her mind just drift in thought. A lot had happened that day, and many emotions were felt. Beverly felt as though she had to protect, defend, forgive, understand, and yet be kind, caring, polite, and respectful to someone that did not treat them with the same respect. As they got to the room, they felt it had been an exhausting day, more than any other day. They felt defending their mother was not what they went there to do; however, Aunt Katie made them feel the need to constantly protect her in death. Diana knew she had more information about their lives, "but she is not willing to share it with us out of bitterness. It is sad to see someone hold a grudge against her own sister even after she has passed on." Beverly believed "these kind of people will answer to a higher power eventually, and it is not for us to judge them." They went to sleep knowing they pursued every possible option available with their Aunt Katie respectfully, even though she was unwilling to share with them as family.

It was Monday, November 19, 2012, and they went directly to breakfast as they knew Margaret would be waiting to hear if they had located Aunt Katie, and if so, what had happened. There was their table all set up by Mark, hot coffee brewed, and Diana had her half-cut tea as usual. As they ate, they began telling Margaret about Aunt Katie and how they found her home by accident. That was really just a fluke that Diana wanted to go down a road that had barricades. Who would think that would be her street? No one but Diana, the big sister. Then they had to let Margaret know how they stood at the front door and how she slammed the door, knowing who they were as Diana had introduced them. They did not go into the whole family personal situation but let them know it was not the most inviting visit they had had so far. Beverly and Diana wanted to just leave it like that out of respect for their mother.

They had talked to a lady at the restaurant that asked them if they had been to the Maryland room at the Bel Air Library. She also spoke of many documents, newspapers, etc. from the 1900s were kept in the Aberdeen Room; however, it was closed on Monday and Tuesday. Of course they were leaving on Tuesday, but they drove by and wrote down the information from the door so that they could call to research over the phone.

Diana had to take some things back to the store in Bel Air, so they decided to do that on the way to the library. Beverly noticed as they got near the library there was a Dunkin' Donuts nearby, so they had to splurge as they had not done so in days. There is something about those chocolate-covered cake doughnuts that are irresistible. Beverly had to point out that Diana had two doughnuts, by the way. As they entered the library it was very quiet and busy with students and people reading, researching, so they asked where the Maryland room was. A nice lady showed them to the room. Diana and Beverly saw walls of books and did not have a clue where to start looking. They were trying to find any information on their grandfather Clark. They looked for him in the military; they had already exhausted Ancestry as he never showed up with their grandmother and their father, and his two brothers. They had knowledge from their father's birth certificate that he worked at the APG as a civilian, most likely in ammunitions. However, they found not a trace of him except when they got a divorce. Therefore, they could not trace the family line back to find their nationality. Some of the cousins felt that there was Indian blood in the line as they said their father, Uncle Benjamin, had reddish skin and no hair on his body. However, Beverly and Diana looked at their father's picture, and he had black hair and no reddish skin. It may just remain a mystery, but Diana and Beverly continued to work to try and find him and probably will continue. They found some dog tags with the same name as his; however, they did not know his birth date or where he was born. It seemed as though they had come once again to a dead end.

Beverly and Diana got to the car with the frame of mind that even though they did not accomplish what they came to do, at least they were together. Every minute they spent with each other was getting back what was taken from them so many years ago. They recognized they could not recover all that time, but they were emotionally doing the best they were able to do. This journey together helped fill the void that needed to be filled for so long. They knew it was just a start. Whatever it took, they wanted to recover from the tragedy that began all those years ago. They had accepted the "why" so they could have closure in their lives. Although difficult and heartbreaking at times, they still wanted to move forward to discover each other.

As Beverly drove from Bel Air to Aberdeen, she had the frame of mind that she was not giving up on their grandfather yet. He was the key to finding their heritage, and she thought that there must be someone that knew him. Diana was also thinking that some of their grandmother's family should have known of him.

They needed to keep researching Ancestry through both family lines until they reached a family member that knew of him. Diana was quiet for a few minutes until they got close to the Clarion, and

Beverly could not believe her ears when Diana suggested they pop in the Applebee's for a brownie bite. Actually, the SUV knew the way by now, so they pulled right in the parking lot.

Beverly and Diana had this figured out now; they just ordered water, and what a deal! After the brownie, they had to go to the Rite Aid to get Beverly her eighth bottle of cough syrup and enough cough drops to make it through the night. She really should have gone to the clinic, but she had asthma and never wanted to stop to take the time to go see the doctor. As they were coming out of the drugstore, they got a call from one of the Loper sisters.

They were so excited that Beverly and Diana saw their brother Robert that they wanted to visit with them. Diana explained that they were leaving in the morning. Diana handed Beverly the phone to talk to them so they could make some kind of arrangements.

Beverly was also anxious to see them; however, the only thing she could think of was inviting them for breakfast at the Clarion at 8:30 a.m. Beverly explained that they were expected in North Carolina to a going-away party for her son, Blake, the next evening; otherwise they would stay another day. The girls understood and were happy to meet them at 8:30 a.m. sharp at the Clarion. They had one concern, and that was how they would know them after so many years. Beverly told them not to worry. "We are pretty well known in the restaurant. You will not have any problem when you come in the door."

Beverly and Diana went to the room to start packing as they did not want to do that job in the morning. In fact, they were able to pack a lot in the SUV that night and just leave out what they were going to wear in the morning. Of course, they had to do some laundry, but that led to a problem because it was difficult to get Diana to give up her precious quarters as she collected them. However, Beverly, being her little sister, was able to get a few. It was surprising the way Diana held on to those like they were gold coins.

They both went over the day thinking again about their grandfather and how they could get a lead on how to find him so they could get down that line of descent. They thought that back in the 1800s and 1900s, many times people misspelled their names, also went by nicknames, and when you are lacking important information like their birth date it is even more challenging. Beverly and Diana did not have the makeup to give up; in fact, it had become almost an obsession with them to find out where he and the rest of his family were. That was the last thought as they drifted off to sleep for the night.

It was a great morning on November 20, 2012; they were refreshed and ready to get on the road to Louise and Jon's in North Carolina. However, they had a breakfast meeting with the Loper kids, which was the first foster home Diana and Beverly stayed in when they were abandoned in 1953. They went down to tell Margaret and told her about their guest, so she quickly set up a large party table for them. Beverly explained that she would pick up the ticket for their breakfast complimentary for them. Margaret also let them know that Mark was coming down to say good-bye to them because "he is not working today." He was so pleasant to them and caring, and that was a nice gesture on his part. Just about then a couple of women came rushing over to them and said that they remembered them. They were so surprised that they still recognized Beverly and Diana after all those years. However, they were teenagers, and Beverly and Diana were four and seven, so there was quite an age difference. They began to tell stories of things they used to do that were funny. They remembered them as very well-behaved children. Beverly told them how badly she was punished and made to sit on the toilet for hours as punishment for wetting her pants. The one sister Janice expressed that she felt that sounded like her mother. However, they said the sisters were playful, especially Beverly was always running around happy; they could not understand or remember them getting into trouble. However, the Loper sisters wondered why Beverly and Diana were there for such a short period of time. They had a lovely visit talked and talked, laughed, and joked, and it was like going back in a time capsule. They all said their good-byes and exchanged numbers and e-mails. It certainly was a pleasure to get to spend time with the very first family they met in 1953.

When Beverly went to Margaret to pay for breakfast, she refused to let her pay, which was very kind of the hotel as they treated them with the best accommodations you could ask for in a hotel. Especially the help— Beverly and Diana told their story and had everyone tearing up and just begging them to "come back when the book is published." They told them they all would be in the book and yes, they would come back after to do a book signing, as they appreciated all their kindness and thoughtfulness while they stayed at the Clarion.

Beverly and Diana had one more chore to do before they left, and that was to settle their bill with the manager. Fortunately, the manager was on duty; therefore, they got to meet her face-to-face and explain a little further about their journey and the book they would be writing. They first explained their plight of being abandoned as children in 1953 in Aberdeen and then fifty-six years later, "here we are two sisters together." She began to have tears rolling down her cheeks as they told their story. Beverly explained that she and Diana had learned that "we have been blessed with a wonderful opportunity of being adopted and having loving families of our own, now that we understand our parents just did not have the wherewithal to take care of us." The manager was so happy that they seemed to have some closure from their journey and also got to know each other. Also she noticed they stayed ten days so she was able to take more off their bill, and the sisters were very pleased with the final amount. They thanked her for their generosity and hospitality and said that they would return when the book is published.

Beverly set the Garmin for North Carolina, and they made one stop for lunch at Applebee's to have their usual soup and sandwich. They got right back on the road and arrived at Louise's at 5:30 p.m. before dark, or "Diana would have had my neck, got to keep my big sister happy."

It was November 21, 2012, and they had a good rest at Louise's. Although their room was upstairs and she had the heat on, it was really hot up there as the temperature rose. Beverly explained to Diana, "Tonight we are going to open the window and close the door so there is no draft, and Louise will never know about us opening the window." They went down and greeted Louise as she was always up early and explained that they were going to their old stomping grounds Dunkin' Donuts. They inquired if she cared for anything, and she just wanted them to bring Jon a sandwich from Burger King that he liked with egg and bacon. When they returned, Louise said they were invited for lunch by Kirk and Libby, her daughter and husband. "Will that be all right?" About an hour and a half later, they met them at a sushi restaurant and got a large table in the dining area. They had a banquet of all kinds of sushi and Japanese and Chinese food prepared. There must have been at least four rows of food, and the people were lined up out the door. The food was delicious and so was the company. After lunch, they went back to the Sandersons' home.

Beverly and Diana looked for any chance they could to go shopping. Beverly had to find something to bring back to her son, Scott; his wife, Patty; and of course, her granddaughter, Angelina. So they made a short trip to Winston-Salem and found some things at the Marshalls and TJ Maxx. In addition, they had something from Maryland that they decided not to keep, so they returned them in North Carolina. They moved merchandise from Florida to Georgia, Maryland, Virginia, and North Carolina, and let's not forget California. It was crazy, but they had fun buying and returning. It started to get dark, so they left to get back to Louise's house in time for a late dinner. Louise and Jon wanted to order in pizza, which was unusual for them as normally they liked to dine out. However, Louise ordered a delicious pizza, and Beverly stuffed herself more than she should because at 8:00 p.m. she was ready for bed. She said goodnight to Louise and Jon, thanking them for a lovely day and said she would see them in the morning.

It was again very hot in the bedroom when Beverly got up there; however, she waited for Diana to arrive. When Diana got to the top of the stairs, it hit her, and she went right to the window. She opened the window and found that it did not have a screen, so she looked over at Beverly and asked, "Now what?" Beverly explained, "Don't open it too wide because you have to beware of the flying chickens in this area." Diana quickly snapped her head around and said, "Are you serious?" Beverly gave a nod and told her to shut the door so they did not have a draft going downstairs.

They still were talking in bed about how Aunt Katie had made them stand at that door and then slammed it in their faces. That was her sister's daughters; it just was so hurtful, and she treated them like they were nobody to her. When their natural brother, no matter what she thought, lived with her. Also the way she talked about their mother, and they knew their mother was many things, but why smear her to the children that had just connected with her after fifty-six years? It was hard to imagine how heartless some people could be.

First thing on November 22, 2012, in the morning Beverly asked Diana if she heard the chicken hit the window. Diana jumped out of bed and said, "Oh my God!"

Beverly exclaimed, "Someone better do something about it before Jon goes on the porch for the paper."

Diana swiftly went down the stairs and out the front door, and looked on the porch and in the front bushes for the chicken; there was no chicken to be found. Meanwhile, Beverly was laughing so hard, she was losing control of her bladder. Diana realized what just happened to her and began laughing, joining Beverly and also losing control. They both were a mess standing on the hardwood floor in the hallway, and Louise came out to see what the commotion was all about. Beverly, still laughing, explained, "Just sister stuff!"

They knew that Kirk and Libby were coming over to go out for Thanksgiving dinner around noon, so they thought they would get their usual at Dunkin' Donuts and Jon a sandwich. As they were pulling back up the driveway, the next-door neighbor came over with a piping hot loaf of homemade bread. Louise got out some butter and sliced up that bread, and it was scrumptious.

They sat for a while and talked with Louise about many of her crafts. She had so many projects going at the same time, it was hard to keep up with all she was doing. Louise took Beverly upstairs to a room next to their bedroom, of which she had noticed the door. The room was full of handmade porcelain dolls. Louise even had a kiln and made the faces and bodies and hand-painted them, and how exquisite they were just to gaze upon.

Beverly right away had to buy one for Angelina. Louise was feeling very odd about selling one, and she had hundreds of dolls. They were like her children, and she barely could part with one of them. "She asked me to let her think about it until after dinner, and then maybe she would let me chose one for Angelina." Diana used to sew and make many crafts when Louise and Jon lived in Mexico Beach right around the corner from Diana. They were great friends and enjoyed each other's company so much, and it was sad to see them move so far away.

It was time to ride to the restaurant in Jon's van so they could all ride together. Of course, as you would imagine, everyone was having turkey but not Beverly; she was having salmon, potatoes, turnip greens, and topped it off with pecan pie with whipped cream. It was a lovely dinner but very crowded, so they ate and went back to the Sandersons' so they could talk. They wanted to share their journey with Kirk and Libby as they had not had time to sit down with them.

Beverly and Diana once again started at the beginning and ended up with how happy they were that they were given the opportunities that they had. After meeting some of their biological family, they realized that while they were nice people, "many have not left the town they were raised in or the state." Beverly said, "We now realize our parents did all they could for us, but did the best by giving us the chance for a better life than they could provide. It has taken many years to be able to say that and accept that closure. We are still going through the challenge of getting to know each other as sisters, learning that it does not happen overnight. Accepting not growing up together as sisters, we may never be able to develop the same feelings, but we can only accept what we can have from here forward."

Before Kirk and Libby left, Beverly had to tell the chicken story that she pulled on Diana. They all had a chuckle at Diana's expense with that story. "It is fun pulling jokes on her. For some reason she always believes me." They said good night and thanked everyone for their hospitality and friendship.

Beverly and Diana were tired and went on to bed, and Louise asked if she should turn down the heat. They both nodded in affirmative.

They talked a little about their last day here going to the L'eggs outlet. Diana agreed she could use some things from there also. Beverly said, "Let's set the Garmin up with the address, Diana, in the morning."

It was November 23, 2012, and Diana and Beverly got up early as they had a full day of shopping planned in Winston-Salem. They thought they had gotten up before anyone else; however, Jon was up and dressed, ready to go. Beverly inquired of Jon if he was interested in going shopping with them. Jon chuckled and let them know that he was treating them to a big breakfast. That was fine with them, as long as they just had good coffee. Beverly did not care where she got her fuel so to speak. Beverly reminded Diana to get the Garmin set up with the address from the Internet before they left for the L'eggs outlet. Louise was not feeling up to going out to eat; no wonder, she weighed eighty-nine pounds, if that. Beverly reminded her to pick out the dolls that she could choose from for Angelina, her granddaughter. Louise kind of rolled her eyes as she had a hard time parting with those precious dolls. "But just maybe she will consider one for my little granddaughter that is just as precious to me," thought Beverly. They hopped in the van and down to the Waffle House they went to have breakfast. Beverly could see everyone in there knew Jon, so they figured that the housekeeper Anya probably brought him there often. "Hey, he's ninety! Leave him alone, and let him have what he wants," she thought.

When they returned, Kirk and Libby were there to say good-bye again as they had to go out of town and would not be back in time to see them off. Louise's daughter took good care of her mother and father as children should. Beverly recalled her time when after her mother, Margaret, died; then her father, Harvey Simpson, came to live with her for nine years. In fact, she even took him to California from Florida, when she lost her job, and he was ninety-six years old. Diana had her turn also of helping with her husband Vito's father and uncle. "It is a special time to give back after what our parents gave to us for many years."

They were feeling very happy as they traveled to Winston-Salem again, going over their journey thus far, recalling the people they met, the laughs they have had, information that became clear, and some difficult times too. No matter what, they agreed that it had been eye-opening for them and they would not have done a thing differently. Diana had programmed the Garmin that they had come to trust explicitly to the address from the Internet to 320 Mill Road. As they followed along after getting through town, it seemed strange that they began to go through a residential area. However, they continued down the street and turned the next corner where their destination was supposed to be, and they saw a log house. On the front as they pulled around there was a big sign hanging above the door that said Two Poodles in Paradise. Beverly stopped the SUV and looked at Diana like "what have you done now?" Without a word, they both began to laugh—you know, the one that caused them to lose control—and they laughed harder. "What do we do?" asked Diana They looked up TJ Maxx and drove there as they were going anyway and figured that they would know where the outlet was located.

As they entered the store they looked at some things on a table, still laughing about not finding the L'eggs outlet. Two nice gentlemen overheard them talking and excused themselves and said they lived in town and went there all the time. One of the guys took out a piece of paper and proceeded to draw a map so precise and clear, they were sure he must be an engineer. They thanked them and drove right to the door with their directions. There was a big sale going on, and Diana and Beverly left with two big bags a piece. That was the highlight of the day. They started back to Louise and Jon's, happy and tired. When they arrived, Louise had dinner brought in, and she had picked an exquisite doll for Angelina. The day was just a very fun day, and they were looking forward to seeing Blake in Asheville the next day.

It was now Friday, November 24, 2012, and they are leaving Louise and Jon after the delightful hospitality shown to them by Diana's dear friends. They were truly grateful for their grace to allow them the use of their home as they ventured around North Carolina, looking for their ancestors. They just had to make a right and go down to the Dunkin' Donuts and tell the gang good-bye, and Diana once again got two chocolate doughnuts.

Now they were off to Asheville, where they should arrive around 12:30 p.m. to meet Beverly's son Blake and his wife, Cindy, for lunch.

Beverly just couldn't wait to see him, and at the same time, she knew it would be a long time as he would be serving in the ministry work in Ecuador, where the need was great. Her son served in the Spanish congregation, and when he was in his twenties, he went over to Cuenca, Ecuador, to serve in the pioneer ministry and met Cindy, who served in the full-time ministry.

As you can guess, they fell in love, and he brought her to the States; they married and served in the States for many years. However, Blake's heart was where he could be used more to help where there were fewer to serve in his capacity. Therefore, in January 2013, they finished building a new home on a mountaintop and moved there to serve. Beverly hoped to be able to visit them one day soon.

They arrived right at the Mexican restaurant at 12:30 p.m., and Beverly hugged Blake and could hardly hold back the tears. Diana had met him and Cindy before, so at least she did not feel like a stranger. Cindy was such a sweet, kind, and loving young woman, and when they looked at each other, you could see the love they had for each other. Beverly felt that if nothing else, it made her feel wonderful that her son had a Christian joyful marriage.

Their lunch was great with all Spanish dishes, which were different from Mexican, as Cindy was quick to let them know. After they finished, Blake asked them to follow him to their apartment so they could see pictures of his new house. They had not checked into the hotel, which was on the other side of Asheville. Blake explained that they had plenty of time.

He had a lovely downstairs apartment way out in the woods, all cedar; it smelled so nice. Blake made them coffee while Cindy brought out the pictures. They all talked about their journey also and the book until the time got away from them, and Blake noted that the party was at 5:30 p.m. They were not informed that it was formal until Blake gave them the invitation, so they had to get on the road to be able to check in and make it to the party, as Beverly was not familiar with that area of Asheville.

They arrived at the community center at 6:00 p.m., and the food was plentiful. It was beautifully decorated with waterfalls and large bunches of shrimp. There were plenty of Spanish dishes; they did not know the names of many, but they tasted delicious. The friends came from congregations that knew Blake and Cindy, and you could tell how much they loved them. "Especially the small children would go up to my son, Blake, and he would pick them up, and they would cry and say how they were going to miss him. It was beautiful to see the love they have for Blake and Cindy." Beverly was tense as she knew Blake's father Luke and his stepmother, Ariel, would be approaching her at any time. To her surprise, they were very pleasant; in fact, Luke spoke more to Beverly than he had for years. It really made it easier for the children, as Beverly never had a problem with Luke or Ariel.

First, they had made a video of each of them from the time they were babies until their age now. It was very well done. They had pictures of Blake and his brother Scott—pictures of them with their father, but of course, only one picture of Beverly was in the video as his stepmother, Ariel, was in the other pictures. In fact, most of the people there did not know who Beverly was until Blake introduced her as his mother. As Beverly watched the video, tears were rolling down her cheeks until she could not bear to stand there any longer, as everyone in that room thought Ariel was his mother. She went to Diana to reclaim her composure and not to ruin her son's party as it was not of his doing.

Next, one by one the ladies, gentleman, children, older men, older women, and teenagers went to the microphone, and with Blake and Cindy standing before them, in Spanish they said their good-byes. Beverly could not understand all the words, but they were heartfelt, moving, loving, kindly spoken, tearful, high spirited, cheerful, funny, and oh, so happy. Blake and Cindy could hardly hold back their tears and their laughter at times. Then at the end, Luke and Ariel went to the microphone before Beverly, as she would be next. Luke was tearful and spoke in English and expressed that "now is time for his mama and papa to speak." You could have knocked Beverly down with a feather. Beverly felt as though Luke had no right to say that, with his mother standing right beside Blake. Beverly was going to say a few words, but out of respect for her son, she thought there was no need to walk up and cause a scene. This was Blake's and Cindy's time, and Beverly was not going to disrupt the jovial time everyone was enjoying.

The party started livening up even more so when one of the friends of Blake, who sang in a popular Spanish band, sang some songs. Then the dancing began like Beverly and Diana had not been introduced to before. Blake came over and asked his mother to dance with him. Beverly told him that she did not know these Spanish dances, and Blake explained not to worry; he would teach her the steps. Diana had the camera out to catch the fool Beverly was making of herself, and yet the happiness on her face was undeniable. It had gotten very cold and Beverly's feet felt like chunks of ice, so she knew that they were not going to last much longer. However, as people began to leave, Beverly could see the loving kindness shown to her son Blake and Cindy for their hard work in serving in the congregation. Beverly could see the excitement on his face. "How happy he is in not only his marriage but in his love of God and serving him in a foreign land." Beverly was very proud of Blake and to be his mother. Blake walked them to the car as Beverly cried and held on to him, not knowing when she would hold him again. However, Blake had a good head on his shoulders and he would do the right things, and Beverly would always love him for that quality.

Diana turned on the Garmin, and back to the hotel they went, up to a very warm room. They both were exhausted, but had not only a wonderful day but a very important day, seeing Blake and Cindy so blissful and joyful together. Beverly closed her eyes with the state of mind not to think about Luke and what he said as she was there for Blake and Cindy, and it was heartwarming to see their happiness.

On to Sunday, November 25, 2012; Beverly woke up feeling somewhat sad that Blake and Cindy would be leaving the country soon, and she didn't know when she could make arrangements to make a trip to Ecuador. Diana got up, and got Beverly cheered up and said, "Let's go down and have a nice breakfast." The breakfast was very nice, and the hotel was full of guests; after talking and relaxing a bit, they went back to the room, and Beverly decided she had another cousin from her adopted family, Caroline, her dad's brother, Uncle Harry, whom she would like to visit. Beverly gave her a call, and when she answered, she could not believe her ears, after so many years to hear from Beverly. Beverly explained briefly what Diana and she were doing on their journey and said they would like to see her. She said she had talked to Oliver, their other cousin, and heard about the book, and she wanted to hear about it also. But she had to do her hair. Beverly explained they were leaving soon, so "We will give you an hour to get ready and see you then."

Beverly was not aware that she had never been told that Beverly was adopted either, so of course, Caroline had to hear the whole story. So Diana jumped right in and helped tell all the things they had discovered. Most of all how they first wrote the letters the same month and same year and how the same social worker in the same office in Bel Air got their letters was very intriguing to people. Diana explained, "In fact, it gives most people goose bumps whenever we tell the story." Caroline was happy for them that they found each other, that they were spending time together, and that they were writing a book about their experience. Beverly talked about old times. When they were kids, they used to come to her house because her dad, Uncle Harry, loved animals, and he had all kinds. He used to take them on horseback rides, and he had a pet skunk. He loved life, and "as kids we were so sorry he died so young because he was so much fun for all the cousins." Beverly said, "I will never forget when the boys decided it was time for me to learn to swim, and they threw me in the pool. My brother Peter came to my rescue." Beverly had to say that ever since that day she did not like her head under water. Before they left, Caroline gave Beverly a little plank with an Irish saying on it as a memento, which she keeps on her dresser. Beverly promised to keep in touch by phone as "we are getting older, and we need to remember our loved ones."

They got a late start to get to Atlanta before dark, as Diana always liked to do; however, they hit some traffic where they drove for several hours at twenty-five to thirty miles per hour. Finally, they decided to stop for gas and at a restaurant to have something to eat and hoped that maybe by then the traffic would get moving. They enjoyed a nice lunch, which took their time, and got back to the highway, and most of the traffic was moving normally. Finally, at around 8:00 p.m. they arrived at Lynne's house (Diana's daughter), and Diana said, "No matter how tired you are, you better get ready to rumble because here come the boys, Gianni and Paul." Those two little guys were so sweet but so full of energy, it was unbelievable. Gianni was the older grandchild and was as sharp as a tack; he remembered everything you told him. He recalled from over a month ago that Aunt Beverly liked white cheddar Cheez-Its. He told his mom to get Aunt Beverly some because they didn't have any for her. Beverly and Diana played with the boys until they had to go to bed and they were exhausted. Gianni had school in the morning, and Dianna, Lynne, Paul, and Beverly would be going shopping until Gianni got out of school.

On Monday, November 26, 2012, Diana and Lynne took Gianni to school, and on the way back, they stopped at Dunkin' Donuts and got their usual, except they had no chocolate glaze. What Dunkin' Donuts is ever out of chocolate-glazed doughnuts? That was an essential! The sisters showered and dressed to go shopping with Paul in tow. No sooner were they in the car riding about twenty minutes than Paul was fast asleep in his car seat. Diana stayed in the car, and Lynne went with Beverly in Marshalls to return something she had got in Maryland. Lynne shopped around while Beverly stood in line as it was November, and people were starting to shop already for Christmas sales. Lynne and Beverly got to the car just as Paul woke up, and Lynne suggested they go to a Mexican restaurant which she liked on the other side of town. Lynne had a Toyota four-door small, compact car, and she scared the pants off Beverly and Diana the way she drove. Now Beverly had to agree that everyone in Atlanta area seemed to drive the same way; therefore, she was just keeping up with the traffic. "However, we can get from one place to another rather quickly. No worries if Gianni's school is across town, and we are just finishing lunch. We will be there in plenty of time without a doubt," said Lynne.

Lynne picked up Gianni from school, and as a treat they took him to the park. They all got out; it was a beautiful warm day, not like the cold days Beverly and Diana had been used to having. Gianni loved the slide, so Aunt Beverly watched him go down the slide over and over again. In the meantime, Paul got on the swings, and Lynne swung him for a while; then he ran around in the grassy area. It wasn't before long they both were tired out and went back to the car.

While they were driving, Gianni spoke up about a concern he had about his mother remembering to get the white cheddar "Cheez-Its" for Aunt Beverly. Lynne let him know that she stopped right after dropping him off from school and picked them up. The night before he had asked Aunt Beverly her favorite flavor, and she said, "White cheddar." Gianni had such a good memory, and that included numbers and birth dates; he knew the states by heart and memorized words to popular songs on the radio. So there was no doubt he was not going to forget about those "Cheez-Its". He right away found them and started chowing down on them before dinner. Also, Beverly had a special treat for them after dinner. They sat down ate their dinner and were ready in no time for their treat, which was a giant bag of M & Ms.

Diana and Beverly packed their things and put them by the front door as they had to get an early start to beat the traffic around Atlanta. The boys were tired, and they got their bath early and went to bed too. Diana and Beverly were sleeping in Lynne's bed as her husband was a pilot and was away. During the night, they were awakened by first someone at the foot of the bed, then on Diana's side, and then back at the foot, crawling under the comforter between Diana and Beverly. When they woke in the morning, there sleeping peacefully was little Paul with his sandy blond hair. Who could resist him!

They gave Gianni a big hug and said good-bye. When Lynne took him to school, the sisters packed the car, rather Beverly packed the car because she was picky about how the car was packed. She preferred to do it herself. Lynne came back, and they said good-bye and got on the road at 6:45 a.m., leaving enough time for the stop at Dunkin' Donuts right on the corner where they had to turn.

It was November 27, 2012; with their favorite coffee and tea in hand and the Garmin set, it was "Florida, here we come." It was a bittersweet journey, they thought, as it was winding down. Diana and Beverly had so much to talk about on the way back. Sometimes there were quiet times where both had time to think thoughts of their own. They learned a lot about each other on the trip, and that was important. It had been many years since they had spent any time together. They had great laughs, did some goofy things, got stuck in crazy places, could not find their way, but they did it without a harsh word to each other. Beverly and Diana had done an enormous amount of research and had more to do. But what a joy it was to share the experiences of their first years together. Beverly was happy that they met so many people along the way that were willing to help them and work with them on their journey in any way they could. Diana felt like the old parts of their family had become new to them. "It is a blessing that we may never have known if we had not gone on this journey." Beverly and Diana had a lot to be thankful for to be able to go on this journey and pursue their dreams and to have been safe.

The sisters were getting anxious to get to Florida, so they stopped and had a quick lunch so they could get back on the road. By this time, Vito was starting to call, and that meant "When are you getting home, questions start. Then when we get there we will have to tell our story all over again," said Diana.

Actually, they arrived at Diana's around 3:30 p.m., so they made good time. Vito was happy to see Diana. Just as she had thought, Vito wanted them to sit down and tell him all about the trip. First of all, as they had been sitting for hours, they decided to get the SUV unpacked, and then "we would be glad to sit down and talk. Because once we sit, then we might not get up very easily," remarked Diana.

They did talk to Vito for hours and gave him as much information as both of them could think of until he was on information overload. Beverly was really tired from driving and just mental exhaustion. Vito took her suitcase upstairs for her, which was so nice of him. Beverly remembered pulling back the comforter and slipping under the soft sheets, laying her head on the soft pink pillow, and then falling asleep.

It was November 28, 2012. Beverly woke up to the smell of coffee; at least Vito drank coffee as Diana only had her half-cut tea. First thing on the agenda was to take Bruno, her dog, for his doggie walk around the neighborhood. It gave Beverly and Diana time to relax a bit from the trip while they were still bubbly with excitement, about how they would begin to write the book. Beverly explained, "There is something much more pressing we need to discuss before the writing of the book." Diana looked a little puzzled but let Beverly explain further what was on her mind. Beverly said that while she had her quiet time she had been contemplating her decision as to whether or not to make the move back to Florida. She expressed her heartfelt feelings to Diana. After a wonderful trip, where they both bonded incredibly well and the desire to once again have her own place, she had decided to move to Mexico Beach to be near her. Diana, of course, was concerned about Scott, Beverly's son. Beverly was too, and agreed that it was going to be difficult to leave him and Patty but most of all her granddaughter, Angelina. They had started doing so many things together, like Beverly would take her to the gym, ballet, shopping, in the pool, and to "PetSmart" to look at the animals. However, Beverly thought that they needed their space as a family as much as Beverly did, and she appreciated Scott coming to her aid when she was very sick with MRSA. Beverly would always love her son Scott for his kindness and generosity and could only hope he will understand it was what was best for his mother.

The sisters arrived back at the house, and Diana had to tell Vito, "Beverly has decided to relocate here to write the book." Vito said, "Great!" He had some ideas for the first chapter. "How about we celebrate?" Vito announced he wanted to treat them to the Outback. Beverly and Diana took the quickest showers on record because when "Vito offers to pay, you better put things in motion quickly before he changes his mind."

When they arrived in Panama City, Beverly announced she needed her tenth bottle of cough syrup and some cough drops. As they pulled in at a shopping center, Vito was getting anxious; they parked in front of TJ Maxx, not realizing that the drugstore was way down the end. Vito motioned them to go on, and he would stay in the car. They walked down and got the cough syrup, noticed some shoes in a shoe store. They never should have stopped, bad idea. On the way back, they lost track of where or how far away the car was parked. Now as you can imagine, the Italian Vito was boiling over. "Where are those girls?" Beverly and Diana were powerless as they began to laugh. The more jovial they became, the more they lost their bladder control. A very nice well-dressed lady saw them standing in the parking lot bent over dreadfully, trying to hold back the flow that was about to happen. They saw Vito, and the anguish on his face was undeniable. "Why were Beverly and Diana so cheerfully laughing? They only went to get cough drops," he wondered. Immediately they got bags and sat on them and drove off to the Outback, not saying a thing to their crazy Italian in the back.

When they arrived at the Outback, they made Vito go in and get a table first, but before he would go in, Vito wanted to know what was going on with them. Therefore, they had to own up to what had happened; he could not even process what they were going to do, but they were going to eat. Beverly had dark jeans on, and Diana had those same light gray jeans on, so she was in way more trouble. Diana tied her jacket around her waist, and they walked in like any other patron and had a delightful lunch. Vito knew Beverly loved Salmon, and the Outback made the best, especially when you had it blackened. The company was great and the conversation even more entertaining as Vito told his stories about some of the books he had written. Vito and Diana made Beverly content to relocate there as she would experience family life with them.

Only two days were left; it was November 29, 2012, and once again the smell of the brewing coffee woke Beverly. She knew Vito would be at the table, ready for some enthusiastic conversation. They chatted about how silly Beverly and Diana could be at times. Vito wanted to know if they had the same issues on the trip, and they had to answer in the affirmative. Diana explained that she had never in her life let herself laugh to such degree as they had on their journey. Beverly expressed the idea of them reliving their childhood together. "We think it brought out our youth and made us feel emotions we have not felt in a long time."

Vito, without further interest in that conversation, inquired, "What is on the agenda for today?" Diana chimes in to say she was taking them to lunch to a place called Magnolia's. "It is a quaint little place. They have all fresh-made food, and it is tucked away in the woods where you can hardly find it unless you are familiar with the place." They all got ready and started the thirty-mile ride past Tyndall Air force Base to Panama City. That is one drawback to living in Mexico Beach. Everything is in Panama City, all the shopping and restaurants.

Mexico Beach has no traffic light and twelve hundred residents, and right on the beach. So it is true beach living. If you are a writer, it is the perfect scenario.

They arrived at Magnolia's, and the place was hopping. Beverly had to park across the street, so that was a good sign that the food must be good. It seemed when you got inside there were patrons of all ages and walks of life. The motif was nostalgic and artsy with tall bar stool tables, lovely hanging natural plants, waitresses with do-rags on their heads, and soft Marley music playing. Now this was what Beverly liked—cool, smooth, and extremely intense. The waitress came and explained the menu, which was very pleasant, and she helped them make a choice. After they had absolutely delicious sandwiches, around came a desert cart filled with homemade cakes, pies, brownie turtle candy bar, and flans—anything for your liking. It was an easy choice for Beverly and Diana as they both precisely picked the brownie combination. Vito went with a rather large piece of pie to his liking. Although they were pleased as punch with their meal, they did not want to see food for a while.

On the way home, Beverly couldn't help but think about the wonderful hospitality Diana and Vito were showering upon her. She knew that it would not be like this every day, but she was happy just to know how much fun they were to be with. Then again her mind drifted on the thoughts of telling her son Scott that she will be moving three thousand miles away. Although for twenty years Beverly had lived in Florida, as she had a career, and at that time, she would visit Scott on her vacation time once a year. Beverly thought, "After the book is complete and published, we will make a visit not only to see the family but definitely we will have a book-signing." The best place where everyone shopped near Scott was Paseo Drive in Palm Desert. That would be one of Beverly's goals for the future for promotion of the book.

When they pulled into the drive, it had started to get dark, and we had to take Bruno out for his walk. Bruno certainly let them know that they were a little late getting home from their adventure. It was a beautiful cool night, stars were out, and the moon was shining, so they walked Bruno once again, just talking like two sisters would, remembering they had a lot of catching up to do.

It was November 30, 2012; it was getting close to the end of their journey together. Diana and Beverly spent most of the morning outside talking about plants. One thing they had in common was they both loved gardening. Beverly was outgoing, and Diana was introverted slightly, but when it came to planting and potting, they were like two peas in a pod. "We will never know who we take after, but it does not matter. We have both got the green thumb!" exclaimed Beverly. Diana could not wait until Beverly arrived and they would get to switch plants back and forth. They would start each other plants that the other didn't have, and when Diana went to Georgia, she would bring Beverly back a plant for sure, because that was the kind of sister she would be to Beverly. They both had great plans for potting plants.

However, Beverly asked Diana what she thought of living in an apartment or condo arrangement. Diana explained that "there are very few in Mexico Beach as most condos or apartments are rented seasonal." She suggested that they go to Panama and look around and see some apartment complexes, just to see how Beverly would like the area. They got on the road, and of course, you have to go across Tyndall Air Force Base each time to Panama City. Then Diana took Beverly to the nicest area as she knew how picky Beverly could be about the area where she lived. The apartments they looked at were large enough, in the price range, and very beautifully maintained. As they were driving back, Beverly checked her odometer so that when they reached Diana's, she could see the distance to her house. When they pulled into the driveway, Vito was standing in the doorway with his arms folded with the look he always had when he was hungry. Beverly looked at the odometer, and it was thirty-four miles from the apartments. She knew her answer right then; they were not for her. Every time she wanted to see Diana, it would be a sixty-eight-mile round trip and that was if they did not go anywhere. "Better start looking in Mexico Beach," said Beverly.

Vito did not want to hear about their travels. He wanted to discuss dinner. Diana and Beverly asked Vito if he would like to go to the Olive Garden for dinner. He perked right up and replied that he would even pay. Diana was beginning to wonder about Vito, as he never offered this much, so Beverly spoke up and expressed to Vito that "this must be the way it will continue when I move here permanently." It became exceptionally quiet in the car. Beverly felt she might have stepped out of bounds and it was better to not say anything more. They had a delightful meal with the usual crisp cool salad they offered.

On the way back, they stopped at Sam's club to get a large piece of salmon so they could cook their last meal at home while watching the Alabama–Georgia game. Beverly got to thinking about the porcelain doll for Angelina and carrying that on the plane safely, so on the way home, they stopped and got a rolling suitcase at TJ Maxx to put the doll in. Beverly could put the bag under the seat on the plane.

As they drove back, Vito just wondered aloud, "How many times have we stopped at the TJ Maxx store?" Beverly and Diana looked in surprise, wondering why he would even ask as they only went two times while he was with them. Then it came to them that he was sitting in the back, and behind him and all through the house he must have noticed the TJ Maxx bags. Diana spoke first and explained, "Oh, just a few times."

It was the last day, December 1, 2012. Beverly got up feeling very anxious about going home. First, leaving Diana after being with her every day for more than a month would be difficult. However, as Beverly gave more thought to explaining to Scott her decision to move all the way across country to Florida, she realized it would be challenging. Scott had a good head on his shoulders, although he had a sensitive side that would be touched, and Beverly sincerely did not want to cause unnecessary stress on the family because of her decision. "We will have a family discussion and converse like adults and come out with a manageable solution for all."

Diana took Beverly around the corner and showed her a brick home they were building that would be perfect for her. However, the neighbor, who was the watchman of the neighborhood, owned the home and was tough to deal with even on simple things that came up. However, he was out of town, so when he came back, Diana would get his number for Beverly to call and see if it was in her price range. In the meantime, Beverly was going to get on the Internet and check out the rentals, call Diana with the addresses to look at them, and call Beverly back if they were nice. Beverly could do the negotiations over the phone. Actually, that was exactly what they did as soon as Beverly got home.

Once again Vito was ready for lunch, and right on the beach in Mexico Beach they had a place called Toucans, where all the beachgoers hung out. Vito said that they had the best fresh grouper caught every day, and that sounded right where they should go, even though they were having salmon for dinner. The waitress sat them by the window looking right over the gulf with the cool salt breeze blowing softly, and you could hear the gulls as a thirty-foot Chris craft fishing boat was cruising along, headed out to the island. They ordered the grouper sandwich and of course, half-cut tea. The company was great and the food delicious.

Now it was time to pack Beverly's suitcases, and that was going to be a job. She knew she had bought quite a lot more than she had brought. However, she had bought an extra suitcase, and now was time to test her packing skills. It took two hours to pack, and the suitcases were bulging out. Beverly could hardly bring them downstairs to get them to the car. When Beverly got to the airport, she realized they would charge her extra for the weight; she didn't realize at this point just how much.

Diana had started dinner when Beverly was packing; she had made a beautiful luscious-looking salad, and she had some sweet potatoes baking in the oven. Beverly could hardly control herself, as she loved salad, and that looked impressive. Diana asked Beverly how to prepare the salmon on the grill as Diana had one in her kitchen. Beverly put the spices that she used at home and then seared it on the grill, when the potatoes were done and were ready to go. The game was on and so was the food!

What a game it was! Alabama won and would play Notre Dame, and Vito was proud because that was his team. It was time to say good night and thank Diana and Vito for their wonderful friendship, and Beverly tearfully and warmly hugged them and said she will see them soon.

CHAPTER 9

When Beverly awoke, she had mixed emotions, thinking about leaving her sister after such a wonderful trip and time of experiencing what it was like to have a real sister. However, Vito had the coffee ready, and her flight was at 7:00 a.m. So there was no time for fooling around. Beverly gave Diana a big hug, and they both walked to the car to say good-bye for now. It was bittersweet as Beverly pulled out, seeing Diana wave and Bruno jumping by her side. Beverly yelled out the window, "Keep looking for a place, I will be back soon." As Beverly was going down Route 98 toward Panama City to the airport, it was quite foggy. It was a warm day, and it was going to be a hot day as she reached the desert in California. Beverly had purchased the cheapest fare she possibly could, and that was a bad idea. It turned out to be a ten-hour flight. Never again! As she arrived at the airport, she parked the rental and took her bags, which she could hardly put on a cart herself, and went in to have them checked. Much to Beverly's surprise, her extra weight was gigantic; it was an extra fee of $300.00! Beverly knew she had purchased a few gifts but not the complete TJ Maxx store. Without a word, she handed her card and smiled at the girl behind the desk and explained, "This was a journey of a lifetime."

Beverly boarded the plane with the porcelain doll in tow as she was most concerned about getting that back to Angelina in one piece. From one plane to the next Beverly seemed to sit next to a talker. The question would come up where are you going, or where have you been? Then the conversation would lead into the story of Beverly meeting her sister after fifty years and going on a journey to find their roots. Almost without fail, the whole rows all around were listening. The next comment to Beverly would be "you should write a book." Of course, then Beverly would explain further that she was moving from California to Florida just for that reason—to write a book and be with her sister. Needless to say, all Beverly's time on and off her flights was taken up by conversation about her life history. She began to consider the impact their story would have on the readers. Beverly was very much convinced that she was pursuing the dream that she had always had to tell her story and help others to understand that you can go through tragedy and still find a respectable life.

Patty and Angelina were waiting at the airport in Palm Springs around 10:00 p.m. to pick Beverly up, and it was so great to see the family. Angelina was so giggly and happy her Oma was home. The first question Beverly had to ask was "How is my little dog, Buffy?" Angelina explained that she really missed Oma and she would be waiting at the door for her. Buffy was a ten-pound Yorkie Maltese mix that used to belong to her father; however, he could not care for her anymore. They got to the house and had so much to talk about; then again, Beverly was so tired that all she wanted to do was go out to the casita and sleep. Beverly gave Scott a big hug and let them all know that "we can talk over coffee in the morning."

After waking up with a little jet lag, Beverly opened the door to 110-degree weather. Beverly right then remembered what she did not miss about California. That temperature was something that Beverly in three years never was able to grow accustomed to learning to enjoying making it her home. This next decision in her life involved her children, and it was not going to be easy to let them know of her plans to move back to Florida. There were a lot of interesting things to share from the journey about Beverly's ancestors that Scott would like to hear. Scott worked from home and was constantly behind his computer. He was a computer whiz; however, he was like Beverly in that he was obsessive in getting his work completed.

The days were very full with explaining about all the relatives that they got to meet and their adventures of trying to find gravesites and farmhouses. Scott expressed that only his mother would knock on stranger's doors to find a relative's house. Beverly was convinced Scott was feeling her emotional state as she spoke about her journey. Beverly was more high spirited than she had been in a long time. She now had a goal in mind and was going to put that goal in motion. However, there was a lot of work to do. Beverly and Diana had spent a lot of time on Ancestry to assist them in locating parts of the family, which would lead them to what nationality they were from their birth parents. Their biggest roadblock was on their father's side. Beverly and Diana were able to find their grandmother and her family; however, they were not able, to this day, find anything out about their grandfather on their father's side. They knew his name from their father's birth certificate and approximate age and where he worked when their father was born. He did not show up living with the family at any time. Beverly and Diana were not giving up; even after the writing of this book, they would still be striving to find their lineage.

Beverly began to look on the Internet and found places in Mexico Beach and Port St. Joe. She called Diana to look at these after she came home from volunteering work. Diana went to the realtors and acquired the keys; she then rode out to the different locations, knowing how obsessive her sister was, to check them out for Beverly. Diana called back after her inspection and answered, "The way you are, that is not for you." Nonetheless, Beverly kept looking and came upon a stilt home that looked nice and had a large porch for many plants; pictures of the inside showed three bedrooms and two baths. "This looks like something that might work." Diana went over to see it and explained, "If they paint, you probably would like it, however, if you don't mind the steps." Beverly thought that it would give her some exercise.

Beverly called the realty and worked with Harmon Realty to finalize the paperwork and see if they were willing to paint the entire inside as Diana felt it needed painting. They agreed. Beverly completed the transaction over the Internet and sent them a check, letting them know that she will be arriving on March 1, 2013. Beverly thought for a minute, "This is major." She had to sit down and tell her son Scott before she went any further. Beverly felt that the proper thing to do would be to sit down alone with him and explain how she wanted her own place, would like to be back in Florida with her sister, and that California was just too hot and expensive for her to live there alone. Beverly made Scott's lunch and asked him to join her and shared her deepest thoughts and feelings about leaving. She told Scott how much she appreciated him helping her when she was so sick with MRSA and having infusions every day. But now she felt they also needed their own privacy, and she would like to have a small place to be able to have her plants and do her potting like she used to do. Scott understood but was concerned that this was quite a big move over three thousand miles. Beverly understood his concern, but she explained how important it was to write this book to finally have closure in her life after the tragic things that she had shared with Scott happened so long ago. Beverly went on to explain that she wanted to be able to share that with her sister, and hopefully, Scott could comprehend that.

Scott was very understanding and wanted to know when this move was taking place. Beverly explained how she had already found a place and secured the house. She felt she would be moving by the end of February. Scott expressed how he was not going to like not having his homemade bread every other day. "Oh, and what about your bread pudding? Who is going to make that for me?" Beverly explained that she already made a copy of her recipes and put it in Patty's cookbook. Beverly and Scott hugged as they will both miss each other very much.

Beverly had an enormous amount to get ready for the movers to pack for her. However, her first task was to call her brother Peter to get him to fly out and drive back with her. Then she would fly him to Tampa from Panama City. Peter and Beverly loved road trips and got along great! In fact, it was Peter that had made the three-thousand-mile trip out from Florida to California, so who better to bring Beverly home? However, their father was now ninety-seven and was not doing well. He was living in Arlington, Texas, with their brother Warren, as he had moved from Washington as he did his ministry work. This detour would be a nine-hour trip out of their way; however Beverly and Peter felt like this might be their last opportunity to see their father alive. It is sad to say that only three months later he passed away quietly in his sleep.

Beverly called Peter, and he was definitely up for the adventure. He got his ticket, and Beverly would pick him up about three days before they would leave, at the Palm Springs Airport. Patty and some others had planned a going-away party for Beverly, and Peter was invited also.

Everything was starting to fall into place. Beverly started acquiring boxes, tape, string, and plastic boxes to pack with. She had things stacked everywhere in the house, garage, and outside by the casita. Out by the casita was all rock around the pool area and Jacuzzi. Also there was a putting green to the right of the casita and a large tree where Beverly kept her wooden potting bench, all her plants, pots, and hose.

Beverly went out to begin to pack up her pots and tripped over the hose. She flipped up in the air and came down on her right shoulder and leg. Beverly lay there for a few minutes in so much pain, yelling for Scott, knowing he could not hear her pleas for help. She dragged herself over to the potting bench, pulled herself up, and dragged herself in excruciating pain to the door.

Scott came rushing over as he felt powerless. Beverly, weak and defenseless, explained what happened. Scott called an ambulance and assisted her to a chair until they arrived. Beverly felt like if they could just twist her knee back in place, everything would be fine.

When the four handsome, rugged guys, arrived Beverly started to feel better. She said if they could turn her knee, maybe it would help. The guys put her on the gurney and took her to the hospital, laughing and joking with her all the way.

As soon as they did a CAT scan of the knee and shoulder, they realized she had torn the meniscus and torn her rotator cuff. Beverly requested something for pain, and they gave her morphine. Immediately the pain subsided, which helped a lot. Her knee was swollen, and they fitted Beverly with a knee brace and shoulder harness and sent her home. Beverly had instructions to see an orthopedic surgeon right away. She called their recommendation for a surgeon and made an appointment for the next day. Beverly was using crutches and had to depend on Patty to get her there.

After seeing the doctor and having an MRI his recommendation was that Beverly needed a whole new knee. Beverly was beside herself. "This is not happening, not now!" She asked the doctor, "What is the alternative to surgery?" The doctor explained, "Not only do you have a torn meniscus, but arthritis has caused the other side to deteriorate to the point it needs replacing." Beverly asked if he could give her something for the pain for now until she could make a decision as to what to do. Beverly decided to call her rheumatologist that she put all her faith in and asked his opinion and what his thoughts would be. She made an appointment and got to see him, and he took one look at her and exclaimed, "What happened?" Beverly brought the films, and he looked at them. The doctor said, "I can give you a shot that will last about three months. Then when you get to Florida, you see an orthopedic surgeon and get another opinion."

Beverly was thrilled with his opinion; he gave her a shot in the knee and shoulder, and immediately the pain was gone. Beverly gave the doctor a big hug. She had to tell him she was moving back to Florida, so they had to say their good-byes. She would really miss him as he was a very knowledgeable doctor, and he would surely be missed. Beverly got home, and now she could do some real packing, although she was nervous with that knee. She did still wear the brace for her shoulder and knee when she was packing and took time to put her knee up to rest. Now the thought came to her, "The seventeen steps to the new house in Mexico Beach." Beverly called Diana to tell her what happened, and she of course wondered what to do about the steps. Actually, as the doctor said, Beverly needed to exercise to get strength in the muscles around the meniscus. "Therefore, we are going to go with the same house. Just wanted to call to let you know, even falling and having to have surgery will not hold me back."

Before getting too far along, Beverly had to make some time to spend with her friend Rose. She and Rose have had so many good times together. She was one person Beverly would truly miss and never forget their friendship. They made arrangements to go to their favorite sushi restaurant, and what a fabulous meal they had. It was delightful, and the conversation was profound. They discussed all the good times and hit on some difficulties that still loomed around both of their families. Beverly and Rose decided they will always call and e-mail so those conversations would continue—sometimes intense, maybe even a bit playful. As Beverly and Rose parted, they did not say good-bye, just "you will hear from me soon," and "we'll talk a few times a week as good friends should."

Peter arrived right as he was supposed to, and the day was sunny and quite cooler than it had been. Beverly took him to the house, and of course, there were boxes everywhere except in the kitchen and living room, where the party was going to be. Scott and his uncle, Peter, got to catch up on a lot of old news as they had not seen each other in three years. Beverly had been in contact with the movers, and everything was pretty set for them to start packing in one day. Peter and Beverly would go to pick up the truck with the trailer to pull her van the next day so they could begin packing. This was going to be an enormous ride across country once again. Actually, this was Beverly's third time, as she did it one time in her motor home. However, Beverly explained, "If you have ever gone Route 10, you know it is an extremely boring ride. Sorry folks that live in those towns. It's not your fault there is no scenery in between the towns."

Patty and the gang put on a spread for the party, and everything was magnificent. The food was tasty, and the guests made it all come together so nicely. Although she didn't like to leave her family and friends, Beverly knew she was doing this for the right reasons. She was making a big step in her life and her sister Diana's. It may be bittersweet for some but the right thing for others. Beverly felt everyone really was exceptional and put themselves out to make her going-away a special occasion.

The next morning, they got the truck, trailer, gas, blankets, and locks and brought them back to the house, and there was Fabricio and his sons, ready to work. Beverly gave them the walk-around as to what things were hers as most were marked, and let them get at packing the truck. Fabricio gave Beverly a four-hour estimate, which she thought would be impossible. She had a full bedroom set, dinning set, and full desk and den set to be followed by at least hundred boxes.

Beverly had to take Buffy for her last grooming before they left. Therefore, while they were packing the truck, she took her down and dropped her off at the groomer. Beverly and Peter came back, and Patty had picked up some lunch, so they all had a nice lunch while waiting for the guys to pack. They chatted away about how much "Scott will have to get used to not having Mom's cooking and watching football with him." It was enjoyable to be able to cook for her son again and for the whole family. Beverly enjoyed cooking and had not done much since her father moved to her brother's. Also, when for almost two years of having MRSA she could not tolerate much solid food, so she did not do much cooking then. Beverly ate mostly rice and noodles. Therefore, she had already started on a diet before she left, as she had gained a lot of weight, but needed to continue when she arrived in Florida after having all that family cooking.

Actually, the time had come, and Fabricio took five hours, only one hour over, to Beverly's surprise. He did do a great job of getting everything into the truck and also filling the van. Beverly paid Fabricio and thanked him for all the kindness he had shown her since she had been in California. Then came the time to say good-bye to Patty and Angelina. That was tough. They hugged and tearfully said how much they would miss each other; somehow it just didn't seem to be enough. Beverly went to put her arms around Scott as they both broke down in tears. They both expressed how hard it would be without being together, but both said they understood. It was difficult for Beverly as she had thought that she would retire there. "However, things change, and it is hard to accept that change sometimes. But you know, the love never changes."

Beverly and Peter pulled out of Indio, California, and were on to I-10 at around 1:00 p.m. They were headed east for the long ride to Florida. They had picked up Buffy and had her seat in the middle, so she was ready. They had snacks and water. Beverly let Peter know that she would not drive after dark as she had a problem seeing. He said that was fine with him. Usually, they would eat breakfast at the hotel, have a light snack, and because we stopped early, they would have a big dinner. Beverly and Peter both liked the Hampton Inn, so he would watch for those on the map and pick out the place for dinner. Beverly thought they had a good system going. Peter would gas the truck, and Beverly would run her card. Peter kept trying to pay, and Beverly told him it was all on her. "Therefore, keep your wallet in your pants. Your money is no good."

After the second day of driving, they had to start taking a different direction to go to Dallas area to see their father. It was nine hours going this way, but it was well worth the trip. As they got closer to Arlington, they spoke with Warren to get directions to the home where their father was living. Beverly was concerned as she had a thirty-six-foot truck and trailer towing her van and did not like tight spaces. However, Warren directed her down a residential road to a beautiful home, but how was she getting out of there? Beverly parked at the end of the road and walked to the home about halfway down with Buffy and Peter.

They were greeted at the door by some lovely ladies, who welcomed them in to see their father right away. This was a beautifully decorated home; it was clean, smelled fresh, floors were polished shinning, and everyone happy and smiling. Beverly was directed to the back, and there sitting in a chair was Dad. He exclaimed, "Well, hello there, Buffy!" Beverly realized how much he missed his little dog. She put Buffy on his lap, and his face just glowed. It was such a pleasure just to see how the expressions of cheerfulness came over his face. Beverly and Peter leaned down together and gave him a kiss on his head still full of hair at ninety-seven.

It wasn't too long before Warren and his wife Peggy came in, and they all were happy to be together as it had been quite some time. At least they could all three be with Dad together, probably for the last time.

Beverly and Peter stayed and talked with the family for several hours as they were going to just go have dinner and find a hotel for the night to leave in the morning. Beverly felt Dad had lost quite a bit of weight since she had seen him, and he was having more trouble eating. Warren explained, "He just wants soft foods. Although he likes steak, he can't chew and swallow to get it down." Warren and Peggy had a previous engagement with some friend who came in town unexpectedly; therefore, they had to leave. Beverly and Peter wished them well, and it was always good to see them, even though it was only for a few hours.

Dad's dinner came, and he was refusing to eat. So Beverly sat and fed him his dinner. She had him for nine years and knew how he could be. Beverly got him to eat almost all of his food. Then he was ready for bed. They waited while the nurse put him to bed. Beverly leaned over to give him a kiss, and he said, "Will you keep this boy straight when I go?" He then told Beverly that he wanted to go to sleep but he wanted to know "if it's okay to go." Beverly told him she understood that he had a good long life, he had been a good father, a good husband, and yes Beverly would keep peace with the boys. Dad just squeezed her hand as if to say "Everything is okay now." Peter bent over and gave him a kiss as he drifted off to sleep.

Not too far down the road they found a hotel as it was getting dark; however, spending time with Dad was more important than dinner. By the time they got parked and went to the rooms, it was really late. Beverly and Peter grabbed a snack and went to bed. In the morning, they met at breakfast, and it was an impressive one. Peter and Beverly were hungry and needed to get back on schedule. They ate and filled up the truck, and down the road they went, knowing that they had spent quality time with their father. Although it might be the last, it was special to see him smiling, happy to see Buffy, still walking, full head of hair, and kidding with the nurses. Beverly thought to herself, "That's our dad!"

The rest of the trip went much the same. Beverly drove and drove and drove until they hit Route 22 and came across to Route 98. The first night they stayed at Diana's, and then she arranged for some help to come and unload the truck for Beverly. Diana had also found a washer and dryer for Beverly, which looked almost new. Beverly was there with the movers and directed them to put the boxes in the rooms according to the designated writing on the box so that she could empty them. Peter decided to drive instead of taking the plane; therefore, they drove him to the airport and picked up a rental car the next morning. Beverly gave him a big hug and said, "I really don't know what I would do without you." He always came to her rescue.

It took Beverly days to unpack and get all her things put away. All her furniture fit just right. Going up and down those stairs began to irritate her leg, and before long she had to find a doctor to give her another shot. After consulting with him about surgery and showing her MRI, Beverly let him know about having MRSA for almost two years. He discussed with his partner, and neither felt they wanted to operate on Beverly. He also recommended, "Exercise and try to build up the muscle around it and try to wait as long as you can for a shot." Beverly had some therapy, did exercise, and was six months between shots.

As the months went by, Diana and Beverly went crazy with the potting, exchanging, starting from each other's plants and were just having a great time. Then they traveled to the next little town Apalachicola, a quaint town loaded with antiques, small bistros, and potting places. Diana and Beverly made a day of it, had lunch, and hit all the stores that carried plants, looking for new species. By the end of the day, the car was filled with all kinds of plants, pots, hangers, and anything they saw along the way that they felt they could pot. Beverly and Diana were in their element when they were with their plants and getting their hands in the soil. This certainly helped bond them closer than they could have ever imagined.

One of the first pieces of furniture Beverly needed was a sofa. Diana took Beverly to practically every store in Panama City. Beverly finally landed at a sale at Hanks furniture. Having been a general sales manager in the automobile business, when Beverly had to make a purchase, her selling skills were her best asset. She would go into the store and let them know what she used to do as a profession, and they would bring out the manager. Beverly would negotiate with him and get the best deal possible, as Diana sat by the front door, embarrassed. However, Beverly got a beautiful recliner sofa, delivered from a very nice gentleman, and was treated with great respect and felt like she got the best price for her money. She went home happy and said she "will purchase from there again."

After being there and just getting acquainted with the area, Beverly and Diana knew it was time to settle down and start doing some research for their book. They still had some ancestors to locate and paperwork to put together. Beverly started taking notes on their feelings from the time they were left home alone, found each other in 1982, then reconnected in 2012, and then made their journey to find their roots. Finally, she ended up with Beverly's trip back to California, finding a place to live in Florida through the Internet, and moving to Florida. Here is where the story really began for them, so to speak. Now Diana and Beverly were going to put together all the good things and bad things that happened through the years in a book to share with others. Beverly thought, "Some may have gone through similar pain such as ours and may be helped as we have by others."

Beverly and Diana wanted to pass on their feelings and compassion to everyone that has been through adoption, and allow them to have great strength and courage to accept their challenges to fill in the blanks of their history.

CHAPTER 10

The Summary

They exposed that thousand-pound gorilla; therefore, now he had no power over them. Beverly and Diana opened up and spoke about their feelings, about the experience of being abandoned and never knowing why, but always searching for the answer. They also had the burning question as many adoptees' have, should they pursue looking for their biological family. Diana explained, "When we first found each other, it was the happiest time in our lives. Although we had our own families and did not share much time together, we still began to build that bond. However, you have to accept the fact that, you were not raised together and had two different life styles, which makes things complicated. Just to know that you can see and touch that person that you longed for is sometimes hard to understand that this is reality. We are grateful for the time we have and are building on our relationship every day."

As they pursued finding out why their parents just walked out of their lives, it was hard to understand, after they had their own children, just how their parents could leave their little girls. Beverly, especially, had feelings of hatred for her biological mother, which was a concern for a Christian to have those feelings. However, when Diana met her mother, it was impossible for Beverly to bring herself to meet her and forgive her as Diana had done. Beverly and Diana had those lingering questions, like why did you leave us? However, she had no answers. Diana ended up getting hurt as she could not get the affection she wanted from her mother or answers as to why she just left them. They began to realize their issues were their issues, but they were not going to let them define who they were. Beverly and Diana could not let that part of their life go without finding out why.

Time goes by so quickly, and you never forget about your past as that sting will always be there. Beverly and Diana both learned in therapy that "you have to put all those things in a box, put them on the shelf, and don't take them down. Therefore you will be able to deal with the constant memory of the abuse you had been through when you were children." Beverly and Diana had taken the box down once to find each other in 1982, and now in 2012, it was their final attempt to find out why they were abandoned.

Beverly and Diana felt sometimes when they were adopted that they lost their birth family, and they were never allowed to go through the grieving process of losing their family. Beverly hid her adoption from her friends and did not talk about it, as she was ashamed. Diana had low self-esteem as not only her parents gave her away, but her foster parents sent her back. Beverly and Diana felt when they were adopted they had to show gratitude to their adopted parents and try to please them for adopting them. Adoption can be painful. Beverly and Diana carried the constant burden of why they were given away by their parents.

Even though Beverly and Diana had these feelings most of their lives, they were going to try again to get the answer as to why they left them home alone with a six-month-old baby to care for as they were young children themselves. Was it possible they had a reason? Beverly and Diana finally in 2012 went to Marsha this last time to make the effort to see if it was possible to get the records that would show what really happened in 1953 that caused their parents to walk away. There must be a record. Beverly and Diana knew that in 1982 when they were reunited, nothing was available to them. However, all these years later, after the death of both their parents, there must be a release of the records that can help take the burden and pain away as to "why?"

After they reconnected with Marsha, she fully understood their fight to finally get the answer to why. Not knowing herself if the answer would be there and then dealing with the disappointment, she forged ahead on their journey. Beverly and Diana understandably were happy they did not get the documents with the information they acquired in 1982. They realized the sensitive nature of what they learned in 2012;

they could not have accepted it fully when they first met. As children that were adopted and had good families, Beverly and Diana did not search for their biological family to hurt their adopted family in any way. That was a fear, however, Beverly had to face with her mother, but the drive to find Diana was so great that she had to fulfill her desire to find her. As it turned out, her mother was very fond of Diana; she was just concerned that Beverly would get hurt and meet Arlene, her mother.

When Marsha read those documents and then was able to call them with the good news of what really happened, Beverly and Diana had a burden lifted from their shoulders that had been there for years. It was apparent that their parent had left them, Marsha read to them how for two long years they kept them in foster care, would not sign off to allow them to be adopted, as they were trying to make arrangements to take them back.

Unfortunately, they could never work it out because lack of education and work, and they did not have the "where with all." Beverly and Diana had tears streaming down their cheeks as Marsha read to them as they realized that their parents did want them back. That was all they wanted to hear! No matter how bad it hurt that they just walked out on them, it was good to know that they came back. Beverly and Diana explained to Marsha how finally they had the answer to their question. Beverly said, "We can't tell you the difference that it makes to know you weren't just a throwaway kid. Our parents made the effort to come back for us." Although they did not have the circumstances to keep them, Beverly and Diana felt that was a blessing.

Their biological parents gave them the opportunity to have a better life than they could have ever given them. "We are sure it was difficult to make that decision, as it took two years to sign away their rights," said Diana. However, Beverly and Diana would not have been able to experience the many opportunities they had if their parents had not made the right decision.